REVOLT ON THE TIGRIS

Crises in World Politics

TARAK BARKAWI
JAMES MAYALL
BRENDAN SIMMS
editors

GÉRARD PRUNIER
Darfur: The Ambiguous Genocide

FAISAL DEVJI
Landscapes of the Jihad

MARK ETHERINGTON
Revolt on the Tigris

AHMED HASHIM
Insurgency and Counter-Insurgency in Iraq

MARK ETHERINGTON

Revolt on the Tigris

The Al-Sadr Uprising and the Governing of Iraq

Cornell University Press
Ithaca, New York

Originally published in the United Kingdom by
C. Hurst & Co. (Publishers) Ltd, London.

First published 2005 by Cornell University Press

ISBN 0-8014-4451-9 (cloth: alk. paper)

Printed in the United States of America

Librarians: Library of Congress Cataloging-in-Publication Data are available.

Cornell University Press strives to use environmentally responsible suppliers and materials to the fullest extent possible in the publishing of its books. Such materials include vegetable-based, low-VOC inks and acid-free papers that are recycled, totally chlorine-free, or partly composed of nonwood fibers. For further information, visit our website at www.cornellpress.cornell.edu.

Cloth printing 10 9 8 7 6 5 4 3 2 1

For Emma, Anna and Orde

CONTENTS

ILLUSTRATIONS

between pages 144 and 145

Chaos: the provincial border crossing between Iraq and Iran at Arafat, near Badrah

Interpreter Majed Mayat al-Kureishi

Blackhawk helicopters over the Tigris, departing from the CPA base in Kut

Timm Timmons with Iraqi children in a school classroom

Ukrainian armoured personnel carrier, Kut

The author with Gen. Sergey Ostrovskiy, commanding the Sixth Ukrainian Mechanised Brigade

Followers of Moqtada al-Sadr demonstrate at the front gate of CPA Kut, 4 April 2004

Ukrainian sniper returning fire, 6 April 2004

Kut CPA team and security teams, 7 April 2004

US Army Lieutenant-Colonel Mark E. Calvert, May 2004

'The Villa' (CPA base, Kut) after occupation by Moqtada al-Sadr's militia, May 2004

Inauguration of new Province Council building, 26 June 2004

ACKNOWLEDGEMENTS

This is an account of a nine-month period after the 2003 war which I spent in the Iraqi provincial capital of al-Kut, serving as head of the small Coalition Provisional Authority (CPA) team charged with overseeing Wasit Province, two hours south-east of Baghdad and adjoining Iran. It is a necessarily narrow view of a much broader endeavour, and is not designed to be an authoritative account of Iraq's recent political evolution or CPA's part in the process.

My thanks go particularly to the Iraqi and international members of the CPA team in Kut with whom I shared this experience. It is to them that I owe any success we may have had. We could not have functioned at all without our Iraqi staff, whose wisdom, kindness and courage gives me cause for optimism about their country and its people. I thank my highly able principal interpreter Faraz Faisal Maqsosi, and particularly my adviser Majid Mayat al-Kureishi for his untiring assistance at the time and subsequent patience in answering my questions. Both men taught me a great deal. CPA team members Timm Timmons, Neil Strachan, Colin Coyle and Rob McCarthy helped me with recollections and photographs. I pay tribute to the professionalism of our Control Risks Group security details, and particularly to Russ Pulleng and Robert Pease, the leaders of my first security team, who were with us from beginning to end. We drove many thousands of miles together.

I am grateful to Major Andrey Lischinsky for assisting me with detail regarding the Ukrainian Army, and to U.S. Army officers

Lieutenant-Colonel Mark E. Calvert and Major Christopher P. Taylor, then of the 1st Squadron of the U.S. Second Armored Cavalry Regiment (Light), who kindly answered my questions concerning the Squadron's operations in Kut in April–June 2004.

Dr Brendan Simms encouraged me to write this book, and his encouragement and guidance sustained me in the process. I am very grateful to him. Dr Tarak Barkawi gave me sound advice at the outset. I am indebted, too, to Dr John King who read the manuscript and provided valuable comment.

I thank Christopher Hurst, Michael Dwyer and Maria Petalidou of the publishers, Hurst and Co., and Sebastian Ballard for executing the maps. I am grateful to Eddie and Sharon Parks for their hospitality during the editing process, and to Nigel Race who first introduced us.

My partner Emma Morgan's decision to make her way across the Kuwaiti border to spend Christmas with me in Kut in 2003 is perhaps the best illustration of her courage and of her unwavering and unequivocal support to me over the years. I owe her more than I can easily say.

I have changed some names in the text and omitted others where I judged that to do otherwise might endanger the people concerned. The opinions expressed and any errors of fact are mine alone.

May 2005   MARK ETHERINGTON

ABBREVIATIONS

CJTF 7	Combined Joint Task Force 7
CPA	Coalition Provisional Authority
CRG	Control Risks Group
DFID	Department for International Development
DOD	U.S. Department of Defense
FCO	Foreign and Commonwealth Office, British
FRL	Former Regime Loyalist
FPS	Facilities Protection Service
GC	Governorate Coordinator
GST	Governorate Support Team
ICDC	Iraqi Civil Defence Corps
IGC	Iraqi Governing Council
INC	Iraqi National Congress
IRAQREP	UK Special Representative for Iraq
KBR	Kellogg Brown and Root
MND C-S	Multi-National Division Central-South
PMO	Project Management Office
RPG	Rocket-Propelled Grenade
RTI	Research Triangle Institute
SCIRI	Supreme Council for the Islamic Revolution in Iraq
USMC	U.S. Marine Corps

Iraq

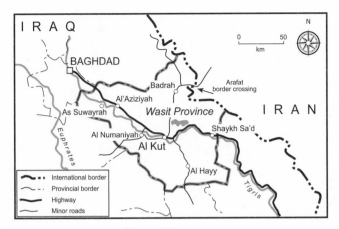

Wasit Province

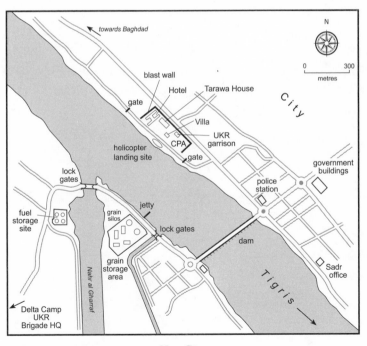

Kut City

INTRODUCTION

It is the unvarying bleakness of much of Iraq's southern flatlands that makes the presence of the Euphrates and Tigris rivers, winding south-eastwards to the Shatt-al-Arab and the Persian Gulf, so arresting. Their importance to the country is impossible to exaggerate: in summer the water is diverted through myriad capillaries to farms and smallholdings along their banks, or channelled in concrete watercourses to distant plantations whose palm groves loom on shimmering horizons. It pours luminous and untrammelled from ancient pumps that shake in a haze of blue exhaust or arcs through holes in long-perished hose, forlornly patched with rag. This process of cajoling water from these ancient water-ways always seemed to me a devotional act, an historic affirmation of a link between Maker and Man that needed no missionary intermediary: for the Shi'ia of southern Iraq see the hand of God in everything.

Perhaps it was this primacy of the elements that had imbued them with an innate and fatalistic conservatism, a quality doubtless compounded by years of persecution under Saddam Hussein. The Iraqis of the region seemed at once to long for change but were unable to allow themselves the guilty excitement of expecting it; and to kick against the bondage of occupation while simultaneously avowing that Iraq was incapable of self-betterment. They wanted, I thought, a miracle; but almost without exception none saw themselves as part of the solution.

In the heat of a June evening thirteen months after the end of the 2003 war, and three weeks before the Coalition Provisional

Authority (CPA) dissolved and handed power to an Iraqi government, I sat on the steps of the CPA's first-floor offices in al-Kut,
Wasit province, looked over the expanse of the Tigris and wondered what we had achieved. A hot and insistent north-west wind
blew through the compound: past the car-bomb defences at our
back gate and the squat menace of 'Be Sensitive', our sentinel
Abrams tank; through the thick stands of reeds at the river banks;
around our shattered buildings, through the date palms and out to
the old British-built barrage beyond. The three flags on the roof—
Iraqi, American and British—flew taut against their restraining
halyards. Our small team was a long way from home and at that
moment I felt the isolation of every mile.

Much of what I saw that day reminded me of our efforts and
prompted me to question our accomplishments. I looked across the
river to the agricultural silos and, further left, to the small police
station, and wondered what had changed. The fire-tug sat at its
moorings near the lock as it had since our arrival. The camouflaged
tanks of the oil storage site partly obscured the hangars of Delta
Camp, one of Saddam Hussein's former air bases, some 4 km.
distant and now the headquarters of the Ukrainian brigade and a
U.S. cavalry squadron. There was an insistent sense of immobility
about it all, as though our meetings and proclamations, our measures and targets, were symptoms of a broader delusion. That steady
wind mocked any sense of advance; indeed, the very idea of achievement appeared irredeemably subjective—who, after all, was to
judge us in the end? The wind lifted the sand from the road and
momentarily obscured the antennae and machine-gun barrels on
the Humvees of the U.S. 1/2 Armored Cavalry Regiment's Quick
Reaction Force. I watched the soldiers gather their playing cards
and find shelter.

Even now, I do not feel I can adequately describe Iraq, or even
our province, in a way that makes sense of it all. I remember the

seasons: the desiccating heat of summer and its remorseless punishment of all movement and initiative; the darkness and incessant
rain of winter as we walked our perimeter in the fog, searching for
weak spots and waiting ceaselessly for attack; and the seasonal
floodwaters of spring and autumn sprawling across the desert to a
come-hither horizon. I remember the wetlands of southern Iraq
from the Blackhawk helicopters, the cattle-egrets scattering behind
us and the door gunners' machine-gun belts in the evening light;
and the cold beauty of silver and red tracer commingling during the
attacks.

I do not remember much of myself. When I assumed my task as a
Governorate Coordinator in al-Kut, Ambassador Paul Bremer had
said that the job resembled being a 'DC' (District Commissioner).
The task, it seemed to me, demanded an assertion of personal and
national principles that in the twenty-first century verged on arrogance. My reservations about re-assuming a quasi-colonial mantle
caused my American friends some amusement. If the first prospect
of living a colonial fantasy possessed any schoolboy allure, this
feeling was quickly eclipsed by a sense of acute and burdensome
responsibility. With this came a typically post-Empire cargo of
introspection, and I used to wonder, as I gazed at my province through
the armoured glass of a Land Cruiser, whether so reluctant a governor was really worth protecting. But modern Iraq, six months
after the 2003 war, was no place for self-doubt.

1

ARRIVAL

Operational experience, particularly the kind derived from conflict and war, is largely unknowable by those who have not encountered it. No amount of reading or conversation can be successfully distilled into a synthesis of the events described. There is a stubborn and largely invisible fault line between every layer of reporting and decision-making in these instances, magnified by distance, culture and the number of participants, which leads inexorably to inefficiency and misunderstandings. In short, the very complexity and breadth of recent international interventions to re-fashion the world in our own image militate against effective and timely execution of the task.

It is ironic that I imagined, flying north-west from Basra in a British Royal Air Force (RAF) Hercules on 1 October 2003 to assume my duties as a Governorate Coordinator in the Iraqi province of Wasit, that our failure to assemble a coalition of major powers to prosecute the war and manage the aftermath would in the end lend us operational advantage. The manoeuvre war had finished five months earlier. The fact that we had a small—if powerful—team whose axis rested principally on American and British political and military commitment would surely relieve the existing Coalition of the need for broad and time-consuming consultation, enable us to move fast, and devolve power inexorably downward where it belonged. In using this unprecedented opportunity to

achieve success in theatre we might then recapture the political consensus we now so demonstrably lacked.

I suppose there was a kind of arrogance implicit in these reflec-
tions: a sense that our setbacks and failures in the Balkans, particularly, had been rooted in a peculiarly somnolent European
diplomatic tradition. Formulating foreign policy on the basis of the
lowest common denominator had been a frustrating business. It is a
cliché that the United Nations has largely failed to capitalise on the
opportunities presented by the demise of the Soviet Union; certainly the Security Council had proved fatally divided over Iraq and
Saddam Hussein's flouting of their Resolutions, and this apparent
paralysis suggested a more pervasive malaise caused by moral tor-
por among some of the Permanent Five. Even the RAF load-master
now striding among us in the evocatively shaded hull of the aircraft
wore a T-shirt that said 'Operation Iraqi Freedom March–April
2003—next stop Paris'. If I had spoken to the U.S. Army officer
seated half-asleep at my side he might have said that we had tried the
time-worn international recipes of negotiation and cajolery, and
that they had led us down a hole—nothing, he might have added,
would rouse Europe from its sleep and now was the time for action.
In breaking free of these perceived constraints I believed that an
opportunity to demonstrate the operational benefits of a lean and
battle-tried partnership, based on a revitalised British-American
alliance, now beckoned.

Destiny's call always sounds slightly louder in a military aircraft,
and its volume increases with speed, proximity to the ground and
the number of weapons carried. Military equipment imbues perfectly ordinary journeys and events with a delusory sense of pur-
posefulness and power, and no recent armed interventions had
caused sufficient casualties on our side to moderate the effects of the
drug. Even eight hours waiting in a white plastic chair at Basra
airport between connections had not deadened my nerve endings.

Now, fifteen years after leaving the British Army's Parachute Regiment, the wail of the Hercules' four turbo-props fired that old cocktail of sensation within me: I remembered the race down the fuselage towards the parachute doors, the green light and the night outside, heavy with equipment and purpose. Watching the southern Iraq desert scroll beneath our wings I was conscious that I would encounter substantial difficulties in the months ahead, but could conjure up no requisite human reaction. Rather, this flight, so redolent of past experience, produced in me a sense of confidence that verged on abandonment.

In September 2003 such confidence appeared far from prevalent in the British Foreign and Commonwealth Office (FCO), which had struggled from the outset, like other government ministries and departments, to honour the pledges implicit in Britain's participation in the war. There remained much uncertainty about the facts on the ground, and Iraq was an unpopular cause among the British intelligentsia. Britain had probably not felt so politically exposed since the 1982 Falklands war, and the grounds for military intervention in Iraq were a great deal less clear-cut. My impression at the time was that the government was under considerable pressure; and that the Foreign Office had recruited me, a private citizen, with some reluctance, having failed to find a serving diplomat for the task. It may of course have been that few wanted to go.

I walked to Whitehall through the autumnal beauty of London's St James's Park and approached the Foreign Office past a statue of Clive of India and Churchill's Cabinet War Rooms. In these predeployment briefings in London my new employers had been unable to furnish much more detail than gossip and the media had already provided. I met Henry Hogger, our former ambassador in Syria, who was to become Governorate Coordinator (GC) in Basra; and a former deputy head of Mission from Nairobi, destined to be GC in Kirkuk. In a series of meetings in the Cabinet Office, the Foreign Office's Iraq Policy Unit and the Department for International Development we eyed each other warily, our discomfort alleviated only by the chocolate biscuits and cups of tea that the British government habitually assembles at moments of national crisis. We were told there were eighteen Iraqi provinces. In each the Coalition Provisional Authority (CPA), charged with running the country under Occupation Law until a satisfactory transition to Iraqi authority could be made, would establish a civilian Governance Team, headed by a GC. Four of these provinces would be British-led, and it was intended that the rest, possibly with one or two exceptions, would be American. I would answer to the head of the Coalition Provisional Authority, Ambassador L. Paul Bremer, as his representative in Wasit province. Wasit was south-east of Baghdad and its provincial capital was al-Kut, two hours from the city by road and adjacent to the River Tigris which runs south to the city of Amara. The team for which I was responsible would be largely British, though I would have an American State Department deputy. It would number no more than eight people, of whom only he and I had so far been named—the others had yet to be found.

There were two aspects to this plan that surprised me. The first was the issue of governance capacity. Clearly the Governance Team was small for the task, if that task was in essence to impose the will of the Coalition on the population while transition was effected. Early seizure of civil initiative is essential in circumstances like these. In Kosovo we had fielded thousands of civilian experts to oversee every aspect of administration, and installed an office in every major town. While security concerns were clearly a powerful constraint on efforts to replicate this entirely in Iraq, I thought this deficiency an error. I was unaware at the time that the Governance Teams were themselves a recent creation—the U.S. Department of Defense had previously intended to rely only on the military units already in place. Given the size of the new team now mooted for this province and others like it, much of the governance burden would clearly rest by default on those 1,600 Coalition troops already present, who retained the traditional military advantages of coverage, communications and logistics. In Wasit these troops were Ukrainian. It seemed unlikely at first sight that a Ukrainian unit would possess sufficient experience of civil-military operations to undertake complex governance tasks effectively.

The second concern, linked to the first, was security. Iraq was clearly dangerous. In the months following the end of the war the Americans had lost a further 180 dead and 850 wounded.[1] On 19 August 2003 a bomb at the United Nations (UN) HQ in Baghdad had killed a number of senior UN staff members including the Special Representative, Sergio Vieira de Mello, and my friend Fiona Watson. I had been unsettled by their deaths and by Fiona's in particular; and the risk that had shadowed much of my working life suddenly seemed more real. Many found it difficult to accept that the UN could be targeted in this way; indeed, were wholly unable to fathom the motives for the attack or understand the kind of people who could carry it out, so vicious did the assault appear against an organisation that had opposed the war. If the bomb profoundly shocked the UN and effectively ended its presence in the country, it arguably illustrated too a more general public ignorance of popular attitudes in Iraq, and specifically of the devastating effect of UN sanctions on ordinary Iraqis. The attack greatly retarded efforts to broaden political participation in handling the Iraq problem. The British government, among others, found it more difficult to find people of the requisite experience for the task and felt unable to order its diplomats to take part, relying instead on a 'trawl' of the Civil Service for volunteers.

[1] These figures refer to US casualties in the period 1 May–1 Oct. 2003, and include non-combat cases.

From the outset the British national requirement to carry out efficiently the tasks of political re-structuring and physical reconstruction in Iraq, and of ensuring the safety of the staff dispatched to do so, created an important systemic tension that was never fully resolved—indeed it could not rationally be resolved. This sprang, I thought, from intellectual confusion: Britain was clearly a key political partner in Iraq—though its physical and financial input was dwarfed by that of the Americans—but the country seemed to shy away from the responsibilities this role logically conferred. The British had made it plain that the safety of their people was of primary importance, but it remained unclear how this imperative was to be reconciled with the urgency of the tasks at hand. Inescapably there was a job to be done and it could not be done without risk. Yet taking risks with their civilian staff was anathema to the British government. While this was clearly laudable, I thought it unrealistic. With the invasion of Iraq and our assumption of the associated political and military burdens we were, whether we liked it or not, neck-deep in the risk business. This pre-occupation with safety betokened a sense of national timidity that seemed ill-suited to the probable demands of the expedition on which we were now irrevocably embarked. The fact was that Britain remained deeply divided over Iraq, and these divisions went to the very core of the government.

This anxiety had led to spirited discussion about how best to place British forces and assets in Iraq post-war. Some suggested that British policy would be best served by concentrating soldiers and civilians in a single area—the south—thus creating an environment for which Britain might be solely responsible. Clearly this also implied enhanced national control—the underlying concern being that American policy and tactics might otherwise impinge on British interests. Foremost among the dangers posed by this concept in the eyes of its detractors was the possibility that Britain would thus

isolate itself from U.S. funding and broader largesse. When asked
my opinion I could see the logic of the argument, but thought it
altogether eclipsed by the greater danger of establishing a largely
autonomous Britain-by-the-Sea when the aim, however difficult to
achieve, should clearly be to create an integrated command.

Inevitably there was a compromise. An area under overall British
military and political command was created in the south, but com-
mingled with other contingents. Of the four British Governorates
two, Basra and Nasiriyah, were under the over-arching British
military aegis in this area, and a third, Kirkuk, was in the Kurdish
area in the U.S-led north. Only one, my own, was placed in 'Central-
South', a sector neither British nor American. This distribution of
assets seemed eminently sensible, and consistent with the British
stake in wider success, but inevitably complicated the issue of protection. This was mitigated to some extent by the provision of a
security team of four people and two civilian armoured vehicles,
paid for by the British government, to each of the four British Governance Teams. *In extremis* however, Britain would be faced with the
difficulty of assuring the safety of its staff in Wasit without a British
or American military unit on which to call. I am not sure that this
eventuality was ever properly considered; rather, it was just another
administrative detail among many that seemed naturally to fall to
the 'military'. I add the quotation marks because the military forces
in Iraq were fast becoming a mythological cure-all for every gap,
and there were many. In truth, the 'military' and the military were
very different entities: the separate contingents varied substantially
in ability and resources, and all were spread thin.

The principal moral danger of taking part in great endeavours is
the human temptation to be an onlooker rather than to assume the
active and evaluative role for which one has been employed. The
majesty of the event at hand conspires against objectivity. This is
compounded in my case by a stubborn reverence for the British

Establishment. As a colonial child, brought up in the Arabian States of Kuwait and Qatar in the 1960s, I caught the ragged ends of Empire. We stood for the National Anthem in the Hubara Club in the Kuwaiti oil town of al-Ahmadi on Friday film nights; we had curry lunches at the Cumberland Yacht Club; and I was impressed by the lean, sun-tanned sailors whom we helped entertain there during regular visits by Royal Navy warships. A colonial's respect for British institutions was inculcated in me that I have been wholly unable to discard: a visceral need to belong to the club matched only by later, commensurate, surprise at the antiquated and unimaginative thinking one was apt to encounter within. At boarding school in England I dutifully tried to accept that an education in Kent was more exciting than the deserts of Arabia, and surreptitiously studied grey 1970s Britain from the rain-streaked window of my classroom in the hope of catching a glimpse of the Imperial spark. I was eleven years old. I had expected to meet Winston Churchill, Admiral Lord Nelson, Keats and Shelley in the Heathrow airport arrivals lounge, and never quite got over the disappointment of finding that they were all dead.

Six years in the Army, arguably the most successful of all of Britain's public institutions in the post-1945 era, restored much of my faith in the British brand. I was neither militaristic nor some post-Empire jingoist: the Army simply appeared to me in those dismal years to provide a national repository for those standards of courage, confidence and fortitude that I had once so admired. I do not suggest that the Army's officer-training benchmarks were ever necessarily met by our small band of uncertain cadets when we first encountered them at the Royal Military Academy in Sandhurst; but the key is that we all knew what they were, we thought we knew what they meant and we had all volunteered for the task. The Army was not very good at compromise: one either completed a run in forty minutes or one did not; one was either able to both strip and re-assemble a machine gun in the dark or one was not. Excuses were not tolerated, no one was cuddled afterwards and the atmosphere was unambiguously competitive. This lent a stark and uncompromising clarity to our performance evaluations that verged on the brutal; and doubtless Sandhurst's enforced and arguably simplistic egalitarianism occasionally stuck in the craw of graduate botanists and the like who privately wondered whether there was more breadth to their abilities than this.

The Army's espousal of group achievement and the virtues of moral courage produced some confusion in my mind about the proper place of the individual. We British appeared at once to laud the historic virtues of teams against the imposing back-drop of the vast colleges and other institutional fabric that made up the Academy, yet also to deify the individuals who had led them. To achieve individual profile thus appeared a bewildering mixture of hubris and conscience. In accepting the former definition one had also to accept the notion that the country and its legions were led by men and women of great wisdom, on whom it was logically wrong to press oneself or one's opinions; if the latter, one ought rather to accept that all systems require intelligent opposition and fine tuning to ensure integrity. Understandably the ramifications of this second course created anxiety among senior officers in an Army absorbing large quantities of graduates. A visiting brigadier, fresh from the 1982 Falklands war, confided in us, his audience of credulous cadets, that he would rather take non-graduate than graduate officers because the last thing he wanted was some fresh-faced philosopher mulling over his commander's plan of attack; and all graduate cadets were ritually warned of the dangers of 'intellectual arrogance' by small groups of (presumably non-graduate) officers for whom the spectre of insurrection from within by disaffected botanists seemed only too real.

How many times since then have I declined to write what I think, or hesitated before an open microphone at one conference or another for fear of disturbing an imaginary *status quo*? In Bosnia-

Herzegovina, as a British Foreign Office secondee to the European Community Monitoring Mission 1992–5, I saw the overwhelming preponderance of Bosnian Serb military power in the first years of the war and their habitual shelling of city centres for the stark injustice that it was, but duly took my place in the line of British apologists for them without a murmur of protest. Shortly before my leave periods, I would ring the Foreign Office's Eastern Adriatic Unit and ask whether they wished to debrief me in Britain. The answer was invariably 'no'. 'Fool!' I would say to myself, cheeks reddening, as I replaced the hand-set. 'Of course the British government knows the situation here.' The country, I knew, would be awash with British intelligence agents disguised as small hillocks, the ether sieved relentlessly by groups of dedicated servicemen and women, their product even now being weighed by the glittering minds of Whitehall. Reassured and slightly embarrassed I would try to sleep in our house listening to the flat concussion of heavy shells in the adjacent districts, the shrapnel fragments clattering down our tiled roof and the keening of sirens, assured that all was right with the world. Only after the war did I realise what I had witnessed and resolve to have the courage of my convictions thereafter.

From the moment when our Hercules banked steeply to begin its spiralling operational descent into Baghdad International Airport through the layers of warming air, the sun flickering intermittently at me like a faulty arc-light through the opposite window as we completed each gyration—from that moment to my arrival in al-Kut five days later, I thus fought my yearning merely to enjoy the awesome spectacle of a major military commitment. A British Parachute Regiment soldier who had fought in the Falklands once told me of his feeling at the time that he was taking part in his own B-movie, and felt obliged to script his own utterances accordingly. So it was with me in those opening minutes in Baghdad: Apache ground-attack helicopters hung like sinister insects far out over the city, describing menacing circles; Blackhawk general purpose helicopters roared low in pairs across ranks of parked aircraft, their passage marked by tiny dust-devils at the margins of the runway; and everywhere there were people in uniform shouting and getting on and off trucks as an endless succession of aircraft took off and landed. Sensations merged into one another—the roar of fork-lifts and the whine of turbines; the heat and cloying dust; the clatter of rifles and equipment; the clang of tail-gates; the chatter of radios; endless shouted instructions above the din: 'Move over there please; no—over *there*. Put your bags down. Where are your flak jackets? Do you have a ride?' An American soldier walked me to the car park with elaborate and unexpected courtesy. How long had he been in Iraq? Four months. Had he been home? 'Nope. And my wife is three months pregnant. Do the fuckin' math, man.'

The Green Zone, some 30 minutes' drive from the airport on fast roads, is a large complex the size of a small town, containing elaborate palaces, ceremonial gates and broad avenues that once housed the Ba'ath Party elite. The signs of war-time bomb damage were everywhere. Roofs slumped tiredly into empty swimming pools, and exquisite wrought-iron gates topped with gold-leaf hung broken from their hinges. Plastic bags and other litter flew like pennants from the razor wire over walls and entrances. Red aerosol daubs on the brick walls warned of mines or unexploded shells. This was a secure area, defended by the military at choke-points and bridges on the perimeter. It now housed the Coalition Provisional Authority, an array of liaison organisations, a military hospital and fighting units. The diversity and splendour of these buildings was extraordinary, given the poverty of the suburbs through which we had just driven. The 'Palace', the CPA headquarters, was a sand-coloured building some 350 metres long and two stories high with three separate pillared entrances overlooking gardens and fountains. It had once been used by Saddam Hussein, who had placed on the roof three vast stone heads, helmeted and heroic; the CPA later judged these inappropriate and removed them. Inside were echoing corridors, carved doors and marble halls, with vaulted roofs and chandeliers. In one room a large mosaic depicted a salvo of Iraqi rockets rising majestically heavenward in almost mystical assault on an unseen foe. Behind the palace heavy pillared balconies overlooked a palm plantation, now studded with hundreds of Portakabin accommodation containers. In the middle was a large swimming pool where American soldiers leapt whooping from the diving boards. There, as helicopters clattered low over the palms and 4×4s hissed endlessly up and down the roads, I lay slightly self-consciously on a sun-lounger and studied my briefing pack.

The prophetic quality of Power-Point presentations is justly celebrated: the vivid colours and clever title sequencing soothe the mind and painlessly inoculate the reader against the hazards of chance. Reading this establishment plan for Governance Teams under the palm trees was both surreal and relaxing. Each was to have a Governorate Coordinator and a Deputy; a Political Adviser; a Media Officer; a Facilities Manager; and Projects and Administrative officers. A group of engineers called the Governance Support Team (GST), administered by the local military unit, would provide technical assistance to the projects effort. Other potential additions included a medical officer, a computer expert and what the Americans called a 'Foreign Area Officer', a trained military linguist with local knowledge. An internet link was already in place. It was a system called 'Internet in a Box', originally designed for Afghan schools, consisting of some six computers and a satellite link. A full allocation of vehicles was on order. Each step towards full establishment was set against a chronological bar-chart in yellow and green. Barney Miller, an articulate former U.S. Army Ranger, talked me through it. We were already six weeks behind.

My private rule in assuming any new job of this nature is to keep my mouth firmly shut for a week, while learning as much as I can. First impressions are often wrong and international organisations,

particularly those combining civil and military elements, are politically complex. I was surprised by the composition of the proposed
team: already concerned that it was too small, I saw that there was
no rule-of-law component—no obvious expert who might review
the work of the police and the courts. This had been a hard-learned
lesson in south-eastern Europe—this foundation, this bedrock, is
generally thought essential. Without the rule of law it is very difficult to initiate civil reform, and the tenets of Occupation Law
were unlikely to prove a suitable remedy in the long term. Barney
said that the military would be responsible for the daily oversight of
police and judiciary, which I thought a curious notion—one generally tries to separate the law from the gun in the public mind
because such connotations are counter-productive. While we were
clearly an invasion force turned occupiers, labels which no amount
of sophistry could disinvent, we clearly needed to re-brand ourselves at some stage.

The small British administrative office on the second floor of the
Palace appeared chaotic, and I thought it lacked grip. I was concerned that Kut, falling just between the British sector in the south
and an American sector in the centre, would receive neither the
requisite support nor the political attention that might fall to its
better-connected counterparts. Nor was I convinced that we had
done our sums in security terms. Despite British insistence that no
British Governorate site would be occupied that had not been
checked by British security staff first, no such check had been done
and there appeared no immediate prospect of one. It was also clear
to me that when the two-vehicle security detail that had been
assigned to us arrived, it would quickly prove too meagre a resource
for the job, forcing our small team to advance on a narrow rather
than a broad front because there were insufficient vehicles to de-
ploy the team to maximum effect. I made this point, but sensed
resentment in the room at what was probably seen as abrasive

insistence on corralling resources for Kut. I was conscious of how it looked but privately discomfited by what I saw as complacency.

It is often difficult to question security measures without implying that one is simply afraid and somehow not up to the job. Pride is the root cause of many errors. The head of the British office gave me an emollient smile and said 'I think you'll find Kut very safe.' I fumed gently. The same might have been said of the Somme before the battle. Of course it was safe—we hadn't started work. I then attempted to draw communications equipment—there was none. Feeling that I had some claim to preferential treatment given that I was going to the field, I asked for the roster of those who had already drawn equipment. No such roster existed. I had never before encountered such implicit profligacy—clearly Britain was under more pressure than I knew. There was no set equipment scale—it all appeared rather *ad hoc*. The head of office finally gave me his Thuraya satellite phone, and I drew an additional base station sat-phone in a small attaché case. When I got to Kut I opened it with a small surge of proprietary excitement, only to find it had no antenna. It was my fault for not checking.

Despite such administrative difficulties, it was clear that Britain had carefully considered how best to protect its civilian staff. It was the only member of the Coalition that insisted that its nationals, particularly in Baghdad, travelled in armoured civilian vehicles. It had sub-contracted, at great expense, a British security company to provide these and armed protection teams to operate them. This undoubtedly saved lives, and substantially enhanced the capabilities of the CPA offices so equipped.

In insisting on these provisions the British Foreign Office had made a sensible and courageous decision. It is not often that the average British citizen in such circumstances is better looked after than his or her American counterpart—but in Iraq it was invariably so. My American Deputy was to be left with little but his wits for most of his time in Iraq. In October, however, these new vehicles were not yet present in sufficient numbers to meet the needs of the proposed CPA structure, although they were being bought from production lines as fast as they could be built and often air-freighted direct to theatre. Given British security strictures, this deficiency had begun to dictate the speed at which Governorates could now be staffed, at a time when this establishment process was seen as an over-riding priority.

Tension between operational demands and security safeguards is not unusual, though the fact that Britain was the only member of the Coalition to insist on such strictures inevitably complicated movement around the country. At this relatively early stage, the CPA was afflicted with a sort of systemic nonchalance, and Britain's preoccupation with such measures was probably thought fussy by others. A British citizen was invariably issued with a Kevlar helmet and flak jacket and asked to read (and later sign) the understanding about armoured travel. They might then find themselves marooned in their Baghdad offices because armoured vehicles remained so scarce as virtually to preclude general staff from leaving the base. This deficiency was to remain a significant constraint on headquarters personnel, and contributed to a slow erosion of understanding among them of conditions in the field.

My first impressions of the CPA were of a large organisation with unprecedented resources locked in logistical rather than ideological struggle. Much of its daily business appeared to consist of establishing and administering itself in the provinces and in the centre, rather than persuading the population of the merits of its intervention. There had been insufficient violence nationally to alter this approach. Clearly there were towns in the so-called 'Sunni Triangle' (an area dominated by the minority Sunni rather than Shi'ia Muslims) west of Baghdad, such as Fallujah or Tikrit, in which the Coalition faced significant opposition and in which death or injury were features of daily life, but these were regarded as anomalies. There were large swathes of Iraq in which there were no incidents at all.

Such regional variations, some of them pronounced, had affected CPA policy. The irregular pattern of incidents and this kind of asymmetrical local reaction to our presence lent itself to analysis in purely Manichean terms, particularly in light of the ruthlessness evident in incidents such as the UN bombing: clearly, the argument ran, there were small elements of Iraqi society sufficiently opposed to us as to admit no response but military defeat—and these calculations tended to focus minds on these military problems, and preclude early consideration of the concerns of an Iraqi majority that had so far proved both supportive and quiescent. This, in retrospect, was complacency and stemmed largely from a belief that our role as liberators, amplified for the sake of our national electorates, represented a currency whose validity was infinite. One should remember that this period was one in which the CPA's tenure in Iraq remained open-ended—there was no deadline imposed for transition between it and an Iraqi governing entity. I and my phantom team-mates thus had no idea how long we would be required to remain in Kut.

I walked the corridors of the Palace awash with sensation, anxiously clutching pieces of paper from each of my rushed meetings like talismans, unsure of what to do with myself, uncertain of my role and anxious to start for Kut. The command arrangements, at least, seemed admirably clear. There were two principal points to which I should report: Governance, the political wing of the CPA, and Operations, headed by Andrew Bearpark, a British friend whom I had known in both Bosnia-Herzegovina and Kosovo. These two chains then reported upward to Bremer.

The military chain of command was separate. The American four-star General Ricardo Sanchez, based in Victory Camp in west Baghdad, had some 165,000 troops under his command in a group-

ing known as CJTF 7—or Combined Joint Task Force 7—of which
140,000 were American and 9,000 British. The Americans ran the
Kurdish region in the north of the country and the centre, based on
Baghdad. A new Polish command ran 'Multi-National Division
Central-South' (MND-CS) from its headquarters in Babil province,
immediately adjacent to the city of Hillah. This Divisional area had
formerly been run by the Americans and was the area in which
Wasit province belonged. The British ran the south.

Andrew Bearpark, CPA Head of Operations and Infrastructure,
was a former Personal Private Secretary to Margaret Thatcher and a
passionate free-marketeer. He was a UK government contractee,
and the only member of the Palace complex to be given special dis-
pensation by Ambassador Bremer to smoke in his office, which he
did with enthusiasm. He told me that the issue of command chains
in the field had become contentious. There were four CPA regions
in Iraq, devised to match their military counterparts: South, South-
Central,[2] Central and North. Each had a regional head, which provided over-arching civil authority. Each had been asked to help
create the Governance teams in the provinces that fell within their
regional boundaries, and then to relinquish the political lead and
revert to the provision of programme and administrative support;
in South-Central, for example, Wasit was one of six provinces that
together formed a swathe running east from Jordan to Iran. This
establishment task was now virtually 'complete, yet the Regional
Centres, having produced the Governance teams, had been reluctant to relinquish their roles and now sought to interpose themselves
politically between teams and Baghdad. This was not my understanding of the way in which I was to operate. Iraq was simply too
large and fragmentary to impose layered political control of this

[2] The military referred to this area as Central-South, and this is the form generally
used here.

kind, and the boundaries delineating CPA South-Central con-
formed to no Iraqi political structure. So far this squabble over
chains of command had been fudged, and Ambassador Bremer had
balked at ruling on it. Andrew had gone as far as he could, and
hinted that the British lacked traction in such matters given that this
was an overwhelmingly American operation.

It had been arranged for me to make a formal call on Ambassador
Bremer. I thought his title, 'the Administrator', marvellously bland.
It gave no hint of the extraordinary powers he enjoyed; indeed it
removed all gravitas from his role. The contrast with the grandeur
of his surroundings—unavoidable, given the tastes of his Iraqi predecessor—was acute. He sat at the centre of the Palace at one end of
a long room behind double doors, in a suite adjacent to a dome of
dizzying height and guarded by soldiers. The acoustics of this atrium
faithfully relayed every step and whisper, and hence imbued entrance to these offices with a subtle dramatism which I rather
enjoyed. At the opposite end of this room was a second set of double
doors, behind which was the British representative, Sir Jeremy
Greenstock. Between these two offices sat their respective staffs—
security, military advisers, personal assistants and private secre-
taries. Tom Krajeski, a charming and cultured State Department
official from the Governance office who had done a great deal to
make me feel welcome, took me in.

My immediate reaction on meeting Bremer was that Britain does
not generally produce people of this kind. It is clearly absurd to
suggest that he might command a better education or mind than his
putative British counterpart—no nation has such a monopoly. Yet
he appeared to combine a rare mixture of attributes that struck me
as peculiarly American. Of youthful appearance, medium build and
tanned, with a luxuriant head of hair, he exuded tough self-confidence and carried himself like the athlete I was later told he once
had been. He was casually dressed in an open-necked green shirt

and tan trousers. It was difficult to say whether his U.S. Army desert boots were affectation or gave the lie to it. Here, his clothes suggested, was a man suited for all roles, be they in Bedouin camp or boardroom. I wondered whether the power of his position—he was after all the ultimate authority in the country—had somehow bred the man; or whether America, at the very apogee of its power, had created him herself. He was above all an executive, and resembled, I thought, the CEO of a large American company having a few sales difficulties in one of its more far-flung divisions. There was one more thing that struck me, and this was perhaps a peculiarly British reaction: there was something a touch inhuman about Bremer, as though this professionalism, with its firm dry handshakes and quick formal smiles, had somehow drained away his humanity. One felt he would be a difficult person to get to know.

The meeting was brief and workmanlike. Clearly conscious of the guilty frisson of post-colonial excitement among the British in Iraq, Bremer compared the task of Governorate Coordinator with that of a British colonial District Commissioner. What was needed was the broadest possible participation of Iraqis in the political and physical re-fashioning of the country. Where there was no civil society it should be created. Where we had established sets of regular interlocutors we should now add others to broaden and re-invigorate political debate. Councils should be established in towns and villages where there were none—Iraqis should be given a stake in the democratic process. There was a caveat—there should be no elections. We were not ready for them because the requisite safeguards were not in place. I listened, both inwardly mesmerised by the job he described and slightly appalled at its scope.

I refrained from questions, left the office and closed the double doors behind me. Tom Krajeski handed me a letter of appointment from Bremer and a sheaf of reports, before wishing me luck and returning to Governance. Entirely free of pomposity, remote, probably unforgiving of error, and somewhat unclubbable, as the British say—a man who would not mix or invite one for a beer in the evening: these were my impressions of Ambassador L. Paul Bremer III. I wondered what the British Foreign Office thought of him.

One of the points about the British, I often explain to American friends, is that the cult of the amateur is historically important. Calm under-statement is also essential. One should not be seen to try too hard at anything, or ever to claim competence in any sphere at all. This gets the British into all kinds of difficulties, particularly when applying for jobs. A friend of mine insists that the only correct response when asked if one has any interests is to look one's interlocutor straight in the eye and firmly reply 'None whatsoever'. The late-nineteenth-century British Prime Minister, Lord Salisbury, once characterised his view of British foreign policy as floating gently downstream in a boat and putting out one's oar at intervals to avoid collisions.

Although the Foreign Office has changed, this appearance of studied indolence survives in some quarters, particularly among its more senior staff. My experience has been that, irrespective of the matter at hand, one's Foreign Office interlocutor will always convey the sense that vastly more pressing things are afoot, and thereby that you yourself are rather unimportant. As I have previously explained, I am only too ready to believe that this is true. As I was ushered in to see Sir Jeremy Greenstock therefore, among Britain's most senior diplomats and a former Ambassador to the United Nations, I gained the distinct impression that I had torn him away from the planning of a major naval engagement.

We stood awkwardly together in the middle of a large room, the door ajar. He looked at me gravely and with, I thought, a fair measure of disappointment. There was an array of tanned seats in one corner. I was not asked to sit in any of them. He was tall, careful and studied. He had devil's eyebrows that gave him a permanently interrogative air and framed a careful, intelligent face. His entire body appeared to be a giant diplomatic antenna that evaluated posture, expression, mannerisms and speech and radiated his impressions direct to London. When I spoke he listened so intently that I immediately stopped. Here again was a consummate professional, but of a different kind to Bremer. Sir Jeremy, a former Classics teacher at Eton, one of Britain's premier private schools, had been asked to go to Iraq to be Britain's representative—IRAQREP in the shorthand of the day—instead of taking the retirement that was his due after New York. It was rumoured that his relationship with Bremer had been difficult, and that there was no personal chemistry between the two men. If true, I cannot say I would have found this surprising—it was hard to imagine any two people more dissimilar. I had been told that Sir Jeremy's favourite word was 'lacuna', from the Latin for 'hollow' or 'gap', and employed in the political sense. He used the word often in conversation, a foible celebrated by his staff who commissioned sweat-shirts with the legend 'UK Special Representative's Office—It's a Lacuna'. It seemed most unlikely that Bremer—the restless, slightly pugnacious executive that I had seen across the hall—shared this predilection.

Our meeting was brief and Sir Jeremy said little. After a moment an aide entered the room to end my agony, presumably to tell him that forward elements of Her Majesty's Fleet had sighted the enemy. I made my apologies, offered a damp hand-shake and left, discomfited. I doubted that I would remain long in his thoughts. The traditional British welcome hadn't altered much, and the contrast between my encounters with him and our American partners was striking.

On the whole I had always felt much more at home with the Americans than with my own people, but doubt that this was due to any historical or pre-ordained affinity. Indeed, the gulf between this expectation of instant brotherhood between the Americans and the

British and the awkward reality often led to disaffection. As a child I attended the Anglo-American school in Kuwait and grew up with Americans. I had worked for the American oilfield concern Halliburton Services for four years in my teens and twenties. These youthful bonds notwithstanding, I was impressed by the American working practices I encountered on the drilling rigs of the Arabian Gulf. Especially striking to an Englishman was the absence of class distinction—to the untutored eye, at least, everyone simply worked till the job was done, regardless of what it might be. I remember the entire rig crew working until dawn to overcome a drilling problem that had taken us off-line, and the feeling of brotherhood that followed at breakfast. All of the staff on board was American except for me. My memories are of lean, rangy men with a strong work ethic, taciturn, tough and funny. At Christmas time the Company gave us bonuses. There was a unifying, classless, loyalty, and hard work and financial reward were closely linked. I had seen nothing like this in Britain.

Despite this shared experience, my renewed contact with Americans reminded me sharply how little we British generally knew of them as people, and how easy it was to be seduced by crude portrayals of the United States in the British media. It struck me in my first few hours in Iraq that Americans seemed in no way prone to the kind of melancholy romanticism shown by many of their British counterparts about some supposed 'special relationship'. In the American view, any such relationship should be properly founded on results. Where Britain was unable to influence a political or military outcome, it was simply not invited to the table. Clearly this was often the case—America was providing overwhelmingly the most money, people, logistics and raw combat power, and Britain's effort was dwarfed in comparison. It was ingenuous to think that we could bank eternally on some diffuse notion of mid-twentieth-century wartime camaraderie—it existed, of course, but that did not make it powerful enough to eclipse present political interests. Yet time and again one would come across small groups of Britons in thrall to an imagined trans-Atlantic romance bemoaning their exclusion from one process or another.

One had, I thought, to work hard and long at such partnerships, though it is probably true that Britain has to work less hard than most. Despite the fact that a reverential silence settles in my parents' home whenever Franklin Delano Roosevelt's name is mentioned, it is clear that the British-American relationship of 1941–5 was no less fractious than that of Iraq in 2003. It is probably true that national peculiarities complicated understanding—the British were wont to give the impression that, had they only been in charge of Iraq, everything would somehow run a great deal more smoothly. I imagine the Americans found this rather irritating. The British would, meanwhile, rightly highlight the fatal American belief that everyone secretly wants to be an American, and bemoan a lack of U.S. curiosity about Iraq, its peoples and preoccupations. One doubts such complaints are novel.

After my meeting with Greenstock I sat under the vast cupola outside Bremer's offices and watched the surrounding bustle as the business of running Iraq unfolded as an intricate ballet on the tiled floor. In the office behind me was StratCom (Strategic Communications), charged with press, public affairs and external relations. The place was filled with people, each in a partitioned space, with televisions banked against the wall. Their task was clearly pivotal to our success but they reputedly lacked a defined strategy. Near me, security people with cropped hair lounged on benches in black safari-jackets, complete with knives, pistols and short machine-guns. In front a great tide of people, largely military, ebbed and flowed: U.S. Marines in their speckled camouflage uniforms and others in the more conventional garb of U.S. Army and Air Force, walking in groups or singly; Iraqi local staff; grim-faced men in suits, chewing gum remorselessly; slow-moving men in jeans with a pistol bouncing on each thigh; and a kaleidoscope of Australian, Polish and British uniforms. Outside the building an array of armoured 4×4s endlessly came and went, nose to tail, with sirens wailing intermittently. Helicopters surged over the building in pairs to alight at the 'Washington' landing-site within the compound. What all this activity meant and precisely where my own efforts were to interweave with it mystified me. I simply had to get to Kut before I suffocated.

I opened one of the reports Tom Krajeski had given me after my meeting with Bremer. It was from my American Deputy Timothy S. Timmons, who had been in Kut alone acting in my stead as over-arching civil authority for some four weeks. Formerly an Army officer, he was now a State Department official—Iraq was his second posting. His first report dealt with the province's 145 km border with Iran, and specifically with the one border crossing point, Arafat, that fell within our jurisdiction. In sparse and deliberate language Timmons set out the problems: there was neither infrastructure nor leadership and no staff worth the name. There were no rules, and had there been any, there was no one to enforce them. Corruption was systematic and widespread. Customs officials had looted all that the Coalition had left for them, and taken both alternator and battery from the generator: there was thus no power either. Meanwhile a mass of people pushed through the crossing every day, principally to the holy cities of Karbala and Najaf in the interior; an estimated 10,000 of them had crossed the border on the day the report was written. It was, quite simply, chaos—so much so that the Iraqi Governor of the province, a judge and Coalition appointee, complaining that the influx of Iranians had driven up prices, had closed the border. The CPA had forced him to re-open it.

There was something rather nineteenth century about that message, and I fancied I tasted the dust in my mouth as I absorbed each dry and measured paragraph from the Iraqi hinterland. In the air-conditioned cool of the atrium, the impact of that report was the more profound; and, as I looked through the main door of the palace and the portico beyond, the palms seemed fixed in the sullen and immobile white heat of the afternoon. What would I find in Kut, and what would these next months bring? I looked at my frustratingly uninformative map and traced the course of the Tigris with one finger.

I had not gathered the full extent of what remained to be done to establish the CPA office in Wasit, let alone to supervise the running of the province. I had imagined that we were much further advanced with the Iraq project than was now apparent. I was told privately by Andy Bearpark that merely to establish a permanent presence by Christmas would be regarded as a success, though I was determined to do better than that. Kut had rather receded from view since the end of the war because there had been no fighting there, and little had changed subsequently. The U.S. Marine Corps (USMC) had taken the city without major incident during their advance north on Baghdad, and handed over to the Ukrainian brigade in the newly-formed Multi-National Division Central-South (MND C-S) sector in August. Since then we had done little but maintain the *status quo*.

There was also difficulty in defining who exactly 'we' were. It was extraordinary, to British eyes at least, that here was a major foreign commitment for the U.S. being managed almost exclusively by the Department of Defense rather than by the State Department, which one might have assumed to have the requisite regional knowledge, political expertise and language skills. This seemed counter-intuitive, and one would ordinarily imagine that so complex and risky a commitment as the 2003 foray into Iraq would not have been allowed to become the subject of what appeared to be inter-departmental wrangling within the U.S. government. And from what I had seen in my short time in Iraq, the British had not sent their Arabists. Of the four GCs only one, Henry Hogger in Basra, had obvious Middle Eastern credentials. The Governance office had one or two people who had worked in adjacent countries, but my chief memory was of ranks of empty desks. Although I had grown up in the Gulf and knew some Arabic, I was far from being an expert on the region. Certainly I had experience of conflict and post-conflict reconstruction in south-eastern Europe in both political and physical senses, but few of the people I met had even this. It was clear that the experts were not, in the main, here—partly because such people commanded good salaries without having to come to a country which promised an unusually high security risk; and arguably because the American-led Coalition, buoyed by perceived military success against a regime once seen as an intractable international problem, felt that it had no need of advice.

The staffing of this enterprise had been difficult from the start. The end of the war in Iraq had heralded the coming of the sub-contractor. In almost every sphere of CPA endeavour a contractor loomed large. Some wielded considerable responsibilities, and the Halliburton contractor Kellogg Brown and Root (KBR) was perhaps the most striking example of this. KBR was contracted to provide 'life support' to both the CPA and the military: this entailed all contracting work, all catering, the supply of all items from swimming pools to lavatory paper, and the hiring and supervision of local staff. It was a bold idea, and removed at a stroke a major logistical problem for what remained a small civilian operation when compared to its military counterpart. Yet logistics, in the end, underpins strategy, and the fact that this important responsibility had been allocated outside the tactical command of the CPA was to have important repercussions, not least because the thoroughly impressive Halliburton people of my youth had not, in general and to my great regret, come to Iraq either.

In retrospect it is clear that we were spread thin and not expecting opposition. We were not properly configured as an occupation force, and credible military power is an indispensable pre-requisite if one is to re-fashion a regime, particularly one as deeply rooted as the Ba'ath Party. Civil-military command arrangements in theatre were opaque, and distances large. The majority of CPA personnel did not have armoured vehicles, and a number, including many of my American civilian colleagues, either completely lacked protective flak jackets or the ceramic plates that turned them into bullet-proof, rather than anti-fragmentation, vests. There were insufficient numbers of troops in theatre, and the looting and violence that had dogged the early weeks of occupation had given the impression of systemic weakness. This was exacerbated by the attempt to broaden the membership of the Coalition: each new contingent, no matter how competent its individuals, further com-plicated an already complex and varied command structure. At local level there were simply too many organisations in the com-mand chain, each with its own discrete security policy and hierar-chy over which, ultimately, the CPA had scant control. All these things would return to haunt us.

In the excitement of departure none of this actively concerned me. I left Baghdad on the afternoon of 3 October, checking out from the Green Zone's Rashid Hotel and waving goodbye to my South African room-mate, whose unusual task was to look after the private zoo of Saddam Hussein's son Uday. We sped nose to tail south through the outskirts of Baghdad on Route Tampa in two Chevrolet Suburbans. Traffic of all descriptions surged around us. Gaily painted trucks of fantastic design vied with small yellow taxis, each berating the other in strident and entirely routine outrage. The inside lane was clogged with motorcycles, each carrying up to four passengers, and with bicycles sporting coloured lights and a mul-titude of mirrors. Some women were veiled, others not; many of the men wore traditional Arab garb with checked *kaffiyah* head-dress. All eyed us in a manner that seemed impassive, almost leaden. Away to our right by the side of the road, I saw a great mound of discarded and destroyed Iraqi armoured vehicles lying jumbled one on top of the other. Tanks, bridging equipment, trucks and bent and blackened artillery pieces were silhouetted by the evening sun; and a dusty haze, lifted by the wind and turned lurid by the light, gave the scene an almost cinematic dramatism. I wondered at the human story inherent in what we now saw, and wondered too what the Iraqis who swirled about us thought about our destruction of their army. They stared at us as we passed. The smiles I proffered were tentative.

An Australian officer named Chris McHugh drove me south at dizzying speed, with one hand on the wheel and the other on a Beretta pistol. As he did so he issued a running commentary on the road ahead: 'Mosque on the left with a crowd outside. Watch that truck. What's that bastard doing? There's our turning. Is the other car still with us?' The vehicle surged and slowed in cadence, as we wove our way down the road and I affected a nonchalance that made my jaw ache. At Chris's side was a U.S. Army intelligence officer, Captain Sallaye Kakay. Both were from CPA South-Central in Hillah, the Regional Centre that had spawned the CPA presence in Wasit. The most striking thing about these vehicles was that they were thin-skinned, which no amount of bluster could obscure. When I informed the British office that I had found Chris and Sallaye in Operations, and thereby procured my lift to Kut via Hillah, I was immediately asked whether this would be in armoured vehicles. Reluctant to be branded a liar in my first few days as a beacon of hope to the Iraqi people, I had mumbled 'I believe so'. I was burning to get started and unsettled by the anonymity of the Palace's echoing corridors and throngs of people. But there was more to it than that: I felt strongly, as I have already intimated, that Britain needed to get on a war footing in Iraq to do the job assigned to us—as so often, the civil effort could not match the pace of the military, and the lack of determination and urgency exasperated me.

I could not help also feeling that this preoccupation with security suggested a bureaucratic fear of getting into trouble rather than genuine concern for my welfare.

Those who oversaw the Iraq operation should have understood from the outset that civilian casualties were inevitable. I thought it wrong to establish an environment in which this risk was merely shouldered by those leaving the gate. Every time a vehicle departed or a helicopter took off it had to be understood by everyone that the move entailed the risk of violent injury or death. This did not axiomatically mean that the risk should not be taken. The Iraqi project could not simply be placed on hold. Complacency had bred the idea that Iraq was a generally forgiving environment, and that we had time to organise ourselves. We did not. I could not contemplate saying to my new colleagues that I would not ride in their vehicles because British policy demanded armour—a facility not due to arrive in theatre for another week.

As Baghdad receded behind us our horizon broadened to show a vista of flat grey desert, largely unrelieved by anything except occasional mounds, tracks and copses of palm trees. Salt-gatherers skimmed the surface of saline pools by the road, and piled their harvest in pyramids at the verge. The dual carriageway was straight and in good condition and led inexorably south. Encouraged, Chris put on some dreadful music and accelerated contentedly. Somewhere to the west was the Euphrates, and to the east the Tigris. As a child I had been driven along this road from Kuwait by my parents on several occasions. Our destination, Hillah, was a city that had been built next to Babylon, of which the ruins would be visible from the road—as would Uday Hussein's palace, which he had built in the midst of them. It was now occupied by the Polish Multi-National Division HQ. I had long wanted to see the famous archaeological sites of Iraq, but it was dark when we arrived.

Regional Centre Hillah was typical of the sites that the CPA adopted in Iraq. Its base was a hotel formerly run by the Iraqi

Ministry of Tourism which served as accommodation and offices for CPA staff; it overlooked a river which flowed past its front some 100 metres from the hotel steps. Surrounding it was a system of wire and barriers, the whole secured by a sub-contracted security force made up of Gurkhas from Nepal, all of whom had formerly served in the British Army. Typically, too, the hotel did not have enough rooms to house all the burgeoning staff now working at the site, and the overflow was moved to a small container village of two floors adjacent to the hotel and surrounded by the ubiquitous T-Walls. These were sections of pre-fabricated concrete wall of twelve feet high and eight feet wide that sat on a T-shaped base, designed to interlock with one another and to provide protection from small arms, fragmentation and rocket-propelled grenades. They also provided cover from view.

The camp felt like a science-fiction outpost on the barren surface of some hostile red planet. A persistent and unlooked-for image of myself as a twenty-first-century homesteader haunted me during my fifteen hours there and subsequent visits. It was enhanced by the fact of my impending move still further into the interior via this curious staging post. I wondered about Timmons, who must once have taken the same route. Around the compound small generator light-sets whirred noisily, projecting a glow from their towers far out over the palms and river bank. Each of the beams caught a mass of wheeling insects. The sky, despite these intrusions, was glorious. Dogs howled outside the perimeter fence, and isolated gun shots could just be heard from the city. I trudged across the gravel and through a gap in the T-Walls, let myself into my Portakabin container, dropped my luggage on the floor and examined my transit home. I sat on the unyielding bed and, abruptly overcome by the institutional formality of my surroundings—the toy-town sink, the single unusable cupboard, the two yellow hangars, the crisp acrylic shower curtain—surrendered briefly to loneliness.

Mike Gfoeller, head of the Regional Centre and ostensibly responsible for a huge swathe of Iraq, wore a white suit, a broad white hat, an automatic pistol and a sizeable knife with a silver hilt. A large moustache and flowing hair gave him the air of a desperado forced by economic circumstances to find work abroad. He sat behind a desk piled with paper and cuneiform bricks from the Babylon site some 2 kilometres away. I knew him to be a State Department official, who had formerly dealt principally with the countries of the former Soviet Union, but had also spent two years as a student in Cairo. He spoke both Arabic and Russian fluently and had been in Hillah since the end of the war. Hillah served as the focal point for six provinces—Wasit, Al Qadasiyah, Babil, Karbala, An Najaf and Al Anbar, or the 'Heartland' as he called it. The region included the holy cities of Najaf and Karbala, which were shrine cities of particular importance to Shi'ia Muslims.

He said that he had personally selected me; I had been formerly unaware that there were any other applicants for the job. He spoke fast, continually lurching between poles of extravagance and amusing self-deprecation. He began by announcing flatly 'I am the senior State Department representative in Iraq'. To the English ear, this smacked of Taking Oneself Seriously, a monumental *faux pas*, and I dropped my gaze, smiling politely. When I looked up Mike was laughing. 'So you can see what a fucking mess *we're* in'. I thought, as we talked, that he showed the suppressed excitement of someone whose personality, ambitions and task have merged by an unaccountable and happy chance; and that here in Iraq in 2003 Mike and a number of others were enjoying themselves hugely. I liked him, and he showed me kindness and loyalty, though we would not always agree; and the issue of command—bluntly, whether or not he was in my hierarchy—was to dog us from the outset.

He saw our effort in terms that I thought peculiarly American—not simplistic, but with boundaries drawn with darker ink than a

European might employ. What he described was, at heart, a contest between good and evil, a process by which we sought to keep 'the bad guys off-balance' while we re-built the country politically, physically and morally. This would be done, as he saw it, by emplacing three large policy 'anchors' in each of the provinces: human rights, women's rights, and the fostering of tribal democracy in a bid to shape and utilise the inherent power of the Iraqi tribal system. It was not clear who the 'bad guys' were, but in October 2003 a number of assumptions were implicit : they were a small group, who could use Iraq's porous borders to move at will; they enjoyed little or no mainstream support; and they could be defeated.

I was not persuaded by this notion of anchors, and thought it gimmickry. While human rights and women's rights were clearly desirable, it seemed to me that these would be products of any success we had in re-shaping the country, rather than its principal locomotives. I was not against advancing on these fronts, but did not see them as priorities. The tribes belonged in a separate category, and qualified for early consideration by virtue of their imagined power. I was all for co-opting them, if this were judged appropriate, but was less sure that introducing them to the delights of democracy would secure for us the stability we needed in the short term. There is no substitute for control—though we did not have sufficient troops to retain it without public consent—and this control might then permit an environment in which the rule of law might flourish and normality return. Reform and opportunity could then follow.

I was not sure at the end of our conversation that we had a plan worthy of the name. Everything seemed extraordinarily *ad hoc*. This was hardly Mike's fault—we were simply dwarfed by the canvas. My province alone was about two-thirds the size of Kosovo. Given the small size of the proposed Governance Team in Kut and other provinces like it, much of the responsibility for discharging our civil governance and oversight tasks would clearly fall to the military;

and it seemed unlikely in my case that the Ukrainians had the experience to do it. This was not a reflection on their military competence: civil-military cooperation was something on which relatively sophisticated NATO armies had only recently concentrated. We appeared to be assuming that the Iraqi population would give us time to correct our mistakes, and this presumption had often proved mistaken elsewhere in the world. While there are clear dangers in attempting to compare different post-conflict reconstruction enterprises with each other, an invariable feature of such situations is impatience—impatience for justice, for change, for progress. And this in turn prescribes a period in which genuine advance, however arbitrarily defined, will be expected by the public, both in theatre and at home. This window can be enlarged by careful management of expectation and adept public relations, coupled with judicious intervention for maximum positive effect. Inevitably the reverse is also true.

Clearly it was incumbent on me now to sit quiet and reserve judgement, and I did so. Part of the reason for this was the unprecedented role planned for financial intervention. To some extent we hoped to spend our way out of trouble, and Mike's thoughts interested me. His particular genius lay in his ability to extract money from the CPA for his region and to fire it outward for immediate and high-impact use. There would be no other regional head that could keep up with him in the months to come, nor any so willing to delegate financial responsibility when it was needed and cut through needless bureaucracy. All the Governorate Coordinators would be allocated millions of dollars to spend in their provinces, derived chiefly from seized Iraqi assets. That day Mike allocated me $3.5 million and asked that one million of this be spent on the province's police. The idea of employing financial muscle as a weapon on this scale was genuinely new to me. How could it be otherwise? Such money had never been made available in this quick-fire manner in south-eastern Europe. Cash spent on this scale might have decisive effect.

That night I lay awake in my container-bedroom trying to decide whether to turn off my hugely efficient air-conditioner and await death by dehydration, or to keep it running and be woken up every ten minutes by the exultant clatter of the unit's compressor and its malevolent blue light. In the end I renounced both and did two kilometres on the rowing machine behind the kitchen block. The air was thick and damp and clogged my lungs; but there was something soothing about the arithmetical certainties of the stroke counter after the maelstrom of uncertainty through which I had lived during the past two days.

We assembled for departure next morning at seven, with mirrored sunglasses and short Kalashnikov assault rifles clearly *de rigueur* among my escort. Some, one felt, were living out a private fantasy. Chris McHugh had again volunteered to do the driving, but this regrettably meant that he had brought his music with him. A very large former New York police officer and paratrooper, Bruce Hopfengardner, came to the car window and wordlessly placed a large box of moist lavatory tissue beside me. The engines started, and we careered through the protective chicanes of the Regional Centre complex eastwards for Kut.

2

AL-KUT

It is difficult to recapture the blend of emotions that coloured my arrival in Al-Kut on 5 October 2003. The flat-lands of southern Iraq afforded no rock-strewn pass where we might have paused to survey the city that was to be my home. There was no vantage-point where we could gather in that last moment of solitude as the engines of our hard-worked vehicles gradually cooled in the wind, or refuge where one might draw breath and mentally prepare for new and onerous responsibilities. There had been only the open road, flat and remorseless.

My memories of the time are of the heat radiating through the blued windows of the Chevrolet Suburban like a warm liquid as we drove the two hours from Hillah to the city. The landscape was like a vast grey ocean, its flat expanse broken only by ancient palm groves behind low red walls and the sprawl of tumbledown mud villages. Veteran tractors stood on earthen ramps, their starter-batteries long gone. Sheep milled around thorn enclosures. Children sprang from the undergrowth, waving. The clatter of an old irrigation pump would intrude on the hiss of the vehicle's air conditioning and fade. We passed battered traders' vehicles and buses travelling east wreathed in blue smoke; destroyed tanks and armoured personnel carriers beside the road; and, once, a military convoy with goggled and helmeted machine-gunners training their weapons to left and right from the tops of their vehicles. A gunner waved at us as we passed. Huge concrete structures shimmered on the horizon in almost mystical isolation. These, Chris said, were Saddam Hussein's military airfields, now abandoned but piled high with discarded bombs, missiles and other ordnance.

The city of Kut, its presence unheralded save for urchin fuel salesmen with oil drums, a triumphal archway and a concrete façade on which Saddam Hussein's visage was still just visible despite attempts to efface it, had the feel of a staging post rather than a destination. The arch, in faded red brick and damaged mosaic, appeared to promise more than the town could realistically deliver. One did not really arrive in the city—one simply stopped. To the north-west lay Baghdad; and to the south, Amara and Basra. Iran was 80 km. to the north-east. As we drove through the arch two police officers, sitting in the shade, noted our passage without interest. A third was asleep. We had crossed the river Tigris at Numaniyah. It lay now to our right, a ribbon of green water 200 metres across and shocking in its brooding presence in these drab surrounds; and we converged gradually with it as we drove the two kilometers into town toward the CPA site.

Wasit province consists of six districts, each centred on a city. The largest of these was Kut, with some 350,000 inhabitants according to the food ration roll; and the smallest, Badrah, a town of no more than 18,000 people near the Arafat crossing between Wasit and Iran on which Timmons had so recently reported. The province is 120 km. long and some 110 wide at the most, and its north-western corner, in which lies the province's second city, Suwayrah, of 260,000 people, is just 55 km. from Baghdad. There were also eleven sub-districts, centered on smaller areas of habitation, though each formed a satellite to one of the district cities. Ration roll figures suggested that the province's population was approximately 970,000.

We turned off the main road to central Kut, and retraced our course in parallel along an adjacent route on the river bank. It was strewn with debris and ran past an abandoned children's playground. The equipment—small Ferris wheels, swings and merry-go-rounds—had been looted, and the remaining pieces lay canted in the dirt. On the river bank were several reed huts and a collection of boats, including a circular craft like a coracle. Looking upriver, the Tigris flowed straight for kilometres, flanked by thick undulating stands of reeds. Ahead was a barrier manned by Ukrainian troops behind a half-hearted vehicle chicane of concrete blocks, daubed with untidily spray-painted instructions in red Cyrillic. The red and white pole was raised and we swept inside in a pall of choking dust.

Rushing anywhere, particularly with weapons, may give one a fine sense of resolute progress, but the re-acquaintance with reality that must follow can be depressing; and so it was that day. If our complex of former Ba'ath party buildings by the Tigris conveyed anything, it was a feeling of stubborn and collective indolence. A small Ukrainian garrison force occupied a white building beside the main road. Next to it was a half-ruined complex of rooms on two floors and a palm grove. A third ribbed and honey-coloured building known as the Villa provided a makeshift office while preparations were made to begin work on the biggest of the four, named 'Tarawa House' by the U.S. Marines after the Second World War island battle in the Pacific. This was 100 metres long and consisted of two floors. It had been comprehensively looted, apparently, I was later told, by the police after the U.S. Marines' departure. Air-conditioning units had been levered from the wall; door and window frames removed; and even wiring and light switches wrenched from the masonry. One or two windows had survived, but overwhelmingly Tarawa House and the larger complex looked simply derelict.

I sat motionless in the car for a moment. A dust-devil whirled on the river bank, and a stubborn gusting wind blew across the reed thickets in the shallows. Two anti-aircraft cannon had been left by the Iraqis—both looked undamaged and still stood by the river with twin barrels pointing skyward. Discarded ammunition boxes lay beside them. As I opened my car door the heat jumped in beside me like an animal. A small herd of water-buffalo eyed me, impassively chewing. I walked towards Timothy Timmons, my Deputy, to say hello.

Timm had been alone in Kut for a month. I can still see him watching us as the dust cleared, waiting for us to disembark as I was to watch many visitors arrive myself in the months to come. How was one ever to explain adequately the relentless strain and friction of CPA service in Iraq to one's visitors? How many times were we to watch cars depart or helicopters fade from view, frustrated by the growing gulf between Baghdad and its outposts?

Despite the preponderance of U.S. over British effort in Iraq, Britain's supporting role was clearly of political importance to the Americans. Any schism between these primary allies would have been particularly damaging, and it seemed to me that all of us needed to do our best to make it function. I was determined to have a good working relationship with Timm regardless of any difficulties that might arise. We would, after all, have the opportunity personally to test the American-British relationship to destruction during the months ahead.

Bearded, lean, and over six feet tall, Timm looked like the European idea of an American homesteader and I think there was some of that dogged missionary zeal in him. His father had flown fighter-bombers from Britain in the Second World War, and had a ranch in Texas where Timm spent much of his time. Something of that implied toughness and moral strength emanated from him when we first met: it was not difficult to imagine him branding cattle, clearing mesquite brush or pacing a distant fence. He was a first-class horseman and had an encyclopedic knowledge of firearms; had been an officer in Germany in the armoured infantry; and had just concluded a State Department posting in Pakistan. For Timm, I think it fair to say, Europe's broad failure to assume what he saw as its responsibilities in Iraq was difficult to understand—it had lost its moral compass and fallen into a state of drowsy contentment, a condition largely made possible by American support and sacrifice. He appeared immune to the kind of soul-searching to which I was addicted. I doubt if it ever occurred to him to question the American presence in Iraq, not through ignorance of the debate, but because there could be no practical profit in further discussion of something that had already occurred. The Ba'ath regime had clearly been cruel and corrupt, and its extirpation would in the end be seen as a moral good. In many Iraqis he saw the sins of weakness and moral decay, and armed intervention by the Coalition as no more than a benchmark of state failure in its final and most humiliating form. Weapons of mass destruction or no weapons of mass destruction, it was quite clear to him that these were the Augean stables and he was holding the fire hose.

While Timm, I think, saw the American brand of armed vigilance and interventionism as something tantamount to a national vocation, this neither blinded him to America's own failings, nor those of her countrymen in Iraq, who would rightly become wary of giving him the impression that they were impeding the CPA's progress in Wasit province. He was a hard man, and sometimes irascible—doubtless he made his enemies—but in all the time I knew him he was loyal to a fault, led from the front and assumed responsibility unhesitatingly. I could not reasonably have asked for more. I came to rely on him absolutely and we became firm friends.

Only when my escort left that afternoon to return to Hillah did I become fully conscious of our isolation and the extraordinary nature of our task. A heavy, almost oppressive silence settled on the site, broken only by the chorus of frogs from the reeds and the chirp of cicadas. A flight of cranes wheeled in to land on a mid-stream island as I looked out over the river. There was something comfortingly immutable about the measured passage of the water, if only because all else appeared so unpredictable. My arrival in the country and passage to Kut had created an avalanche of sensation that was only now fading, to be replaced by a dull foreboding about the future. We had so much to do. The very dereliction of the site seemed to mock my imaginings.

Timm and I walked the complex, awkward in our new-found proximity, our footsteps echoing from the walls. The Tigris looked beautiful as the evening approached, and great bands of orange and purple soared skyward above the palms on the opposite bank. Bats played in their hundreds over our heads. The site had yet to be properly cleared by Explosive Ordnance Disposal teams, and we were cautious where we stepped. Timm had cleared out the Villa to serve as our temporary office while Tarawa was prepared, and thereby recovered Rocket Propelled Grenades (RPG) and boxes of 20 mm. armour-piercing cannon shells. The former had been given to the Kazakh ordnance disposal detachment billeted with the Ukrainians; and the shells now sat in a lean-to in the yard. In a dusty second-floor room in Tarawa, the largest of the four buildings, Timm showed me our recently-installed Internet in a Box.

I had two official e-mails. The first was from the British Foreign Office's Iraq Policy Unit. It said 'Thank you for your message regarding your intention to travel onwards to Kut. I regret to say that you cannot do so till your security detail and armoured vehicles arrive. These will pick you up from Hillah 10 October. You are not to move to Kut till then. Sorry.' I thought briefly, and then wrote 'I have just read your message of 3 October, together with its injunction against travel to Kut. I see a number of obstacles in complying with your instruction. Foremost among these is probably the fact that I am already there. *Alea iacta est*. Mark.' I then felt guilty.

I explained the situation to Timm, who said 'What are they going to do? Send you to Iraq?' Then, gently: 'Do you think anyone else *wants* this job?'

I had not really thought about service in Iraq in that way before. He had a point. Our assets at this stage appeared to amount to a green thin-skinned Chevrolet Suburban with a cracked windscreen that I had seen outside; an all but derelict former Ba'ath Party complex, complete with a single, poignant truncheon propped up in a corner of one of the rooms; the internet system; a Kalashnikov and two pistols, one of which had no fore-sight; and a signed mandate from Ambassador Bremer charging me to oversee the province.

Actually there was more. In one wing of the building in which we now sat was a Reservist U.S. counter-intelligence team of about ten people, who worked directly to Central-South Divisional HQ in Babil, and seldom spoke to us. Their task was to collect intelligence about threats to the Combined Joint Task Force and the CPA. They were administratively self-contained: they had brought their own linguists and had two unmarked saloon cars which they used to drive themselves around the province. In the Villa, meanwhile, camped a capable and tough American, John Doane, from a sub-contracted organisation called 'Research Triangle Institute', or RTI, which had been awarded the contract to pursue so-called democratisation and civic education initiatives across Iraq on the CPA's behalf. He had already recruited a number of local people to shadow the Iraqi branch Ministries in the city. Finally, on the top floor of the Villa a U.S. Special Forces team, based in Babil, retained two rooms as an outpost for their provincial visits. Timm had signed for the Villa from them, and they had given him some lurid Iraqi furniture.

The second message on my screen was from a man named Cameron in Baghdad, who was responsible for the 'Hundred Thousand Jobs' programme. This entailed each of Iraq's eighteen provinces

enlisting a number of unemployed people to carry out civic main-
tenance tasks via the Ministry of Public Works by drawing on public
funds through a letter of guarantee. All that was needed was to take
the letter to the bank, ask the Ministry office to begin recruiting a
workforce of 7,000, detach a team member to deal with the issue
for a month, and carry out spot checks on the labour force throughout the province to ensure that the process ran smoothly. In reply I
explained politely that I thought this a fine plan, but was less sure we
were sufficiently advanced to take on these responsibilities. I later
received a message from him informing me with subtle menace that
the '100,000 Jobs programme will go on, with or without you'.
This was a considerable relief to us at the time.

For the last month Timm had been living with the Ukrainians in a
tent at Delta Camp, one of Saddam Hussein's former military airfields, and now the headquarters of the Ukrainian Brigade. It lay
across the river on the outskirts of Kut, 4 kilometres by road from
our site. Each morning Ukrainian troops would escort Timm from
the camp to our complex, and in the evening he would call for them
on the radio he had been given and they would send a detail to
escort him back. It was now time to go. Rather self-consciously
I donned the flak-jacket I had been issued, unsure of what I was protecting myself against: Al Qaeda? Cameron? It had been allocated to
me in England, together with a helmet, a net laundry bag, a pair of
suede shoes and some extraordinary sunglasses that looked like
welder's goggles. I do not know who had recommended the issue of
this ensemble—one imagines an obscure research department in
London—and assumed that putting it all on at once was a desperate
act to be carried out only in times of extreme emergency. I once
read the obituary of a British Rifle Brigade officer nicknamed
'Bunny' who apparently used to advance into battle during the
Second World War armed with nothing save a copy of *Vogue*, a chif-
fon scarf and a light coating of mascara. When questioned about

these experiences he would say only that a short halt in no-man's-land provided the perfect opportunity to repair one's make-up.

I became conscious that Timm was waiting for me, and got into the car. He offered me a choice of pistols like a duellist's second. I chose the Russian Makarov because it sounded exotic and the Soviet Union had long fascinated me, and placed it under one thigh while Timm took an Iraqi Tariq. We then wedged an AK-47 assault rifle between the seats together with a copious quantity of magazines. Our chances of retrieving it rapidly in the event of trouble were slight. Our convoy of jeeps, Suburban and a Ukrainian armoured personnel carrier then lurched into the chaos of Kut's rush-hour as the sun was setting behind the river bank, where we sat immobile for some time as a great mass of citizenry washed past us unheeding on foot or bicycle. The images through our cracked wind-screen danced and shook as we negotiated the heavy traffic along the potholed high street on the river bank and then turned right across the Tigris barrage, built by the British in 1935. One did not feel part of the scenes we saw because our security posture had deliberately isolated us from them. The approach to the river was dominated by a large placard depicting the Shi'ia religious leader Ayatollah Mohammed Sadiq al-Sadr. Fishermen manoeuvred their tiny boats and threw their nets in the shallows downstream of the barrage. The two-lane road across the dam narrowed to one where it crossed the old shipping lock.

Everywhere there was confusion. Opposing streams of traffic noisily contested each intersection. A token policeman or two blew whistles endlessly and waved their arms, but most simply watched the chaos around them. The traffic lights worked but no one heeded them; and the lenses blinked amber, red, and green in cyclic impotence over the carnage below. Aided by our armoured escort and some suggestive waving of its machine-gun we made our way through, past the yellow grain silos opposite the CPA site and across the lock gates of the Nahr al Gharraf, a river that branched south from the Tigris. Both waterways had once been navigable but were used in this way no longer.

Delta Camp had been heavily bombed in both Gulf wars. The rubble from the first had been bulldozed to one side, but the latest accumulation still lay where it had fallen. The camp occupied an enormous area, and there were perhaps a hundred separate buildings within its confines. The squat concrete hangars that had housed Saddam Hussein's aircraft still stood, but their orange surfaces were fissured and cracked by the explosions. Some had jagged holes in one corner from which steel reinforcement rods protruded. The aircraft themselves were piled in pieces near the barbed-wire perimeter fence alongside an old and rotor-less helicopter. Ukrainian soldiers guarded the complex and its single major runway. We drove past a water tower on which an American soldier had written 'I love you Diane Honey' within a giant red heart, and an open air cinema with 'Now Showing: Operation Iraqi Freedom—starring the U.S. Marine Corps' sprayed in black on its screen. Defeat of this kind seems absolute when one sees it at close quarters, and I was never to meet an Iraqi in whom there was no ambivalence about the conquest of his country, regardless of his feelings about Saddam Hussein.

The commander of the Ukrainian Fifth Mechanised Brigade, Major-General Sergey Bezluschenko, had been militarily educated in the Soviet Union and had completed the majority of his service in tanks. He had served in East Germany, the Baltic republics and Central Asia. He now shouldered considerable responsibility, stemming not simply from the hazards of senior command in an operational theatre, but also from the fact that he simultaneously spearheaded a Ukrainian foreign policy designed to display the country's credentials as a reliable international partner. This in turn might lend momentum to a future NATO membership bid. Ukraine had sent its troops to Croatia and to Bosnia-Herzegovina as part of the United Nations effort in former Yugoslavia in the 1990s; but sending troops to Iraq in 2003 had been a bold move, particularly given the contentious political circumstances. Some of this boldness was induced: the United States paid each Ukrainian soldier $550–650 a month or some $500 more than a contracted soldier would generally receive at home. For officers the extra amounted to $950–1,200 a month. Ukrainian troops were now deployed across the province, in As-Suwayrah, in Badrah on the Iranian border, in Kut and to the south in al-Hayy.

Multi-National Division Central-South, to which General Bezluschenko's Brigade belonged, comprised 8,000 troops, and included elements from Hungary, Honduras, Mongolia, Lithuania, the Philippines, El Salvador, Bulgaria, Thailand, the Slovak Republic, Nicaragua and the Dominican Republic. It was led by Poland, which had the most troops in the region and thus contributed the Divisional Commander based in Babil, astride the Babylon site and adjacent to the CPA Regional Office in Hillah. The Spanish were the next most numerous, followed by the Ukrainians with some 1,600 troops, 100 armoured personnel carriers and 250 other vehicles. This made them the fifth largest contingent in Iraq. General Bezluschenko had a number of detachments from other countries under command, including the Kazakh ordnance disposal team and an intelligence-gathering Romanian detachment which operated pilotless drones from the airfield. A team of nurses from the republic of Georgia arrived later.

Included in his Brigade was a team of Polish specialists forming the so-called Governorate Support Team, or 'GST'. This was designed to deal with all areas of proposed project activity using the money which CPA Wasit had been allocated, from education and water to sewerage and bridges. The GST was billeted at the military base but its role was to support the CPA; making this distinction had proved problematic among Brigade commanders less amenable than General Bezluschenko. It was unusual to have a GST of a different nationality from that of the attached Brigade—but this contributed to the lack of controversy over command.

Our nascent CPA team was now an additional responsibility; and, whether or not I felt that we yet deserved the attention, it was clear that the General took the burden seriously. Those elements of his Fifth Mechanised Brigade that had not been deployed in the field were housed in rows of ochre tents that stretched not much less than a kilometer and six ranks deep on a piece of prepared ground 500 meters from the main runway. Timm's tent was a VIP model not far from the General's, and housed a fridge and an air-conditioning unit insufficiently robust to counter the late summer heat. There was also a television that showed Ukrainian soap-operas. At each side of the tent were a military camp bed and a cupboard. Rudimentary shower and toilet facilities were provided in Portakabins 200 meters away.

Each evening in those early days Timm and I returned to the stultifying heat of our shared canvas home at the airfield, and talked through the day's setbacks and tiny triumphs. We would then make our way to the General's tent for dinner, greet his guard, and push through the heavy canvas flaps to sit in an array of armchairs on a makeshift brown linoleum floor; then talk to one another while picking at the questionable food on white plastic plates provided by Kellogg Brown and Root (KBR). I would drink cup after cup of sweet black coffee poured by Tolimir, his aide, who had been with the General for years. Major Andrey Lischinskiy, his interpreter, who spoke excellent English, had also known him for a long time. He was a huge man with a broken nose in his early thirties who had been militarily educated in Siberia and subsequently, in the opium-dream world following the demise of the Soviet Union, in America under the 'Partnership for Peace' program. His ambition was now to live in the United States. There was nothing for him, he said, in Ukraine.

The General was short, plump and moustachioed, and spoke no English other than 'good morning', 'sorry' and 'OK', words which he moulded in a multitude of ways to convey a broad range of meaning. He chain-smoked, and we would do our best to deliver decent cigarettes to him whenever we had the chance. He was never anything but charming and kind to us, and we could not have functioned without him in those early days. In his tent was a large wall-chart of the province, whose outline, he was quick to point out, resembled that of a screaming human form with arms stretched 10-to-4 in alarm. He was something of a conspiracy theorist, and attributed an almost supernatural importance to intelligence data. He had a rich sense of humour, but never displayed it when his superiors were in the room, when he would become taciturn and watchful. I quickly learned not to bind him into conversation in these circumstances.

He was subordinate to only one other Ukrainian in theatre, Lieutenant-General Anatoliy Sabora, a lean man with a booming voice and a handshake like a steel clamp. General Sabora was based at Divisional headquarters in Babil but descended without warning on Kut at intervals—a Ukrainian officer once said to me wryly that he was a man with a great deal of 'initiative'. At intervals during the early evening Sergey would be called away to brief a clutch of superiors in Kiev by telephone in bewildering variety—the Chief of the General Staff, the Commander of Land Forces, and other senior representatives in the Ministry of Defence. This he did with complete equanimity, taking his leave of us with a single 'sorry' and an eloquent sweep of the hands. The army was just twelve years old; and if Kiev occasionally appeared anxious and over-eager for news, it was perhaps understandable.

Timm had bequeathed me a close working relationship with Sergey, and this proved central to our early efforts to establish ourselves. His Brigade, it transpired, was something of a one-man band and authority was retained at the centre. Nothing happened without his permission and very little was delegated. I am not sure we ever met his Deputy, and certainly I saw no other signature on any order of significance. Our daily escort was coordinated through him, and when our long-awaited security detail finally arrived he showed them to their tents personally.

He was clearly uncomfortable with his involuntary assumption of both civil and military authority, and this made him somewhat unusual among other forces in Central-South Division. When the Ukrainian Brigade had replaced the U.S. Marine Corps in August before Timm's arrival there had been no-one but the General to pick up the baton of province command in all its forms, and hence no choice in the matter. Now, with the arrival of CPA representatives, it was clear that he wanted nothing more than for the CPA to take the political reins. On the basis of anecdotal evidence from other Governorate Coordinators I felt lucky: some had been forced to vie with their military counterparts for power, which was wholly unsatisfactory. In all my time with the Ukrainians I had no such difficulty. Indeed, they were regarded by many in the CPA as the best Brigade in the Division. Sergey saw his role, with good reason, as holding the fort while we gathered our strength and extended our political reach. Precisely how this was to be done was a mystery to him, but he had faith in us.

Regrettably it also remained a mystery to me. Each night after dinner, I would lie sleepless in my narrow cot vowing never to drink so much coffee again, while wondering how to assume direction of the province with two people. If I allowed myself to fabricate fantastic schemes in the small hours, the truth was that only schemes that one might hitherto have thought fantastic would do. These were extraordinary days. Timm and I held political responsibility for the province—this much was fact, and could not be disinvented, but where were we to start? Then, my mind awash with these thoughts, I would fall asleep.

Just as surely, every morning at 0530 exactly, the Brigade would play the Ukrainian National Anthem loudly over a broadcast system erected for the purpose, and I, provincial administrator-elect, would start awake from a deep sleep in my spartan cot in southern Iraq, with little idea of where to place the marker between fiction and reality. This would be followed by pounding Ukrainian rock music designed to destroy the vestiges of hope; then came the trudge to the shower blocks in the darkness along with the soldiers of the Brigade, and breakfast with the General. At about this stage our tormentors in the Ukrainian broadcasting facility would embark on a lengthy monologue describing armoured vehicle driving techniques.

It was during these hours that Timm and I would produce coffee from purloined ration packs and talk in our tent as the sun rose. We made two early decisions: first that we would channel our early energies into preparing an operating base in the Ba'ath party complex, in which the CPA team might live and work, and second, to make no other plan till we had learned much more about the province and its problems, and canvassed as many people as possible for their thoughts and advice. We had nothing to go on now, and the U.S. Marines had left no body of information on which we could draw. We thus had little choice but to start afresh. These decisions, so clearly sensible in retrospect, felt courageous at the time because everything we had seen in the city so far appeared to clamour for urgent interventionist action in its most muscular form. It was also becoming clear that Kellogg Brown and Root (KBR), our 'life support' contractor, was unnerved by our choice of site.

KBR was unwilling to work outside the perimeter of the Ukrainian base at Delta Camp, where its provincial office was based— this had been intimated to me at Hillah by a grossly overweight

American with his hat on backwards. I had said that it was not possible for the CPA to accrue support for its political policies from within the confines of a large military camp based 4 km. from the centre of town. We needed to be in the community and remain accessible to it—neither of these requirements could be met by remaining at the air base. KBR accepted this justification with obvious reluctance. I could not get them to see that in the timely and efficient establishment of CPA offices in cities like these lay our best hope of strategic security. In the final analysis what we faced was fear—most KBR staff were institutionally unwilling to leave the wire and did so only rarely. This in turn stemmed from a lack of understanding of Iraq and its people that Timm and I were to encounter again and again—in their eyes the fighting in the Sunni triangle was symptomatic of a widespread and general hatred of America and its motives, and Iraq was a fearsome place in which lurked shapeless and unquantifiable dangers. Sadly this reflex of suspicion and mistrust often resulted in self-fulfilling prophesy as we missed the chance to exploit early opportunity. For now this problem was to slow considerably the contracting work in our chosen location.

It was additionally clear that the province had serious problems, although we had seen little but the airfield, the centre of the city and our site. Mains power was intermittent and available for only half the day at most. Wasit generated no power of its own, relying instead on imports from the south. Sewage flowed unchecked in the streets, and collected in ponds in the low ground between the houses and mud shanty dwellings of the city, oozing black-green and bubbling in the heat. Rubbish lay uncollected at every street corner, and the summer wind had blown countless plastic bags into every corner of the city, and far out into the desert. Black-market petrol was sold at each major intersection. Chaos existed at fuel stations. The police clustered in small groups on the steps of their stations and nearby fences like crows. There appeared to be thousands of them, in almost comical disarray, and few police cars. Most policemen had no weapons, and none of the officers appeared to be doing any work. Worse, there was plenty of evidence that they were directly implicated in criminal activity. It was clear that there was no police presence as a force for law and order in the city, and that we were now witnessing an unprecedented test of the limits of social cohesion.

These difficulties represented not so much the illness itself as symptoms of more fundamental dysfunction. The Ba'athist government had been centralists, running the country through parallel branch ministries embedded in each of the provinces. The public sector had been consciously over-staffed by the regime as a method of social control. This centralist tradition had been reinforced by international sanctions because the resultant shortages had made that control more necessary, and compounded by the ruthlessness and paranoia of Saddam Hussein. Now at one stroke this system and the Ba'athist elite that once ran it had gone, and the fear that made this cumbersome apparatus work vanished with it. What we had inherited was institutionalised disorder: the old framework remained but the people who had given it reason and purpose had disappeared, and with them the discipline they instilled. All over the city public services had collapsed. The looting of public property had become a national sport. Cars, sewage and rubbish trucks, army equipment: most had simply been appropriated in the anarchy accompanying the Coalition's advance, driven to the Iranian border and sold.

We could not attempt to treat the symptoms of these maladies because we had neither the people nor resources to do so. If we had possessed the numbers we might have placed advisers in each of the key ministry branches at province level and steered them through this apparent interregnum, or implanted senior police officers in the local force. These things, of course, were done in Baghdad's parent ministries throughout the CPA's term of tenure with varying success, but this option was not open to us, and the Ukrainians were not established for the task. The only option, then, was to co-opt Iraqis into taking control of their own province earlier than we might otherwise have anticipated—but we had to find the right ones. This was more adventurous than it now sounds: after all, the CPA's tenure in Iraq at this point was still open-ended, and there had been no tradition of provincial power under Saddam Hussein. The process would take time and the province's problems would meanwhile continue. In this we had no choice.

To ignore this array of difficulties as we formulated a plan was very difficult because we were daily confronted with them; and as workmen painted and scraped in the stubbornly empty spaces of our would-be offices, their efforts seemed comically insignificant in the echoing vastness of the province and all that needed to be done. I confess that in those early days the spectre of First World War British Major-General Charles Townshend, who had led a British force up the Tigris against the Turks to humiliating surrender in Kut on 26 April 1916, hovered alongside me. Over 12,000 troops had been captured in one of the most significant defeats ever inflicted on the British Army. Some of his troops were buried in war graves in the centre of the city. Recollection of this event was the more insistent because the very foreignness of Iraqi society gave added eloquence to history's warnings. We did not know the country—though my time in adjacent Kuwait had helped—and no obvious short-cuts to knowledge were available. There was no ready point of reference, and we thus could not know whether the problems we now saw had been caused by our intervention or had preceded them. Had we, in a sense, created this society that we were now so quick to censure? Would it—or its rudiments—hang together, or would the problems we had marked in the city push us inexorably into anarchy—and, if so, when would this happen? Was there even a society worth the name to which we might appeal, or were we to be denied even this purchase? Iraq appeared in those first few days impenetrable, and Townshend's defeat at Kut a warning about complacency and presumption.

Recent military history appeared to compound this problem. Some on the American Right appeared to believe that America's hyper-power status somehow absolved it of the need to study history or practice diplomacy—the country was so overwhelmingly powerful, the argument ran, that it needed to do neither. The use of the American air arm and the precision-guided munitions they delivered so effectively had been a *leitmotiv* of sophisticated wars of intervention for fifteen years. In the first Gulf War, in Kosovo and Serbia, in Afghanistan, and recently in Iraq a credulous public had been fed grainy images of alleged pinpoint destruction; believed the tales of war-time heroism and daring written by Special Forces soldiers under pseudonyms; watched increasingly militaristic and flag-waving fare from Hollywood; and concluded, particularly in the United States, that their forces were immortal.

Militarism, admittedly, is a powerful drug. The panoply and latent power of the U.S. armed forces seen at close quarters, particularly the aircraft, is mesmeric. I remember watching an Apache ground-attack helicopter preparing for departure at Babil. It looked like a stylised praying mantis, and shared the same pose: nose-up, predatory and deadly on the tarmac with rocket-laden stub wings like claws and shimmering armoured glass that added to its dispassionate menace. The steady passage of its rotors imbued the whole airframe with an electric energy. Its pilot sat black-visored and remote in the cockpit in his Kevlar seat. Below the fuselage a slaved black 30 millimetre cannon framed by its magazine feeds followed his head movements to the inch. A yellow sticker on his helmet said 'Don't Try This At Home'. Could one see this and not believe, really believe, in one's heart that everything would somehow be alright, after this casual display in a 40 million dollar helicopter by a nation at the peak of its powers? One felt like genuflecting there on the hot tarmac in deference to the technological power of the U.S. military brand, its omnipotent wizardry so novel that a new language had been developed to describe it: a world of gun-ships and recon teams, of Hellfire rockets and 'fast-movers' and of 'Spectre' and fire-fights.

It hardly needs to be said that, despite the seductive and exhilarating power and splendour of the U.S. armed forces their invulnerability is a myth; and the much-vaunted deep-ranging capability of the Apache helicopter, for one, had already been revised in the light of operational experience and mounting losses in the second Gulf war, to a role now described as 'over the shoulder' of Allied forces. One could only wonder how substantial these reverses might have been against a sophisticated enemy. While this latent power was not in doubt, such strength cannot win wars unless it is satisfactorily brought to bear, and this was to be the root of many of our military problems in 2004. Despite all this, the Apache remained a formidably potent weapon in the right conditions, and one for which I and my team were later to be grateful.

The security conditions in Kut were difficult to divine in October. The nights were noisy and gunfire of all kinds was common. Explosions of varying magnitude occurred regularly. The ownership of weapons was virtually obligatory in social terms, and the majority of households possessed at least one automatic weapon, particularly among the tribes. After a wedding a noisy and riotous vehicle convoy of guests would make their way through the streets, firing into the air as they went; the Ukrainians had confiscated an AK-47 from a tribal elder who, with head and shoulders wedged through the sun-roof of his Mercedes clutching a Kalashnikov, had been seen firing magazine after magazine into the air. To discharge a weapon in this way was like a salute, and a mark of respect; and the larger the weapon and the more vigorously it was fired, the greater the respect that accrued.

Such displays were no direct threat to us, though this gun-play resulted in a steady stream of casualties, and made a mockery of any notion of law. The main danger for us lay in direct attack, either at our base beside the river or *en route*—such incidents occurred almost daily in Iraq. If it happened at our base, the most deadly form of attack would be a car-bomb; if on the road, it was likely to be an ambush using automatic weapons and rocket-propelled grenades (RPG) or roadside device. RPGs are also particularly effective against the thin armour plating routinely used by the Ukrainian Brigade in their vehicles, many of which were old and vulnerable compared to those used by other more modern forces. The car-bomb was the primary threat to our security and a horrifying weapon of potentially enormous destructive power: easily prepared, difficult to track and able to carry a great deal of explosive. In the hands of a team prepared to die delivering the explosive directly to its chosen target at the most advantageous time, it becomes still more formidable, in terms of both the enhanced prospects of devastation and carnage and its psychological effect.

Our new base was more or less wide-open. The entrance was ill-guarded, and the rudimentary physical defences easily circumvented. There was no stand-off distance—the first interrogation-point for visiting vehicles was the front gate of the site. Fields of fire were particularly poor; our flanks consisted of the main road into Kut on one side and the Tigris on the other, and there was only a low masonry wall between us and the road. Here a car-bomb could do terrible damage, to us and particularly to the Ukrainians who were billeted closer to the traffic flow. The danger from a car bomb is overwhelmingly flying glass and other debris propelled by the blast. The explosion itself is less likely to kill unless one is close to it. The sentry positions that overlooked these areas of threat were generally exposed, often poorly positioned, manned irregularly and only rarely with more than one soldier.

Explosive was not hard to obtain. There were four major airfield sites in the province, and three of these possessed staggeringly large ammunition stockpiles that had belonged to the former regime. The size of these vast complexes, and the difficulty of securing their 10–15 km. perimeter fences without crippling the Brigade's man-power resources, meant that some were, in effect, open to anyone who wished to enter. Inside, untidy piles of rockets, bombs, explosive cannon shells and missiles lay in blast-shelters and in the open. Even if one discounted these opportunities, there remained in the desert hundreds of war-time emplacements where such ammunition lay discarded after the recent fighting, piled next to long-abandoned weapons. In those sites that had been bombed, as was often the case at the airfields, this ordnance lay strewn across great distances.

Military presence is not of itself security, and we took no particular comfort from the Ukrainian soldiers at our gate. Such a presence can be counter-productive by being subtly delusive, allowing a civilian organisation to abrogate responsibility for itself, perhaps sub-consciously, to others, based on a purely subjective appreciation of capability. Security then becomes an orphan for whom everyone feels a measure of parental responsibility without ever individually mastering the detail and routines that make up the whole and alone provide protection. Both Timm and I had military experience, and some of mine had been in Northern Ireland where bomb attacks were relatively common. We agreed that the CPA would need routines of a higher order than those that presently existed as our team grew; yet we lacked the integral resources to provide them. The Ukrainian presence in our complex in these numbers was a function only of their need to protect us, though they also used the compound as a base from which to mount vehicle patrols. We had influence over them, certainly, through the General, but their individual soldiering skills were not adequate to protect us against the kind of threats that now seemed likely.

The security problem was broader even than this. We were the over-arching civil authority in the province, yet had only the most rudimentary access to the military intelligence gathered in our territory. Nor could we task military assets to collect intelligence on our behalf although, where there was evidence of any direct threat to us, it was issued immediately. This became increasingly frustrating, particularly when our experience and knowledge of the province had begun to eclipse that of the military, whose troop rotations were frequent. For example, there were to be three changes of command in the U.S. counter-intelligence team during my nine-month tenure. We had no security force of our own; for this we relied on the Ukrainians although this was an important and quite specialist task for which they had neither been established nor equipped. Even this garrison force of about sixty was too small to handle a major threat, such as mass insurrection or attack, and we would be forced to rely on reinforcement from the Brigade at the airfield. Finally, the walls and emplacements which we now needed to secure the camp efficiently could only be provided by KBR, which had made its reluctance to do the work clear. This was a serious problem. By delegating so much administrative power to a single sub-contractor, CPA headquarters had unwittingly delegated, *de facto*, a large measure of inherent operational control to it too.

As already described, I have often failed to follow principles which I knew to be right, while clinging to the comforting notion of an omniscient higher order. Plans, particularly in these environments, often go wrong in their earliest stages, pursuing a default course that owes more to the sum of events rather than to any human input, not least because it is at this early stage that overall control of any plan tends to be weakest. In the absence of a supervisory system good enough to detect this and to correct it, a plan assumes a path of its own like a trickle of water, flowing around each point of resistance till it is stopped or channeled in a different direction. As time goes on, an ever more defined path is created, and it becomes increasingly difficult to change. One must therefore be prepared to intervene early regarding apparently small anomalies to prevent major errors developing as a result.

After I had been ten days in Kut there were clearly enough of Sir Jeremy Greenstock's favourite creatures—lacunae—to cause us concern, although this was inevitable in the circumstances. The key for now was how we dealt with them. Clearly security was one such gap, but it appeared that we could eliminate the worst of the weaknesses we had seen. Another was the issue of command arrangements between ourselves and Hillah, which saw us as a subordinate command while Baghdad did not—rather, in the words of Bremer's letter of appointment, I was to 'draw on the Regional Coordinator ... for technical and program support'. Overwhelmingly our present problems were administrative rather than political, but we could not efficiently tackle one without solving the other. A plea to the Foreign Office had now secured the first of our team names, and we hoped that they would begin arriving in the next fortnight. Everything meanwhile was frustratingly linear with Timm and myself submerged under a daily barrage of logistical and technical detail and no time to think. Finally, it was clear that one might as well simply burn a million dollars as buy equipment for the police in their present state. It was hard to imagine a body of men less viable for law-enforcement.

Ironically, although we were to have unprecedented quantities of money to spend on projects, we had not a dollar of our own; and throughout our period in Kut we were to be dogged by the fact that neither we nor any other of the CPA Governance Teams had been allocated an operating budget. The reasoning behind this omission was simple: KBR was slated to perform all the functions that would normally require expenditure. Yet, as rapidly transpired, KBR was often unable or unwilling to perform these tasks, and we therefore ran the risk of being paralysed till this could be solved. The money we had been given was for projects only and could not be used to enhance CPA facilities—yet the security risk to the base was real, and delay in establishing counter-measures was obvious folly.

So far as we could, we adopted a twin-track policy of self-help using the resources we had, while simultaneously requesting assistance from Baghdad. Given that our site would one day revert to the Iraqi authorities, and the urgency of security measures, I allocated project money to site improvement. We had first of all to strengthen the defences at the entrance to our base, and did so by hiring a bulldozer to create chicanes and earth ramps—KBR could not do this because it was not, in its phrase, 'turned on' to do so. We used the same equipment to create a helicopter landing site on the river bank for casualty evacuation; KBR was also unable to do this. In addition we recruited our own local guard force, with the assistance of John Doane of Research Triangle Institute, to provide us with an outer ring of defence that might alert the Ukrainians in time, and at the right distance, if we were attacked by a car-bomb. This guard force appeared with weapons—I did not enquire too closely about their provenance. We needed them. They were students of English at the local University, and some had served in Saddam Hussein's army. Timm took charge of them. Finally, we engaged a local company to make the Villa habitable, because KBR was not 'turned on' to do this either.

Although much of our work in those early days was spent administering ourselves and attempting to persuade KBR to take responsibility for the site, it was clear that this process had to be combined with the political mission. Iraqis had already begun to station themselves at our front gate, gravitating to where the power now was, as they had always done: tribal chiefs, heads of parties, trade union delegates, police officers, contractors—all waited patiently in the heat. I was now seen as the resident solution to a range of intractable difficulties. This was hardly surprising given the wholesale transformation now proposed for Iraq: a market economy in place of a command system, a democratic political framework instead of a dictatorship, and the replacement of a regime of thirty years' standing. In my case the majesty of my notional power was allied with a similarly majestic ignorance of my province, and it was hard to know how best to remedy this deficiency with our two people and one vehicle. If my early visitors saw me for the sham I was, they were too polite to mention it.

In Iraq power had always been something to concentrate in oneself rather than to apportion or delegate. I was to meet one political party after another, each of which demanded it from me like a potion. If I gently asked their representatives what they intended to do with this elixir, they would look at me mystified. Even allowing for the lack of democratic political tradition in Iraq, this fascination with power, allied with the absence of any form of portfolio save the ambition to acquire more, was striking.

The changes the CPA now proposed were wide-ranging and would take time to accomplish. Meanwhile, the Coalition's arrival and its destruction of the Ba'athist system had created a vacuum and considerable tumult. It was the tumult not of street demonstrations and mob rule—though this could not be ruled out—but of a society in flux. For some—the leaders and senior members of the Ba'athist hierarchy whom the Allies had supplanted—this intervention meant disaster and probable ruin, together with the danger of retribution from a population now unshackled. For others—those, for example, who had looted government property and sold it for gain—it had created opportunity. The vast majority simply fell between these extremes and suffered the insecurities and lack of direction of a society adrift in prolonged interregnum.

As we pursued our outline plans in those early days in the province, Timm and I feared that these social effects would rob us of the time we needed to proceed. There appeared a real and constant danger that the province would fall apart before we had gathered sufficient momentum to guide the transition. Each day, as we attended General Sergey's tent for breakfast and dinner, I wilted inwardly as he updated us on the night's events and the situation reports from his sub-units that had come through at the end of the day. The province map in the foyer of his tent was like a malevolent presence, and since Sergey had pointed out its resemblance to a deranged human figure it had become more difficult to ignore. While we were hanging water heaters and trying to download our e-mails on a desperately slow connection, the province and its population writhed in apparent torment, and I had no cure to offer.

Sergey's daily summary of incidents and concerns would be read dispassionately to us by him in Russian, before translation by Andrey. Each untoward event felt like a personal reproach. In the border town of Badrah, 100 km. north of Kut, the townspeople had again ejected their mayor, this time at gun-point. In four major towns there were no mayors at all. The *ad hoc* Council in the sub-district of Hafriyah consisted only of members of a single family. Attorneys were not being paid. There was no fertilizer available and nor was there sufficient grain. There had been three grenade attacks in Kut, and an alleged Ba'athist had been killed by an explosion at his house. The police station had been bombed in Suwayrah. The police had no winter coats. The province needed border-crossing infrastructure.

And so it went on. I inscribed each item carefully in my black notebook, and at intervals would underline a random sentence in the hope of giving my audience a sense of confidence, however fragile. When I thought their attention had momentarily shifted I would write a little note to myself in the margins. They survive now and I am looking at two dated 9 October: one says 'Oh God' and the other 'This is a complete nightmare'.

This daily onslaught began to feel like a fiendish computer game. I once saw an Army medic on television talking about the stresses of his job. He said that when combat began, and he like everyone else was coping with the shock, he would suddenly be deluged with the casualties those early bullets and shell-bursts had caused. Hence, at the moment when he was at his weakest he seemed almost to attract the worst aspects of the experience as the injured were heaped beside him for treatment. That was how Kut felt in those early days—up at 0530 every morning to the Ukrainian National Anthem, cold shower, in to see Sergey for the night's cargo of woe, past that accusing wall chart and into the convoy clutching our useless pistols. Then back again after hours of attempting to secure the tiniest administrative advances at the base, through the traffic, and to Sergey's tent for the day's devastating epitaph on my lamentable progress. I had been in Kut for a week.

I should have been happy to see my new Control Risks Group (CRG) security detail when the team arrived on 11 October, but instead I looked at the matt black windows of the Land Cruisers, their subdued desert yellow colour scheme, their spotlights and winches; at the four men that emerged with their Glock pistols and Hechler and Koch sub-machine-guns; at the radio antennae and raw capability this expensive ensemble radiated; and felt my humiliation the more acutely. My lack-lustre performance to date hardly merited this treatment. In addition to this I felt that English sense of reserve about being 'flash'—I naturally preferred a low and somewhat self-effacing profile, and it looked as though this might be difficult to preserve in future.

I had been doubtful about the utility of employing a sub-contracted security firm in this role, and had said so to the Foreign

Office before my departure from England. I was unable to see how they could be good enough, lacking the operational experience, fine tuning and discipline that were surely essential to the role. Security of this kind had historically been provided by specialist members of the Royal Military Police or Britain's Special Forces, but these regiments were already stretched by a string of commitments of which Iraq was merely the latest and most spectacular. Guarding individuals is actually very difficult—the would-be assailant can choose the time, place and method of assault, and as the old saw runs, has only to be lucky once while the defending team must remain lucky throughout. The central problem was that my role was directly at odds with the requirement: what was now needed in the province was aggressive and energetic leadership by the CPA and as much public exposure as we could manage. Clearly this was inconsistent with core security precepts, which demanded a low profile. The security task was hence a challenging one.

The head of the team was a stocky former British Parachute Regiment soldier covered in tattoos named Russ Pulleng, who introduced himself and asked where the 'Governor' was. I said he probably meant me. Russ looked disappointed, but recovered quickly. He said he expected someone older. I said that given a day or two I could probably satisfy those expectations. We were to establish a close working relationship. He was given to understatement, courteous, and had a ready sense of humour. He was not prone to panic and I never knew him to raise his voice. His tattoos fascinated the Iraqis, who had never seen anything like them before.

I like to think that my military experience and regimental links with Russ helped forge the formidable working instrument that our CRG team was to become. We established a number of principles from the start—the first was that I would always listen to security advice, however unpalatable, but reserve the right to over-rule it. I nevertheless understood that Russ too was bound by the regulations issued by the CRG operations room in Baghdad and had the right to refuse to carry out my requests. This, to his great credit, he never did. The second was that we would vary our routes and timings constantly to lessen the chances of a successful attack. The third was that all movement would be controlled—every journey was to be deliberate and the result of forethought. Finally, we agreed that all visits in the province, wherever possible, would be unheralded. This would enable us to see the province as it really was and preserve security at the same time.

There was a single facet to the CRG support operation that I thought ill-judged. Each team went on leave in pairs for three weeks in every six. The gap was filled by any CRG members available in Baghdad, leaving the original members to fit into a team elsewhere on their return. What this meant was that one's original team was destined to vanish by attrition, and this made no sense to me at all—it meant that we would be secured by a team whose knowledge of the province, its people and its patterns would be cyclically and irrevocably lost. I immediately campaigned to keep our team intact; and fortunately both CRG and the Foreign Office quickly made the requisite changes. Henceforth our team would consist of a pool of six people, all dedicated to the CPA office in Wasit, of whom two would be away on leave at any one time. In retaining the same people in our security teams, together with their detailed knowledge of our provincial towns and roads, Timm and I established a system that may well have saved our lives the following spring.

Embarrassed by my new security profile I may have been, but Timm and I jumped into the back of the cars like schoolchildren as we returned to camp that evening. We lounged regally on the grey velour, and tapped the armoured glass with one surreptitious finger. We had been locked in combat with our own administrative deficiencies, and the daily grind of transporting and protecting ourselves had been a major part of the struggle. Russ and his team enhanced our transport and security capability in one quantum leap forward. The cars were equipped with long-range High Frequency (HF) radio capable of communicating with all other CRG vehicles in Iraq, and particularly with the HQ offices in Baghdad's CPA building in the Green Zone and in Basra in the British sector. Russ was required to 'open' and 'close' with Control at the beginning and end of each working day, and to establish coded reporting lines across our province in order that our location was known. Short-range communication—and communication between the two cars—was carried out by Very High Frequency (VHF) radio, although its range was limited. A satellite telephone provided a back-up system. Each vehicle weighed close to 4 tonnes, and the strain on vehicle components such as engine and gearbox was considerable. The tyres were designed to run flat if punctured and the cars' armour was proof against attack by grenades or gunfire. The vehicles were always used as a pair, and passengers alternated between them; the dark glass made it difficult to know where they were sitting. Each CRG team member was equipped with a pistol and a personal radio. One of the pair in each vehicle drove while the other kept watch, and additionally carried the Hechler and Koch (HK) sub-machine-gun. I had used the HK in Ireland and mentioned the fact to Russ, who simply responded 'Hairdresser's weapon'. I sat back, put firmly in my place as Timm looked out of the window smiling.

The arrival of CRG, despite my blushes, lent strength to our small team in those early days and made us much more efficient. If our first days in Kut had been like establishing a tenuous beach-head on some distant shore, CRG's presence now enabled us to consider pushing further inland. We no longer needed to draw on the Ukrainian Brigade in quite the same way; and if I was still unable to look Sergey fully in the face I felt as though we had at least relieved his Brigade of some pressure.

We were able, a week later, to relieve him of still more. The arrival on 20 October of Sally Bond, a British Ministry of Defence employee who had volunteered to be our Administrative Officer, provided us with the necessary impetus to live in our rudimentary new base on the river. There was never going to be a wholly satisfactory moment to make the leap, and there was much that remained to be done. We had in the Ukrainians a garrison force, and our self-help additions had buttressed our defences. CRG could now provide internal security. The pair of U.S. Army casualty evacuation Blackhawk helicopters based at Delta had made dummy runs at our request into our new landing site, and we had their contact information. KBR had installed a generator capable of running the Villa, and we could eat plated food brought over from the base for the Ukrainians. KBR had also begun work at last on Tarawa House, which it hoped to finish by the end of the year.

The lack of a secure perimeter and protective T-walls remained a serious deficiency, and the base was undoubtedly vulnerable to attack. Clearly this militated against the move—although KBR had promised that the wall sections were due imminently, and our team remained small; yet the dangers inherent in our daily commute to and from Delta seemed to me to eclipse this threat. Every day, morning and afternoon, our pair of yellow vehicles moved to and from the camp. There was not another set like them in the province. There were three bridges that crossed the Tigris in Kut including our adjacent barrage 300 metres downstream, and we had been using them all, but each of them fed vehicles inexorably to the vulnerable single approach road to Delta, a 3 km stretch past the grain silos, across the waterways and into the main gates. There were numerous points from which a rocket might be launched or an ambush initiated and many more where a bomb might be placed. The road was not picketed, and preparations for such assaults could be made with impunity. It seemed to me easier to attack our vehicles on the roads than to attack us in our new base. We elected to move.

When we informed Sergey, his Brigade had been rehearsing for some days for a visit by General Ricardo Sanchez. A plywood dais had been hastily knocked together in front of his tent, and the Iraqi, Ukrainian and American flags now flew from newly-painted flagpoles behind it. A band had been similarly assembled, of which Sergey was very proud. It was not clear to me whether any of the musicians had ever played an instrument before, but Sergey listened to their excruciating cacophony with evident pleasure, puffing vigorously on his cigarette and saying 'OK!' at intervals. Timm said he thought he recognized snatches of 'The Star Spangled Banner' but could not be entirely sure. Sergey beamed.

We agreed to meet regularly, at either Delta Camp or the CPA base. We shook hands, though we were moving only a short distance; but we all felt that CPA Wasit was gradually coming of age. The sense of transition was probably more pronounced for Timm, who had been at Delta for nearly two months. We liked the Ukrainians; they had been very good to us, and we had worked well together. The eerie wailing of Bezluschenko's band and the sight of his rump Brigade goose-stepping past the plywood dais as a brisk wind wrapped one flag after another around the poles, added affection to the poignancy of departure.

3

DEFINING A STRATEGY

'Terrorism' is now a much over-used word, but if it is best defined as a strategy of intimidation, the 26 October 2003 rocket attack on the Green Zone's Rashid Hotel, in the very heart of the CPA's Baghdad complex, was a highly successful example of the genre. The salvo of rockets killed only one person in a crowded building, but succeeded in inculcating a sense of fear and insecurity in the CPA's headquarters staff that was never again banished. The Green Zone was at once HQ and emblem. Its presumed impregnability—its walls, check-points, wire and U.S. troops—now ironically fed a new sense of fear; if this assemblage of defences had once proved inadequate, who could believe in it again? The senior State Department official who had replaced the amiable Tom Krajeski, who had welcomed me when I first arrived, left Iraq after only ten days in-country and did not return, leaving the key Governance office still more stretched. Paul Wolfowitz, the U.S. Deputy Defense Secretary, had coincidentally been in the hotel when it was hit, and this had lent emphasis to a sense of public shock. Wolfowitz was an Administration hawk and an architect of the war; he was reported by Agence France Presse after the attack to be 'visibly disturbed'. Clearly no one was beyond reach, and it was no longer possible to assume that personal security could somehow be insulated from policy. The hotel was evacuated and closed, throwing accommo-

dation plans into confusion. Andrew Bearpark, my friend in Operations, was forced to sleep in the bathroom of his office at the Palace.

Probably the most insistent of the doubts aroused by that salvo
concerned the truth of political claims that the Coalition was
winning the 'war on terror' in Iraq. On the contrary, the impression
was now that we faced an expert, determined and courageous
enemy able to strike at will; and it was this realisation more than any
other that steadily eroded morale. These attacks had a further, more
damaging effect: the defences of the Green Zone, which were
designed to protect its inhabitants, had also deprived them of sensation, and in further buttressing them and tightening procedures
CPA HQ staff began inexorably to lose the ability to accurately
judge the situation outside.

Neil Strachan, our Political Adviser and a British Army Reservist, arrived in Kut later that day with a CRG team from Baghdad. He
had been seconded by the Foreign Office. He too had been in the
Rashid Hotel when it was hit, but seemed unshaken by the experience. Although he was a civil engineer he had spent three years
doing intelligence work—his Reservist speciality—in Germany,
where he had just become engaged to a U.S. Air Force officer. He
was wiry, tough and fit and his quiet manner belied a principled
passion for his work and a steely determination. His only obvious
idiosyncrasies were a hatred of puppies and an inexplicable passion
for U.S. Army combat rations, known officially as 'MREs' or 'Meals
Ready to Eat' and unofficially by U.S. soldiers as 'Mr Es' or
'Mysteries'.

Sally Bond, our Administrative Officer, had volunteered for a
four-month stint in Iraq during the British 'trawl' of its Civil
Service. She had established a set of desks on the Villa's first floor
from which we intended to operate till Tarawa House was ready.
She had travelled little outside Britain, but said that conditions in
Kut were better than she had imagined. Actually these remained

spartan, and the recently-installed lighting and electrical systems in the Villa were still erratic. Cold showers were the norm—I later found that this was because our locally-contracted plumber had connected the hot water tank to the lavatory cistern. Distance and time had not improved KBR's food, which now verged on the inedible.

Power cuts were common, and during these the anarchy of night-time Kut was striking, particularly now that we had based ourselves permanently in the city. Gunfire crackled sporadically throughout the hours of darkness, regularly mixed with explosions, some power-ful enough to rattle windows and doors in the ensuing shock-wave and awaken us. We plainly had no abiding control over the city. The Brigade appeared to confine itself to guard tasks in the town on the banks and other key buildings. We lacked grip because we lacked presence. What was needed was an aggressive programme of foot patrols in the city's streets and alleys, but this was beyond the capa-bilities and experience of the Ukrainians who remained wedded to their armoured vehicles. In this poor security environment we faced two problems: first, and most fundamental, was the challenge to our authority, which if left unchecked would damage both Bri-gade and CPA Wasit irreparably; and second, the unlikelihood of progress on any other front if this lawlessness continued.

We had decided to begin our round of meetings with the Gover-nor, the chief of police, religious representatives and the political parties. From these discussions and contacts we hoped to gain a sense of the situation in the province and how best to tackle its problems. Wasit had seen more turbulence than most: not only had there been a transition from one American commander to another during the U.S. Marine Corps' tenure, but the Marines had then handed over to General Bezluschenko, who in turn now gave over-riding civil authority and the political portfolio to us. One wond-ered what had fallen between the cracks—certainly we saw no hand-over files at any stage.

In Saddam Hussein's day the civil Governor of Wasit had been a regime appointee who wielded absolute power in the city and the surrounding province. Alongside him had sat a senior Ba'athist, responsible for two provinces. Our offices had been the Party head-quarters for Wasit and Maysan, the province to our south. These people were long gone, and the Marine Corps, before departing in August, had appointed a single replacement, a former judge and Chief of the Appeal Court, Nema Sultan Bash'aga. In appointing him they had followed principles used elsewhere for key appoint-ments in Iraq since the war—the candidate should have no con-nections with the Ba'ath Party, be generally accepted as honest, and ideally have suffered in some way under the former regime. Inev-itably the choice was subjective because neither the CPA nor the military had sufficient knowledge to make informed choices, having to rely instead on local advisers who were themselves a mixed bag.

Governor Nema Sultan occupied a cavernous office on the first floor of the walled British-built administration building in the centre of the city. There were two entrances to the site, each one gated and guarded loosely by police. A First World War-vintage artillery piece lay on its side in the yard. His office, entered through large double doors after an ante-chamber where his secretary sat, stretched a full 30 metres from the entrance. On either side of the room was a row of white, high-backed chairs that drew the eye down the avenue thus created towards his desk. This *diwan* or coun-cil chamber arrangement was common and in keeping with the Iraqi tradition of discussing matters of importance in groups, with the most important individuals generally sitting nearest the host.

The Governor was about sixty, grey-haired and moustached, and reputedly knew the Koran by heart. He had been dismissed as a judge in Saddam Hussein's time and had spent the wilderness years farming before his unexpected accession to the Governor's chair. Invariably dressed in a grey suit, he had a large nose, carbuncles and a nervous disposition, and was able to talk for long periods without a pause, dancing around his chosen theme like a boxer. He was stubborn and emotional, and made much of the strain of his post. I do not remember any meeting between us—and we had many— where he did not at some point sigh, reach effortlessly for a suitable Koranic aphorism, and threaten to resign. I made a firm practice of accepting all such offers with alacrity, but this made no difference. We both knew that there was no obvious replacement.

He was flanked on one side by a giant Iraqi flag and on the other by a green fridge over seven feet high which emitted a startling range of gurgling noises. I had not been long enough in Iraq to understand that an office fridge is a badge of rank. I never saw him open it, and for ever wondered what it contained. On the wall next to the fridge hung a huge piece of lurid artwork in yellows and greens, showing a coiled snake rearing on a bed of skulls. Its tongue flickered at a wall composed of bricks, each labelled with one crime or another, and its neck was grasped firmly by a muscular forearm around which were draped the American and British flags. This was not all—every fifteen minutes a garish wall-mounted clock played the tune of 'She'll be comin' round the mountain' for a full twenty seconds, and the button that summoned the secretary activated electronic bird-song from a speaker by the door. This cacophony of noise—the fridge, the clock and the call-button—admixed with the intermittent ringing of the three telephones on his desk and an endless array of people leaving and entering the room, disturbed him not at all.

I liked him and enjoyed his eccentricities, although his failings were to manifest themselves increasingly in the coming months. His love of rhetoric was shared by all Iraqis. When we first met he said that I was welcome and doubly welcome and would always be so; and that I had the chance, with God's help, to leave my fingerprints on Wasit and its people. I said that I wanted nothing more than for the province to govern itself, but would not hesitate to intervene if it did not. He nodded, smiling gently, and said 'Time is more important to you than it is for us.' He enjoyed his job and its privileges—the guards, the office and the Mercedes—but was insufficiently robust to accept its responsibilities. He was, at heart, afraid of the mass of his people, and sought sanctuary in his office and its impersonal documents. The majority of the population were not well disposed towards him—Iraqi society is remarkable for its feuds—and I could not persuade him to travel his province.

As we began our conversation a young man, smiling shyly, poured me a quarter of an inch of glutinous cardamom-flavoured coffee from a curved jug, dark and very strong. It was more powerful by far than its Kuwaiti equivalent, though the ritual remained the same: the empty cup would automatically be refilled till one refused more by shaking it. It would then be passed to another guest. The Governor chose this moment to launch an attack on a collection of his *bêtes noires*. The border, he said, was a mess, and the Iranians were coming across it in their thousands to destabilise the country and attack its institutions. What were Coalition forces and the Ukrainians doing about it? It was wide open. It was we, the CPA, who had forced him to re-open the crossing, and we who were now demonstrably unable to secure it. When these Iranian *agents provocateurs* reached Kut, he continued, they joined forces with political parties which had their roots in Iran. Such parties had no place in a democracy, and had caused nothing but trouble. Many were armed, and most had simply occupied government buildings since the war. This kind of occupation was no better than theft—we had connived at a new tyranny.

This went on for some time. If the Governor's impassioned exposition robbed his argument of much of its force, he was essentially right. The border *was* a mess. Timm had made the problem his own, and his early reports were graphic, but the Iraqis were in no state to take it on and we had insufficient troops to secure it. We were to find that this fear of Iran and an uncontrolled and porous border was a common theme among Wasit's population, but amounted to a fixed phobia rather than a desire for practical solutions. It was idle to speak of the subjectivity of nationalism, or of the impossibility of demarcating ethnic distinctions as one would a frontier. The fact that the Grand Ayatollah Ali Sistani, spiritual leader of the Iraqi Shi'ia to whom the overwhelming majority of Wasit belonged, was himself of Iranian descent was dismissed as irrelevant; and the indisputable reality that at least a third of the inhabitants of this border province had Iranian relatives was likewise denied. What we were discussing owed more to the power of suggestion than to logic, and that power, little diminished by the fifteen years since the end of the brutal 1980–8 Iraq-Iran war, remained very strong.

Having championed a popular cause, the Governor then turned to one of his own. If it were possible to hate an entire district, then the Governor hated the border town of Badrah, its inhabitants and environs with a cold and unyielding determination; and the district's population of 18,000 reputedly detested him equally. The problem was the Mayor. Each district should have had one, and each sub-district a Director, who discharged similar duties albeit on a smaller canvas. There were vacancies in these positions all over the province. Mayors in Saddam Hussein's day were centrally appointed and trained in civil administration, but the majority of these had fled. How the resulting gaps were to be filled, and what powers were to be wielded by future incumbents, was unclear.

The same was true of Councils. There had been no tradition of these before the war in the form in which we now understood them. The Marine Corps had established a few, in a necessarily *ad hoc* way, and in other cases groups of citizens had assumed the responsibility on their own initiative. Such people would invariably describe themselves as public-spirited, while those excluded would castigate them as a criminal band of thieves and opportunists.

The Governor now sought to fill these posts with his own appointees. Many were to prove less than suitable. In Badrah he had appointed a friend, Mohassan Abdul al-Akabi, but after a brief honeymoon period the self-appointed Council with which he was supposed to work ejected him, alleging corruption, inefficiency and autocracy. He withdrew to Kut, gathered a police escort (thus confirming in some measure at least the townspeople's third assertion), and returned to his office in Badrah. The population then assembled an armed citizens' band and ejected him at rifle-point. He returned to Kut, where he and the Governor had a series of crisis meetings designed to return him to his post. The Badrah militia meanwhile, dedicated themselves to ensuring that he did not.

I had some sympathy for the Governor's position. We had rather lost control of the democratic concept in the months since the war, because the political controversy created by the invasion had encouraged unrealistic claims for the fruits of peace. In Iraq elements of the population were wont to interpret the change of regime as a broad mandate for doing what they wanted, and the people of Badrah clearly leaned in that direction. The issue at hand was one of definition: what exactly was a Mayor in these days, and how was he to be chosen? What of the Governor? What were the limits of his power? The Councils that Bremer had asked me to establish were self-evidently a method of broadening political representation, but these too were patchwork and their proposed powers opaque. How, finally, were these entities to interact?

The Governor saw the appointment of Mayors and Directors as his fundamental right, and an instrument of governance. He met them all once a week in Kut, received their reports and issued his instructions. His power to make such appointments—which were salaried—additionally buttressed his own position, and assured loyalty. Each of the Mayors and Directors also had power over the police in their areas, further underpinning the influence of this network.

These methods were open to abuse, but I thought them preferable to the possible alternatives. The Governor's hierarchy was the only obvious control we had over the province, and we were loath to tamper with it until we better understood Wasit. While it was logical that these Councils and the populations they supposedly represented should have a say in the choice of their Mayor, it was difficult to promote their power without damaging the Governor and causing friction that would complicate our task. There are tensions implicit in any democratic framework; and if those between a Mayor and Council are a fine theoretical example of them, it was far too early to attempt any such balancing act, and we lacked the solid legislative basis to accomplish it.

For a judge Governor Nema Sultan appeared particularly partial to the use of force, and brusque in his condemnation of those who questioned his rather uncompromising brand of direct rule. It was clear to me that he now actively contemplated returning Badrah's Mayor for a third time, escorted by the full might of Kut's police force. Rather than preside over a civil war in my first weeks in the job, I thought it best to calm him. I suggested that he went to Badrah and resolved the issue by negotiation, and said that I thought this process should be part of any future Mayoral appointment he intended to make. He nodded perfunctorily in a way that I later learned to be an infallible signal of his intention to do nothing of the sort. I assured him of my full support—with a warmth which, I suppose, indicated to him as clearly that the reverse was actually true—and left for the police station, with the sound of birdsong in my ears as I went down to the cars.

One might imagine, as we did, that the difficulties in Badrah could have been managed by the police; and that any attempt by

armed militia to eject a Mayor selected by the Governor would
ordinarily have been resisted and the ring-leaders arrested. Given
that it was the Governor himself who had urged the appointment of
province Chief of Police Brigadier Abdul Men'em Abdul Razzaq
upon the U.S. Marine Corps, these omissions seemed all the more
inexplicable.

Brigadier Abdul Men'em's office, too, was a thing of joy. Just
inside the door was a large Chinese screen, resplendent with inter-
twined dragons and cranes. As one turned the corner the rest of the
room opened out like a shopping mall. Along its sides were armchairs and low coffee-tables, and a decorative fan on the ceiling
revolved gently. At the end of the room was a large black desk; on it
was a stereo system and beside it were a large television and a fridge.
On a ledge was an expensive Motorola radio receiver in a charger.
None of these electronic appliances were operating; the important
thing was that they were there. The desk was both remarkable for its
size and for the fact that not a single document was to be seen on it.

Brigadier Abdul Men'em, grey hair swept back, sat behind his
desk like a large statue in an ironed short-sleeved white shirt complete with his badges of rank, and ordered tea for us. He spoke with
quiet authority and looked kindly, but there was an air of suppressed
anxiety about him. He was universally acknowledged to be a 'good
man' in a moral sense, but regarded as unable to impose his authority on his subordinates. He was clearly uncertain of me and shrank
from discussion of difficult issues.

He had been a Major of police before the war but was dismissed
by Saddam Hussein. He opened our meeting by suggesting that he
was too senior a figure to be in Kut and should be promoted to full
General. He belonged, he explained, at the Ministry of the Interior
in Baghdad. He could not tell me how many officers he had, or how
many cars; nor was he sure about the number of weapons available
to his force. I knew that General Bezluschenko had put military

police into each of the principal stations, and he had told me that station chiefs were as ill-informed. Brigadier Abdul Men'em wanted more equipment and modern weapons, radios and ammunition. His speech over the next half hour was like a protracted sigh of lament—if only he had these things everything would be fine. As the meeting wore on I realised that his nervousness stemmed from the fact that he was unequal to his responsibilities and feared discovery. Both Timm and I thought that the core problem was him.

Timm was generally ruthless about such things. Anyone who was demonstrably unable to do the job for which he or she was being paid should be replaced. The Coalition had a job to do, and it would be done. I, on the other hand, would hesitate; and, mistrusting the cargo of Western values I had brought with me, would wonder whether I saw the problem clearly enough to take a sensible decision. In Iraq great store is set by appearance: hence the uniforms, the fridges and the elaborate offices. The characteristics of an individual are of secondary importance. The Brigadier, obviously, was weak, and it was hard to believe that much work was done at his desk. We could only guess what his police commander in Badrah was like. His Deputy, Colonel Hassan Thuwaini Mohammed, who had speedily entered the office once he had been informed of our presence, appeared more capable and exerted considerable influence on his senior. He also appeared faintly dangerous. When asked a question relating to detail, Men'em would inevitably defer to him.

Dismissal as a disciplinary measure was unusual in Iraq, perhaps because the concept of position and outward appearance was of such fundamental importance that there was thought to be no transgression serious enough to merit it. The sideways movement of staff was not uncommon, and Iraqis could be spectacularly ruthless with one another if relationships had deteriorated to the point at which insults had been formally exchanged. On the whole, however, the only weapon used against recalcitrant subordinates was verbal discipline. Given that all parties knew that dismissal was most unlikely, such measures lacked bite. When we found, in May 2004, that a senior police officer had directed rebel rocket fire on to our compound during the Sadr rebellion and been wounded taking part in the ensuing assault upon us, his chief confided in me with due gravity that he had 'spoken very toughly' to him and the officer had promised not to do it again.

The sharp dissimilarity between Iraqi and Western ideas about the extent to which one should relate a post to performance was striking. What Iraqis mainly sought was the power of patronage: the key was to ensure that one's group—whether tribe, immediate family or friends—remained in the ascendant. This was regarded as the primary task of each individual member of the clan. The appointment of a senior Iraqi figure often resulted in a flurry of activity in the office in question, as one subordinate after another was shuffled to other posts. The vacant positions would then be filled with allies. In appointing these one strengthened one's position and standing as a man who would look after his own. This might one day result in a repayment of the favour.

What this meant in Brigadier Abdul Men'em's case was that the entire provincial force was linked to his avuncular presence at the centre. The longer a senior figure was in position the more pronounced this effect. It was erroneous to imagine that our reservations about the Brigadier could be focused on him alone—what one actually sought to dismantle was a brotherhood, built entirely around the person of the chief. Actually it was worse even than that because he too would be linked upward to some guardian angel in the Ministry of Interior whose job would be to protect him and to block attempts to move him.

This first meeting with the Brigadier and his Deputy suggested to Timm and me that the gap between their abilities and our public order objectives was very large. Timm, who had a range of cryptic comment for each situation that presented itself, had already declared the policing situation to be 'Hogan's goat'—an utter mess—and prophesied, accurately, that 'we can't get there from here'. While we could merely dismiss both, the problem was much more complex than it appeared, and there was no guarantee that changing personalities would secure the improvement we sought. Although such dismissals might have the advantage of imprinting my authority early, I thought that I would risk appearing petulant because I had no better solution. I was wary, as I had been with the Governor, of inflicting more turbulence on a society I did not yet understand. While what we had was clearly grossly imperfect, it remained a system of sorts. We would take action when we understood better what needed to be done.

The disestablishment of the *ancien régime*, compounded by demonstrably inadequate troop levels, had left Coalition forces with great difficulties in the structural void that followed the end of hostilities. The full array of Saddam Hussein's army and vast security apparatus had been dismantled by the Coalition in May. Coalition troops now had no choice but to fill much of the resulting vacuum, and were tied down in their thousands on static guard and routine law and order tasks in a way that precluded all other activity.

The Coalition had therefore re-established a province police force of 3,000 volunteers, and hastily organised brief training packages for them. They additionally created a Facilities Protection Service (FPS) with the task of carrying out static guard duties at key locations. This force of 1,650 was now run from the former Governor's mansion on the Tigris as a single unit, but was to be divided by January 2004 along Ministerial lines. The Ministry of Finance would, for example, become responsible for the training and pay of those FPS officers now guarding banks, while those guarding dams and locks would be subsumed by the Ministry of Irrigation. At this stage no one at all was paying them, and the FPS was on the brink of mutiny.

The principal difficulty with these security measures was that the Coalition had only the most cursory acquaintance with the people they recruited—it could hardly have been otherwise—and inevitably accepted opportunist elements of the kind most likely to emerge first after a conflict. No great citizens' movement emerged—the vast majority of the educated middle class simply stayed quietly at home. The major problem now was a general lack of supervision. These people, in the FPS and police alike—largely untrained, unarmed, unfit, many of whom were de-motivated and probably corrupt, were to be solely responsible for general law and order in Wasit, but they served as little more than a graphic illustration of the weakness of the province. I did not believe that issuing them with expensive equipment would solve these difficulties. This was not strategy, but a palliative for us; and it seemed clear that human strength and leadership were the key qualities presently lacking.

My chief memory of these October days was of the extraordinary difficulty of discerning truth. Iraq's 'otherness' had been accentuated by its political isolation, and in our attempts to understand recent history, emotions and events we simply lacked purchase. Without this we were unable to predict the future either. I had already accepted that we would never enjoy the luxury of being certain about anything in Iraq, but the comfort afforded by this private acceptance failed to insulate us from the reality we encountered. There was no all-embracing society in Wasit to speak of, but rather a series of camps and cliques—miniature societies—each with its own place. Most were quick to denounce the others, and compromise was rare. Each clique was self-sufficient because it was built around a source or sources of power. Like ancient city-states they traded with one another, made alliances and broke them, declared wars and negotiated peace; and occasionally one vanished because the strength sustaining it had waned. When power was fed into Wasit's ancient system this great flotilla would tremble as it absorbed new realities—and then steadily re-align itself as it had done for centuries.

To speak of 'democracy' as a theme, or of 'Iraq' as a rallying point or social adhesive, was thus less than effective because few Iraqis saw the advantage of thinking in that way. It is not that they were incapable of it, but that they failed to see obvious advantage in abandoning an essentially feudal system which at once embodied fellowship, prosperity and protection for an unknown quantity. Economic, social and local considerations, rather than national ones, governed their analysis. If the prospect of a democratic state is among the world's most potent political rallying cries, it meant little to most Iraqis who simply sought to transmute it into the old currency.

Writ small, this meant that the vast majority of Iraqis whom the Coalition employed saw their task as being to promote the cause of their own clans, however constituted. We naturally asked our interpreters for advice and guidance and they would give it, but inevitably it would be subjective, and once this was known one could balance the replies given by asking a range of other Iraqis for their opinions. Even this would generally fail to produce a weight of opinion one way or the other, because the answer depended entirely on whom one asked and where his loyalties lay. An aspirant senior police officer might be extolled by one high-level delegation after another, and denigrated by the next.

Understanding and expecting partisanship on this scale, and compensating for it, could merely substitute one problem for another. A member of a group who failed to create for them sufficient general advantage from his post risked opprobrium or even expulsion, with all the attendant social implications and risk. Several times in the ensuing months a group of my Iraqi staff would come into my office and plead for the chance to place one friend, or for a single building contract.

The complexity of Iraqi human relations made all appointments a matter of extreme hazard, and exquisite torture to anyone with my predilection for introspection. A group might summon hundreds of supporters into the street within hours to noisily espouse one cause or another, and such 'riots' worked powerfully upon the mind, particularly in these first months when the province appeared so unstable. Of these crowds the majority might be relatives of the subject. Subsequent discussions might, for an outsider, have seemed highly comic if passions were not so dangerously inflamed. 'Mohammed X is a fine man, a strong man, the most honest in Iraq. I should know—I am his brother.' When negotiations were over and calm returned, everyone would smile and laugh at the fun they had had, and I would receive a dozen invitations to lunch.

A citizens' delegation came to see me in October, raucously indignant, about the appointment to Wasit of a new Appeal Court judge, the senior legal figure in the province. They said that this new man would replace a judge of unimpeachable character who had guided Wasit since the war. He deserved better than this: the incomer was a former Ba'athist and 'the people will never accept him'. They looked at me beseechingly. Sergey told me that a group of two hundred had gathered at the Court in protest. I made two days' enquiries which, in retrospect, were less than comprehensive, and elected to annul the appointment. I typed out the first of a series of orders whose language I invented on the spot, beginning 'By the powers invested in me by Ambassador Bremer, the CPA Governorate Coordinator instructs that ...' I dated the letter on our ailing computer as the wind blew through the holes in our wall, and signed it with a flourish. Feeling like a newly-qualified magician attempting a difficult spell, I had the missive translated and delivered to the Governor for action. The new judge left the next day. A few months later my Iraqi friends told me that he was among Iraq's best judges, and that the man he was to replace was corrupt to the core.

In this extraordinary atmosphere of internecine strife and complexity it became ever clearer that the CPA would need to utilise local capacity to its utmost. Only thus might we hope to make sense of this extraordinary quicksand of shifting affiliations and allegiances. Clearly we could not gather this expertise by osmosis, nor did we have time to do so. The province was fragile and the local framework we had seen seemed unlikely to endure.

We needed to assemble Councils in each sub-district and district where there were none, and review those already extant to ensure they were up to a reasonable standard. We also needed to appoint a Province Council that might steer the affairs of the province alongside the Governor, and leaven the autocratic style that had characterised much of his activity to date. We did not yet know what political solutions were envisaged for Iraq but it was clear that a measure of devolution was inevitable and that Councils would thus play a key role.

Meanwhile, we had six districts and eleven sub-districts: Governance in Baghdad had suggested that each should have a Council of twenty people, and that the Province Council was to number forty. This appeared to balance efficacy with broad representation. We were thus planning to evaluate in some measure 380 people under what would presumably be highly contentious circumstances. This, I was quite sure, would rapidly prove impossible. Above all things, I thought it essential that our actions were born of transparent procedure, or I feared that we would be subsequently unable to defend our actions and hence lose credibility.

The idea that the religious leaders of this staunchly Islamic country might assist us in effecting our plans was something we had considered at an early stage. Iraq is predominantly Shi'ia Muslim, particularly in the south, but despite this Iraq had been governed by its Sunni Muslim minority since independence in 1921 and the establishment of the modern state. There was considerable tension between the two groups, not least because the Shi'ia had suffered greatly at the Sunnis' hands. The overwhelming majority in Wasit were Shi'ia, who in turn could be categorised as belonging to one of two groups: Sistani and Sadr.

In Islam great importance is accorded to religious guidance—the word itself means 'submission'. The Koran, dictated by Allah to the Prophet Mohammed, is regarded as a practical handbook for life, and the faithful study the writings of clerics to assist them in interpreting its texts. Each Shi'ia individual chooses a senior cleric whose writings and teaching they 'follow'—this can continue after the cleric's death, though one cannot elect to follow a cleric in death whom one has not followed in life. This process is often more formal than the English verb suggests, and the Shi'ia themselves describe it as 'emulation'. Grand Ayatollah Ali Sistani—whose offices are situated in the holy city of Najaf—is described as *marja' al-taqlid* or 'object of emulation'; and he and the select group of clerics at his side are known as the *marja'iya* or holy sources. They interpret the texts of the Koran and give guidance to the faithful.

Hence 'Sistani' is a label describing the followers of Grand Ayatollah Ali Sistani, and 'Sadr' the followers of the Sadr family. Both Ayatollah Mohammed Bakr al-Sadr and Ayatollah Mohammed Sadiq al-Sadr were dead, the former executed by Saddam Hussein in 1980 and the latter killed by gunfire in 1999, allegedly by Ba'ath party agents. Mohammed Sadiq's youngest son, the thirty-year-old Moqtada al-Sadr, remained a student, but had attracted through his passionate, if occasionally intemperate, pronouncements and his family links a larger following than one might expect, given his youth and status.

The authority and weight of these figures is conflated with the veneration accorded by the Shi'ia to the holy cities and centres of learning in which Sistani and Sadr reside. The Shi'ia recognise twelve *imams* (leaders and guides of the Muslim community) in history. The first, Ali, was killed in 661, and buried in Najaf; his son Hussein, the third, was killed at Karbala in 680. The twelfth *imam* disappeared and is referred to as the 'hidden *imam*' or the 'guided one' *(Mahdi)*. According to Shi'ia belief this *imam* will return to judge mankind who, till that time, will continue to need guidance. Many of the twelve Shi'ia *imams* spent at least part of their lives in Iraq, and four of Shi'ism's most sacred shrine cities are in the country. Two of these, Najaf and Karbala, were in the Central-South region, each some 140 km. to the west of Kut. It was to these cities that so many of the Iranian Shi'ia who crossed our border made their way.

At noon on Friday, the Muslim holy day, thousands of the province's Sistani and Sadr followers would attend the prayers of those clerics whom they thought best articulated their beliefs. The core of such sessions was the cleric's address, which would consist of commentary on both the spiritual and temporal issues of the day. These addresses could be particularly influential—an *imam* has considerable power over his congregation and when he was relaying direct messages from the Sadr or Sistani offices, such power was tantamount to command.

The Sistani in Wasit greatly outnumbered the followers of Sadr, although comparisons between congregations at affiliated mosques could be misleading. It is ironic that the Sistani at once came closest to exemplifying the single unifying theme that the CPA sought, yet combined it with what has been called the 'Quietist' tradition which shunned traditional involvement in politics. Moqtada al-Sadr had subtly criticised this approach, while refraining from direct criticism of Sistani, and in so doing he had successfully fashioned a personal platform comprising a muscular re-imposition of Islamic tenets, nationalism and intellectual opposition to the occupation. This now found real resonance among the poor and disaffected of Iraq, particularly the young, and a widening gap had appeared between the followers of Sistani and Sadr.

At heart in the Coalition, particularly among the Americans, there was an almost visceral suspicion of Islam; and a similarly dark and instinctive fear of the ungovernable and bloody religion-based violence that seemed to lurk like a contagion in the mosques and winding alleyways of Baghdad and Iraq's southern cities. Moqtada al-Sadr now appeared to embody these demons. While no one had sought to proscribe dealings with his lieutenants and followers in the provinces, the CPA remained wary of him. They had reason for this: he had reputedly established his own secret court system in Najaf based on *sharia* or Islamic law, regularly and stridently denounced the Coalition, and had allegedly formed the armed Jaish al-Mahdi (army of the 'guided one').

We faced a dilemma. Logic called for a political and religious alliance. The kind of proselytising cleric that we needed existed in some measure in Moqtada al-Sadr, but he was unalterably against us. Clearly CPA Wasit could not deal with Sadr followers in the same way as we might deal with ordinary citizens, given their stated ideology and creation of an armed militia. Yet simply to ignore their demands and proscribe their activities seemed counter-productive—we needed at least to retain the possibility of dialogue. While the Sistani might theoretically offer us the best chance of a mainstream political-religious alliance to disseminate our message, this was a role they were likely to shun in practice. Indeed Ali Sistani never once met Ambassador Bremer.

I was therefore surprised when Ali Sistani's *wakil* (representative) in Wasit agreed to see us. At first sight Sheikh Abdul Jawad al-Qarawi seemed an unlikely figure of authority. But here, I knew, was the only man in the province who could stop us dead; and the only provincial leader of any hue who could summon the bulk of Wasit's population onto the streets in their hundreds of thousands. I entered his simple office and extended my hand. He took it in both of his and looked me straight in the eyes. He wore a tightly-wound white turban. His eyes, set like green pebbles in the lines and folds of an angular white-bearded face, radiated a lively intelligence. He was reputedly seventy-two. His words were more like an incantation than a greeting. 'God bless you, God bless you, you are welcome here, and you will always be welcome. You will be a cleansing wind. He sees you and he knows your fears. He will watch over you. You have left your family and your home to help us, and God has placed you here at our sides. Thank you, thank you.' As he spoke he raised one hand, wrapped in a coil of prayer beads, and extended a single finger. 'He knows', he said, 'he knows', and smiled with infinite gentleness. I felt a great calm steal over me as spiritual power flowed from him like electricity. Perhaps the impact he made upon me that day merely reflected my need for mental succour after the vicissitudes of arriving in the province; or perhaps my memory of guitar-playing clerics at school had left me unprepared for high religion.

His office was a simple one with just two rooms, in a narrow city side-street near a furniture shop. There were about twenty hard-backed chairs in the room where he had his desk. On the walls were posters of Ali Sistani and a photograph of Sheikh Abdul Jawad praying. He now sat beside me, subsiding into his voluminous robes, and made a speech of welcome which lasted five minutes. He then stopped suddenly. I was clearly expected to speak. I outlined my early thoughts. He looked at me unwaveringly. I then asked a number of questions, and learned quickly that Shi'ia 'Quietism' made this a rather Delphic process. To a general question about law and order he made clear his support for harsh punishment of criminals, and said that a 'river, though it winds, reaches the sea'. To a second question about Sadr followers he said that they were 'clouds, which would be blown away by a good wind'. My concluding question about the police showed him at his most magnificent. He leapt to his feet and thrashed the air with his stick: the police were idle and good for nothing and should be beaten into doing their work. He, Sheikh Abdul Jawad, would make a better policeman as an old man that a hundred of them. He asked whether, the next time I drove around Kut, he could accompany me and use his stick on them. I thrilled to the idea.

I felt invigorated by our meeting and wondered if I had stumbled on an ally. Although my childhood reverence for the grand old men of the Middle East had owed something to English romanticism and youth, I felt it within me still; yet accompanying it were the same frustrations that had consumed me at the time. Arabia and its people had then seemed impenetrable, and Iraq now no less so. My brain seemed cluttered with European attitudes, as though the light and sounds of the country were fated only to drip into my mind through a clogged filter. I wanted in the coming months to do more than merely reiterate received thought. I felt I needed to prepare myself mentally and physically for what awaited us or risk failure.

Ramadan is one of the five Pillars of Islam and consists of a fast that lasts a lunar month, designed to remind the faithful of the travails of the poor. Neither food nor drink is to be consumed between the hours of sunrise and sunset. A practising Muslim will rise and take breakfast before dawn and eat a large meal after sundown. This mixture of asceticism and fortitude, combined with the sense of fatalism that seemed to colour all Islamic thought, intrigued me. Ramadan was imminent; and I thought that, in taking part in the fast, I could at once explore a culture of which I knew little at first hand and better understand the province and its problems.

Of provincial problems and emergencies there appeared to be no end. I had recently noticed something else about the Iraqis—their love of rhetoric meant that they regarded the chance to deliver bad news as God-given. Research Triangle Institute's local employees, whom I had asked to brief me about the provincial economy, did so uncompromisingly and with every sign of enjoyment. We sat in an unlit council room in the Governor's building, under a painted wall-map of the city and its river. A pigeon cooed from the air conditioning duct behind my head. The work of each branch Ministry in the province was described by its RTI 'shadow'. The first spoke. There was little or no industry. The province was essentially an agricultural area, fed by the Tigris and the thousands of ingeniously fabricated waterways that drew from it. The only manufacturing site of any importance consisted of a Soviet-built 1960s-era textile factory in Kut that employed 3,000 people although it needed only 2,000. It was designed to run continuously in three shifts but the third had been abandoned because of power shortages. It belonged to the government. Given that we were now the government, it belonged to us.

The second speaker rose like a funeral director. Fuel supplies in Kut hinged on three separate petroleum products: gasoline, diesel and heating kerosene. Some of this had previously been supplied by pipeline from Nasiriyah, to the south-west, but the pumping station had been sabotaged. Here he allowed himself a brief smile. All three products were now brought in by road. The province's stocks and reserves were generally kept in a tank farm south of Kut and sub-distributed, but shortages were now acute. The shrinkage of heating oil stocks, particularly, was regarded as liable to cause social instability as winter began to bite. Timm had reacted speedily to this threat, commandeering trucks from all government departments to make the fuel run to Baghdad, but we barely kept pace with demand. Rationing was probably inevitable.

The third man announced contentedly that the power situation was, if anything, worse. The province was among the hardest-hit in Iraq because it generated no power of its own. Instead, electricity was imported from the cities of Baghdad and Amara. Baghdad had little to give, being hard-pressed itself, and the power-lines to the south had been stolen for their copper. Their pylons, robbed of the stabilising weight of the cable, lay capsized and crumpled by the road-side. The CPA had recently let a contract to a private company to refurbish and guard these lines, using the local tribes, but this was likely to take months.

Education was next. There were 619 schools in Wasit, two technical colleges and a university, all serving a population of 175,000 pupils. The vast majority of the schools were in poor condition, and many had suffered war damage. One school I visited later in the week had mortar bombs stacked next to the playground. There was a shortage of desks and chairs. The old curriculum had been outlawed but no replacement had been issued.

On it went. Each set of unsettling figures was enunciated like a dirge by a succession of lugubrious RTI employees. Three-quarters of the sewerage system in Wasit was open channel and flowed directly into the Tigris. The system for distribution of food and gas was ailing, crippled in part by its own centralist complexity and resultant vulnerability to the effects of war. Flour in Wasit, for example, was distributed through 479 separate agents, and gas bottles through 1,349. The courts needed refurbishment. The judges were of varied quality. The police needed training and had no equipment. The Facilities Protection Service demanded salaries.

I saw that lacking industry we also lacked political power, because there was no economic show-piece to which we might devote quick-impact money and technical support. There was nothing obvious to re-vitalise, and the thousands of agricultural smallholdings in the province were no substitute. Although it was difficult to make an accurate assessment of the scale of unemployment, it was clearly high, and the agricultural base caused large seasonal variations in the figures. The structural and economic problems that emerged began to take on a clear shape. Whether it was our invasion, the years of sanctions, or the decades of chronic underinvestment by Saddam Hussein in Shi'ia areas that had caused these difficulties was largely irrelevant: we were the government and it was inevitable that the average Iraqi would waste no time in making such distinctions. The CPA in Baghdad battled with formidable economic problems: subsidising food alone was costing $5 billion a year, and fuel subsidies added $4–5 billion to this figure. Each drained an Iraqi annual budget totalling some $13 billion.

Throughout October the security situation had steadily worsened across the Central-South region as a result of rising tension in the holy city of Karbala. Followers of Moqtada al-Sadr had taken over mosque and government compounds, rejecting the CPA's authority over the country, and established a *sharia* (religious) court and a prison in the city centre. The Jaish al-Mahdi militia carried weapons and drilled and recruited in plain view. Thirty-five people had been killed. It was estimated that a million pilgrims had visited the city in the second week of the month. A segment of this swollen population supported Moqtada al-Sadr's aims, but most did not. Passions were inflamed, and the possibility of mass violence appeared acute. An attack on the mosque was now being considered, but it was unclear whether the Polish could be relied upon to support it. There was pressure on the Governorate to act, but no agreement among the CPA or the military on the kind of action to be taken.

The debate on the subject had divided the Coalition. In Central-South, the area most directly affected, the CPA pushed hard for Moqtada al-Sadr's immediate arrest, believing that delay would allow him to grandstand further and broaden his popular appeal. This mission was not welcomed by the Polish-led Multi-National Division, who feared the public reaction and knew that the patchwork peace-keeping force under its command was ill-equipped for the muscular public order task implied. The Ukrainians, for example, had no mortars, artillery, tanks or helicopters and only the most limited intelligence-gathering capability; indeed Ukrainian officers often vowed darkly that they would one day wreak vengeance on the committee that had designed their Brigade.

The rest of the CPA was cautious, and the British particularly so. Given that the British sector had a large number of Shi'ia, their opinion carried weight because it too would have to deal with the effects of arrest. The British view was pragmatic: the situation was messy but manageable, and seizing Moqtada al-Sadr might further destabilise it. It implied, gently, that the U.S. instinct for action should be resisted; and some Americans in Baghdad, for their part, chafed at what they saw as Britain's failure to grasp the nettle.

Meanwhile the gamblers' odds on the prospects of arrest lengthened and shortened daily. We had no secure communications systems. All the Governorate Coordinators were operating on their private e-mail accounts and would do so till the CPA was dissolved. This meant that no classified information could be passed and that one could not be politically briefed without travelling to Baghdad. The FCO had toyed with the idea of supplying classified systems to British-run Governorates, but had done so only in Basra. Meanwhile the six of us in Central-South agreed a basic code—an e-mail from Hillah with the subject line 'Traffic accidents' would be the signal that an arrest was imminent. We would then decide how best to respond.

The most welcome effect of this continuing debate was the surprise allocation of two more soft-skin vehicles to us, together with four U.S. Army Military Police whose primary role was to protect Timm. In our case we had a British-supplied CRG team who looked after him too; but it was sobering to think that this was the first formal protection allocated to my American colleagues in other Central-South Governorates.

To leave these crisis meetings and travel the province entrusted to us was often a relief. The heat of late summer had begun to dissipate, and grey skies had become increasingly frequent. We now initiated a comprehensive programme designed to visit every district and sub-district, and every Council, Mayor and Director. We would try and reach two to three Councils per day, although this was something of a race because Iraqi working hours were generally 0800–1400, and scrupulously observed. During Ramadan these hours were shortened to 0800–1300, to allow for the effects of fatigue brought on by the fast.

Neil Strachan and I had agreed to do this tour together. I now awoke each day before dawn, dog-tired, and drank a two-litre bottle of water before watching the sun come up over our palm grove. I then wrote for an hour or two in my room before joining Neil in the cars for the day's journey. The first few days of the fast were hard, and the proscription of fluids hardest. I had lancing headaches, and Neil, whose metabolism demanded that he ate hourly, devoured one ration pack after another at my side. I thus saw my fast as Ramadan Plus, a form of religious ordeal which Neil had elected to make a torment. Majed Mayat al-Kureishi, one of our earliest recruits as an interpreter, had given me a set of dark wooden prayer-beads from Najaf, inlaid with silver. I kept them with me constantly. The scent in which they had been immersed lasted a month or two, and my memories of those days are of that perfume, and a growing leanness of mind and physical resilience as we drove thousands of kilometres along the roads and tracks of the province and immersed ourselves completely in its affairs.

Wasit, except for rolling low hills on the Iranian border, consisted of a flat plain bisected by the river, and a fast road running through it from Baghdad to the next province of Maysan and on to Basra. Astride this carriageway were four of the province's major towns and districts, from Suwayrah in the north-west through Aziziyah and Kut to al-Hayy; here lived most of its population. Of the remaining two, Badrah was to the north-east at the border, and al-Numaniyah was a short distance west across the Tigris *en route* to

Hillah. We went to each district, followed by its sub-districts. We did not announce our plans, and in most sub-districts could not have done so because there were no telephone links.

In the province's second city of Suwayrah three men sat idly on a broken bench outside the old administration building. The city, only 55 km. from Baghdad, was closer to the capital than to Kut, and in Sergey's opinion it was the most turbulent town in Wasit. There had been a Council, the men said, but it had dissolved because its members had been threatened. When we asked who had made these threats they looked glum. After a while one said 'Ba'athists' and the others nodded. A silence ensued. They looked at us with undisguised curiosity. We left to find the police chief. He was not present. There was a Mayor, but he was out. In one sub-district we found a Council of six who were all related to each other; and in another a Council of one, a magnificent-looking tribal chief who kissed me on both cheeks and then described a wave of car thefts in the area, adding that fortunately this was no longer a concern. Heartened, I asked why. 'We have killed them' he said. After a moment we asked some questions about the Council. It existed, he said, but met irregularly. When did it meet? When he called for it. How was it composed? Of his friends from the area. Each of them was allowed to bring one other friend.

We drove back to Kut in reflective mood. Had CPA Wasit been flying a battle pennant that day it would have looked rather frayed by the afternoon. Inwardly, I was appalled by the magnitude of the task ahead. How was our small team ever to generate sufficient energy in a province this size to solve these problems? Our CRG team drove us stolidly southward as Wasit effortlessly absorbed our tiny strivings. We would need to start from scratch.

In any post-war deployment of this kind one would expect to have a civilian presence in each major town, with its own transport and local staff. These sub-missions would provide knowledge and direction, and report upward to headquarters at province level. Alongside these one would embed equivalent military sub-units to support these groupings and work alongside them. At this point, six months after the war, CPA Wasit consisted of four international staff and two pairs of cars, dealing with seventeen Councils and a population of just under a million. The Ukrainians could not have satisfactorily picked up the baton: merely communicating between ourselves was hard enough—it is doubtful whether they had more than a dozen English-speakers in their ranks—and certainly the Brigade had no experience at all of political reconstruction. The gulf between the capabilities of this formation and its American equivalent was significant. This lack of political momentum at an important time was damaging and robbed us of political power when we most needed it. It was not merely the result of insufficient troop numbers; the fact was that many of the units we had in Iraq lacked, through no fault of their own, the experience and tools to do the job.

As the year wore on one was often to hear the cliché that we, the CPA and the Coalition's military forces, were involved in 'a race against time' in Iraq. I had always thought this evidence of a lack of substantive thought, because the object of the race—indeed its very purpose—was so rarely articulated. If we were racing against anyone, it was Moqtada al-Sadr and insurgents for the support of ordinary Iraqis. To pursue the metaphor further, we were neither in condition for the race nor properly equipped for it; and we did not always have a full view of our competitors or their preparations. In such circumstances the individuals in our small CPA team had inevitably to work under great pressure, and each person's importance to the whole was magnified because there was no room for redundancy—we had only one person in each slot. This was true throughout the CPA command chain. From the Governorates in the provinces up to Governance in Baghdad HQ, everyone was under pressure, and staffing gaps were common.

Gradually reinforcements arrived. In November Malcolm Russell, our Media Officer, appeared; he was a Second Secretary in the British Foreign Office, aged forty-nine, who had previously been a member of the FCO's office in Baghdad. Although he had no direct media experience he was clearly intelligent and would doubtless prosper—much of the work at hand was common sense. He was accompanied by Tom Dobinson, on contract from the British Department for International Development (DFID), who was now to be our Facilities Manager. These two now took their places in our make-shift office and accommodation block on the first floor of the Villa.

The build-up of our team remained slow, though the FCO were generally able to fill British team slots faster than the Americans. If our team was never to match the full majesty of the coloured charts I had been shown by Barney in Baghdad, it nevertheless reached a form of full strength in January, three months after my arrival. My American colleagues in other Central-South Governorates were much harder-pressed. One of the main reasons for this was that the Regional Centres refused to transform themselves; when asked by Baghdad Operations to spawn provincial Governorates and revert to an administrative and technical support role, they could never quite bring themselves to do so. No one insisted. As 2003 wore on these Centres, intent on securing the staff and equipment to underpin their vision of their political management roles, effectively fought their own Governorates over staffing and logistics. This tug-of-war was profoundly damaging, and meant that neither Regional Centre nor Governorate was able to build its resources quickly enough to do battle coherently.

The order in which the Kut team appeared owed much to the difficulties of recruiting people for work in a country now associated indelibly in the public mind with violence. Administrative and facilities staff should ideally be dispatched at the outset of any deployment so that the build-up of the team—inevitably logistical and administrative in character—can be properly supervised. Media, in normal circumstances, was a portfolio neither more nor less important than any other; but in Iraq it was pivotal as a means of social engineering that might persuade the population of our merits, counter the pronouncements of our enemies, and above all compensate for our deficiencies in design.

Kut had a television and radio station just 300 metres up the Baghdad road; not every province had this infrastructure. Both worked, though their range encompassed only the city of Kut and its environs. This covered 25–30 per cent of the population and enabled us, theoretically at least, to formulate a message and push it home efficiently. The television station, like all others in Iraq, transmitted a centrally distributed 'feed' from Baghdad, but had been allocated one hour each day to broadcast its own news programme. It was on this hour that we now intended to focus.

Projects were another social lever which we thought particularly important, and Timm and I had talked through the ramifications endlessly. We were allowed to draw, for now, on $3.5 million, and apart from Mike Gfoeller's partiality for early police expenditure, we were theoretically allowed to spend this as we chose. This was a lot of money in Iraqi terms, and we had high hopes for the political capital that might accrue. We had sat with the twelve Polish engineers that made up our Governance Support Team (GST), and asked each in turn for his view of sectoral priorities in the province with a view to creating a projects plan. Yet it quickly became clear that spending such a large quantity of money wisely was going to be difficult. The most cursory examination of the requirement showed that the disbursement of this sum was, in essence, a logistical obstacle. First, no table of sectoral priorities existed, and few of the GST had been outside Kut. We would thus need to make one, or risk the kind of impulsive reactions that we wanted to avoid. Second, all the engineers had so far been forced to travel together because the Brigade had found it difficult to allocate a pair of vehicles and the requisite security detail to each of the twelve. Also, they did not possess enough interpreters. One reason, in other words, why no sectoral evaluation had been done was that the Bridge and Water engineers had, *de facto*, been forced to sit through the Doctor's meetings about artificial limbs; and the sewerage expert had become, as a travelling companion of our Agriculture man, a local authority on grain silos. The other reason was security—the engineers simply did not feel comfortable travelling the province at will, and feared the consequences of their profile: they would not be hard to recognise.

We concluded that we could not spend the money in this way, and decided to dispense with this cumbersome procedure. We would hire local Iraqi engineers to do the work, matching them to the specialist roles present in our GST, and use the Poles to run each of the 'cells' so created from our office. The large American four-wheel drives that had been issued to us, complete with orange lights on top of the cabs, were soft-skin and conspicuous: we would accordingly buy half a dozen battered second-hand saloon cars in the market in colours and styles that would allow them to blend in locally, and allocate them to Ministries when we had finished with them. Our Iraqi engineers could then drive themselves to their sites and dispense with interpreters and security. The digital photographs, they took would provide us with much of the routine information we needed, and we would check progress ourselves at intervals. We could thus employ local people, reap the political benefits of philanthropy, enhance local capacity and train future project managers. The main difficulty for now, however, was that our projects officer, another DFID contractee, was not due to join us till January 2004, and the project planning alone threatened to swamp us.

While we wrestled with the administrative and technical detail of project money, media and Councils, Neil's earliest task had been to map the complex structures of political parties and tribes in the province. Although there were areas where the two overlapped politically, these groups generally disliked one another; each competed for power, and neither would share it. Ideology too played its part. The tribes believed they embodied all that was good about Iraq and Iraqis. Their chiefs described themselves as men of chivalry and tradition, whose lineage stretched back over centuries. They were men of the law, who administered discipline in their clans and communities; they were friends to the Coalition; and, most importantly, they were men of their word. To the political parties this was nonsense: in the modern world the tribes were an irrelevance, anxious only to perpetuate a self-aggrandising feudal order of resolute self-interest. Something new was needed—perhaps secular, perhaps religious but certainly devoid of tribal influence.

There are about 100 main tribes and countless sub-sets in Wasit. The majority is Shi'ia, some are Sunni and a handful is mixed. The large tend to look down on the small because power is everything; and one, the Rabi'a, looks down on each of the others, regarding itself as the most regal of the tribes and the father of them all. Every pure-blood Iraqi (as they describe themselves) belongs to a tribe; Iranians have no tribes and are denigrated for this, among other things. All tribal people have loyalty to their tribes, but its strength varies, and today the hold of a tribe upon one of its members tends to centre upon traditional rites of passage like birth, marriage and death. Few of the tribes that I saw as a child in Kuwait that were then nomadic remain so; and my memories of hunting with them and their hawks in the desert, of Bedouin meals in open-sided tents, and of the men afterwards bathing their faces in the smoke from smouldering sandal-wood, are all that now remains—the reality has gone.

The dilemma we and the broader CPA faced in calculating to what extent we should lean on the tribes was not new, and did no more than replicate the indecision of the British during the 1920s

Mandate. If the tribes possessed greater influence then than now, the key questions remained unchanged: how much power did they really have and how was it to be measured? And how might it be used? That same indecision could be seen in the young Iraqis who worked for us. What the tribes principally offered was protection, and their main sanction was its withdrawal—a powerful tribe conferred on its members virtual impregnability from any form of attack or criminal act. The price for that protection was the imposition of tribal custom and law, and the issue at hand was whether one feature of the package was worth the other. As the threat from Moqtada al-Sadr's followers increased and death threats were made against CPA employees, the tribes increasingly instructed 'their' interpreters to leave our employ, which many of them did immediately. This might seem a curious moral retreat, given the tribes' much-vaunted resistance to external interference in their affairs; actually it merely shows the power that Sadr's followers were able to wield over ordinary Iraqis in combining Islam with nationalism. If one concluded from this phenomenon that the tribes were actually weaker than they appeared, a recent CPA poll appeared to buttress the idea: of 1,531 people in five Iraqi cities only 1 per cent of respondents said that they would vote for a tribal party; 4.8 per cent that they would vote for a party of the same tribe but 95.2 per cent that they would not; and 98.6 per cent that they would not comply if ordered to vote in a particular manner by a tribal chief. Conversely, one might as well say that the cities were not the best of places to canvass tribal loyalty given their overwhelmingly rural roots.

Tribal law existed in awkward proximity to national government, and where there was a clash of interests, it was given precedence by them over the Iraqi legal code. The fear of tribal retribution, or 'qawama', might constrain a policeman from making a traffic arrest because the arrested person's tribe could hunt him down, deeming it an insult to that tribe. If a member of a tribe were killed, whether by accident or design, the man responsible could be legitimately killed by the victim's tribe unless mutually agreed blood money were paid within a certain period. Despite this violent culture, the charm, courtesy and hospitality of the tribes was often to bewitch those CPA staff who encountered it, and colour our thoughts of them with an unwarranted romanticism. They were generous and kind, passionate and colourful, and I now regard some tribal chiefs as friends. Yet the tribes, motivated by profit and advantage as they had always been, never took up any cause but their own and praised us as enthusiastically as most of them had once praised Saddam Hussein. They were, as one of our interpreters once said, 'men for all seasons'.

One of the great natural phenomena of which I never tired in Wasit was witnessing an altercation between a tribal leader and a political party representative. The former would enter the room wearing flowing gold-trimmed robes like a galleon in full sail, and, arm outstretched in ritual denunciation and eyes flashing, decry the shallow opportunism of would-be provincial politicians, their lack of history and their plastic clip files. I had watched such men wade alone into aggressive crowds of a hundred or more. Each knew, as the crowd did, that even if he were alone on this occasion, his tribe walked as surely alongside him. His political party opponent, in Western garb, would sit trim-bearded and bespectacled with his pen and paper and document wallet, and look on his tormentor with gentle, condescending disdain, mixed with a touch of anxiety; for if the tribes, for all their espousal of tradition and history, were unable to see that these were their death-throes, their power for now remained.

Indeed, so sure were the political parties of their place in the future of Wasit and of Iraq that they had felt no need to make plans. Each claimed many thousands of supporters, and some many more. Some were convinced that their suffering under the former regime,

if nothing else, qualified them for consideration now; and each routinely claimed that failure to satisfy the political yearnings of its
group would have the most serious consequences. When the CPA
first began to meet the political parties, rhetoric of this kind further
compounded its sense of foreboding about Iraq, from which followed weakness and a desire to accommodate rather than to stand
firm. This was a general political temptation in the Coalition: our
ignorance bred fear, and that fear derived from a combination of our
darkest imaginings about 'fundamentalist' Islam, violent political
agitation, and the knowledge that, despite our political posturing
abroad, we were an ill-constituted and small force engaged in a
risky enterprise.

Some of the largest parties, like the Supreme Council for the
Islamic Revolution in Iraq (SCIRI) and Dawa ('the call'), combined
Islamic precepts, a history of opposition to the former regime, and
apparent strength in numbers. Others such as the Iraqi National
Congress (INC) claimed a legitimacy that derived largely from the
Coalition's encouragement of them and the hope, which later
proved ill-founded, that the population would rally to such exile
opposition groups. The Communists in Wasit appeared workmanlike, pragmatic and well-organised; the two Kurdish parties, while
supportive of us, were not major players. There were perhaps
twenty-two parties in Wasit, although this number ebbed and
flowed; and all worked somewhat loosely together, particularly
when they felt that demands made collectively would further a
general political aim. Yet the heart of political life in Wasit consisted
largely of a handful of them, who generally saw the establishment of
a government on Islamic precepts—or at least one that did not
conflict with them—as the only rational future for the country.

Given that there had been no election for decades, it was impossible to estimate accurately how much support each party might
reasonably claim. It was also difficult to separate some parties'

assumed political power from the armed strength of their military wings, on which they had relied during the years of struggle. SCIRI, for example, had the Badr Corps, effectively a small army. This had now allegedly been disbanded and the Badr Corps was to become the Badr Organisation, but one instinctively doubted the truth of such claims. Was SCIRI's claim to power in Wasit founded on genuine grassroots support for its political aims or on the fear of retribution?

Some parties, SCIRI included, had appropriated government buildings and now used them as offices. The CPA, lacking the confidence to confront them, dealt instead with problems thought to be more pressing. Our relationship with them was further complicated by the fact that, in some areas, unauthorised party-based militias had proved better able to confront lawlessness than the Coalition, and had thereby attracted greater popular support. Yet that same 'five cities' poll that had cast doubt on the reach of the tribes now appeared similarly to undercut the parties' claims: only 2.4 per cent of the 1,531 people polled admitted to being members of a political party, and only 16.4 per cent currently supported one. While such figures are not as persuasive as they appear—fewer than 2.4 per cent of the British population are members of political parties either—it appeared that Iraqis looked neither to their tribes nor to the parties for national leadership. Meanwhile it seemed to us premature to give away power, either in Councils or anywhere else, to groups simply because they demanded it. While we clearly needed to work with the parties, we had no intention of working for them.

Throughout this period of our preliminary research Neil Strachan and I drove for hour after hour through the unremitting flat expanse of the province, discussing such problems; and I would watch Wasit glide past the plate windows, my impressions and thinking concentrated by the Ramadan fast like light through a lens. In many such journeys and chaotic meetings we tried to gauge the extent of tribal and political party support among the population. In some areas a political party clearly dominated our *ad hoc* gatherings, while in others none figured at all. In the hinterland tribal influence was strong. At the end of each day we would draw to a halt in the dust of the compound, and Timm and I would sit after dark before the remains of dinner and catch up on events.

He, assisted by Sally Bond and Facilities Manager Tom Dobinson, had meanwhile been fighting a protracted battle of his own trying to establish order at our site. Although Kellogg Brown and Root had now assumed some responsibility and started work on Tarawa House, dealing with them, as former British Prime Minister David Lloyd George once said of future Irish President Eammon de Valera, was like trying to pick up mercury with a fork. In essence the company did not want us in the city because it did not want to be there itself, and the many daily frictions and difficulties of our working relationship stemmed from this single fact. I could not see how we could function effectively having given up so much administrative power to a contractor.

On 6 November KBR ceased work altogether on the compound; it withdrew the two international staff who had commuted daily from Delta and its Iraqi workforce, and refused to allow them back till our guard force was enhanced. We still did not have our perimeter T-Walls, and perversely KBR would not now put them in place because of the claimed insecurity of the site. We were now in the position of being effectively held hostage by our contractor, which by withholding the concrete defences that could alone secure the site against car-bombs—the central threat—now prolonged the very security deficiencies that precluded it from resuming work.

Meanwhile we and the Ukrainians were exposed to the resulting danger. I was privately deeply worried because I, probably alone of our team, knew from direct experience how vulnerable we were and how devastating a car-bomb attack would be. The logical move was to withdraw to Delta, which is where KBR had wanted us in the first place; yet doing so would cause us to lose hard-won momentum, which at this juncture might prove politically fatal.

Timm and I had long expected to be attacked, and made our plans as best we could. Security was poor. Karbala remained tense, and the atmosphere explosive. On October 27, the day after the rocket attack on the Rashid Hotel, there had been a wave of car-bomb explosions across Baghdad. Thirty-five people had been killed and 230 wounded. On 28 October two Ukrainian armoured vehicles were ambushed in the north of the province with mines, rockets and automatic fire. The warheads went through the armour as if it had been tin-foil. The Coalition continued to suffer a steady stream of losses fighting an enemy who appeared ever more implacable: on the same day a U.S. tank was hit in Baghdad, killing two American soldiers and wounding one, and a U.S. post in Kirkuk was hit by five rockets.

In the first half of November the nights had turned cold. The river now generated a clinging fog, to which our grossly insufficient security lighting lent an other-worldly glow after nightfall. Each night I walked our weak perimeter, sometimes alone and often with Timm. Much of the complex remained in darkness. Few of the Ukrainian soldiers watched their arcs of responsibility; those at the gate often lit a brazier and clustered around it, having placed their weapons against the wall of the guard house. Several times we found them asleep. I could not, try as I might, get them to understand that we would have only one chance when our time came. I had asked the contingent commander to place a heavy truck across the entrance at night, but this could not be done till his vehicles had returned from patrol at about 2130 hours; and meanwhile we lay wide open but for our tiny force of local guards.

On November 12 a car-bomb killed nineteen Italian Carabinieri and nine Iraqis in an explosion of horrifying force in Nasiriyah,

190 km. to the south of us. In the myriad small details of the tragedy one saw the chain of seemingly unconnected events that so often lead to human disaster. Overwhelmingly the incident confirmed to me that the risk to outposts such as ours was real, and that nothing less than the most ruthless attention to detail and to procedure would suffice. If we were not actually at war, it had certainly begun to feel that way.

4

TAKING CONTROL

The enemies ranged against the CPA and its military partners in the winter of 2003 remained frustratingly invisible. The fact that Saddam Hussein was still at large lent them cohesion in our minds, however delusory that impression may in fact have been. His persona served as a rallying point for dissent, and effectively constrained ordinary Iraqis from cooperating with the Coalition through fear that he would return to power.

The CPA's implicit appeals to the Iraqis for support were largely negated by this spectral presence, and his televised exhortations to violence had a powerful effect on the popular mind. Very few supported him, but the great majority feared him, and the effect was often the same. Most of those whose engagement we so sorely needed stayed at home, fearing the hidden dangers of public profile. This absence of the political centre left a vacuum in which fringe groups and opportunists could flourish without opposition. Finding local people willing to take civic responsibility in any leadership role was extremely difficult and this precluded the creation of local political momentum, not least because we were not alone in competing for their attention.

There were in Wasit perhaps half a dozen groups that might have opposed us; and so difficult was it to separate civil society—such as it was—from the militarism that had characterised Saddam Hussein's reign, that one could not exclude the prospect of armed resistance or attack from any of them. Weapons and ammunition were freely available and the majority of males had military training. Nor could one satisfactorily divide one category of possible malefactors from the others, or salve the fears of one without inflaming the passions of the rest.

In one group lay the Islamic political parties, whose principal political objective at this time was hounding Wasit's remaining Ba'athists, who themselves formed a second group. The Islamists, particularly, lacking any manifesto or plan, found that they were able to garner public support in this pursuit, while the Ba'athists, now lacking a livelihood and alternatives, were forced at least to consider armed resistance as practised by their more committed colleagues. These last formed a third group, branded Former Regime Loyalists (FRL) at the time. There was a fourth, consisting of people whom one might simply call opportunists, who would use violence for personal gain. Actually, one could as readily have applied this label to all of them. I did not sense that the province was yet playing host to those who could be called professional terrorists from outside the country, but Baghdad was only 55 km. from our northwestern townships on a fast road, and the notion that they would not intervene seemed absurdly optimistic, particularly as Coalition pressure began to bite in the capital. The attack on the Ukrainians on October 28 seemed a portent. Sergey told me that he and his soldiers had found passive night goggles at the scene, which suggested an assault of some sophistication. Ironically the Ukrainians possessed none of these themselves.

When I looked at my first death threat I tried to establish in which category my would-be assailant belonged. It was couched in a U.S. intelligence document and detailed my fate in a series of terse paragraphs: 'Who', 'What', 'How', 'When' and so forth. It reminded me of the British board game 'Cluedo', in which you are supposed to establish who had been murdered, by whom, where and how—for example, 'the Colonel, with a hammer, in the study,' and so on. In my case it was to be a member of the Sunni Muslim Sa'dun family, employing a rocket-propelled grenade launcher and automatic weapons at a time of his convenience. There was a photograph of a square-jawed member of the family looking fixedly and with obvious determination into the camera. I showed it to Timm, who congratulated me and seemed disappointed that he had not received one of his own. Bob, the new head of our CRG security team now that Russ was on leave, appeared wholly unmoved, saying merely with unanswerable logic that his team continually operated as though such threats existed. Sulking slightly I returned to my room. I would receive two more.

Moqtada al-Sadr's platform of principle made his followers potentially the most dangerous of all. In rejecting CPA government and proposing one of his own based on religious precepts, he encouraged closer public examination of us. Whether or not we had ourselves created the unemployment, shortages, corruption and decay that made the lives of so many Iraqis a misery, we were now seen as responsible for them. The quiet Sadr clerics we had met in our travels round the province sitting at the back of various Council meetings had treated us with courtesy, and answered our questions unfalteringly. Their questions were more difficult to parry at this point seven months after the war when public patience had been eroded. Why did we tolerate this police force, which was so clearly incompetent? Why was there no electricity? Why were there fuel shortages? How long did we think the population would endure unemployment at present levels? In proposing an alternative form of government they had signalled their intention to impose order where we had failed to do so ourselves.

These difficulties were institutional, complex and hard to solve, and compounded by a police force which was at once a problem in its own right and one that exacerbated others. The idea that Sadr's people should quietly intervene to sort things out was at least arguable among many of the people who were directly affected by these deficiencies. To what extent this heralded broader discontent was hard to say. It remained difficult to assess numbers—the Sistani insisted that Sadr were transient 'clouds' and untrustworthy, and belittled their possible impact on events; yet Moqtada al-Sadr's followers claimed dominance in several of the towns in the province.

Among the areas in which they had a following was Zubadiyah, a half-hour's journey north-west of Kut. There was a Council in the city but it was unpopular, and its head was seen as an American stooge. Both Sergey and I had been invited to a '*husseiniya*', a religious building in the town, to hear the case against the existing structure, and in our ignorance walked straight into a crude political ambush. The area around the building was crowded with people, who jostled and shoved at the entrance. A cleric played the 400 people within like an orchestra. We were shown to seats at the front, and at once given a memorable display of religious-political demagoguery. The Sadr *imam*, who had arrived only ten days before from Baghdad, resembled a turbaned Rasputin and harangued the crowd through a microphone: 'Do we want this Council?' The standing congregation, of whom not a man was over thirty, roared 'No!' Again, 'Do we want this Council?' 'No!' 'Do we want to change this Council?' 'Yes!'

The effect on the mind of this potent mixture of Islam and parish-politics, particularly expressed in the heated atmosphere of a small and crowded building whose walls reflected a barrage of sound, is pronounced. It is also curiously difficult to look dignified without one's shoes. Neither Sergey nor I should have been there at all, and in attending we had made the error of offering ourselves as political hostages for twenty painful minutes. I noted with anxiety the number of people the Sadr cleric had mustered, together with the absolute control he appeared to wield over them. With hindsight, one can see that the most interesting aspect was that he could gather no more than that number in a sizeable town, and that the absence of the mass political centre from the political arena had left it free for groups like these to appropriate. This distortion of my perceptions taught me a core lesson—so often in Iraq it is what has *not* happened as a result of an event or trend that is instructive.

I believed that what we had seen that day was an outpouring of popular anger against the Council, and agreed that we would examine the cleric's proposals to leaven the existing structure with newcomers. Yet we lacked a system for doing so, and I would have preferred to dismantle the Council and start anew than attempt difficult value judgements without adequate intelligence. There had already been violence—the Council building had been sprayed with Kalashnikov fire the previous night. I rejected his attempts to have the proceedings filmed, and only when I threatened to abandon discussions did he agree.

His insistence on filming our talk was consistent with our early appraisal that the media were central to Moqtada al-Sadr's cause. The television station in Kut had so far provided the principal source of contention between us and his followers. The hour available each day for programming was contested—they saw this as their chance to screen Sadrite religious debate, while we saw it as our opportunity to nurture the educated middle class whose support we craved. Malcolm, our media officer, was often called upon to rule on programme content, but meanwhile the twenty-six-year-old Sheikh Abdul Jawad al-Issawi, whom we believed to be Moqtada al-Sadr's main leader in the province, would arrive without warning in the television studio and alternately weep, harangue and threaten the manager till he screened his chosen material, which was often inflammatory. We would then ban him for a fortnight. In this way we maintained an uneasy accommodation.

Two days after the Nasiriyah bombing a Foreign Office security assessment team consisting of Baghdad's resident security adviser and the CRG operations officer travelled down to Kut at speed, allegedly at the British government's behest, and asked us what we needed in order to secure ourselves. Bob Pease, our alternate Kut CRG team leader while Russ was on leave, was a British national who had spent most of his adult life in the French Foreign Legion. He was a hard man, and a professional, who spoke fluent French without a hint of a French accent, and was wont to lapse into this unique language without thinking. I had sat down with him the previous evening and asked him to assemble a list of our principal needs for the site.

In Bob's estimation and my own, we were vulnerable because we lacked a professional guard-force, military or civil. The Regional Centre in Hillah had sub-contracted Gurkhas, and it was planned to extend this measure to the Governorates; but there was no date fixed for its establishment in Kut. Meanwhile it was clear to us that we could not solely rely on the available soldiery for our safety. The key was to stop any attempt to run a car-bomb through the gate, and thus we asked for a small security team of no more than four to six people, complete with a machine-gun, with this as their only task; two aerosol-style fog-horn alarms to alert the staff on the base to danger; and a simple boat and outboard motor in case our exit from the base was blocked and we needed to get out across the river.

None of this ever came. Instead I would receive at intervals from Baghdad messages like (and I paraphrase) 'Be careful of your security during x period. Complacency kills.' These irritated me profoundly because it was clear to me that the complacency of others was much more likely to kill us than any theoretical shortcoming of my own. At intervals, after a major incident in which there had been casualties, the British would circulate a message to all their staff saying that they would quite understand if anyone now wished to go home. In response to my recent death-threat from the Sa'dun family, which had now made its way through the system, it was suggested that I should 'lower my profile'. How this was to be done as a British GC in Iraq with two yellow cars and a mandate to oversee the province was not explained.

These messages did not give me confidence that we had done our homework, or possessed the resolve to push the Iraq project through. I did not believe then that the British office in Baghdad understood the circumstances at Governorate level, and I am now sure that they did not. I believed that our leadership structures were flawed on the British side, and that what we needed was someone capable of satisfactorily combining diplomatic and military strategies. I was not persuaded that the British Foreign Office could do this alone.

These conclusions felt rather heretical at the time, particularly given my institutional loyalties. I worried much more about hierarchy than Timm, who recognised the structural shortcomings of the CPA and its partners like an old friend and moved unsurprised and unhesitatingly to fill the gap, uttering his war-cry of 'Hogan's goat'. The truth was that we were almost completely alone in every sense: money flowed in and our reports flowed out, but this was the sum of our strategic traffic. Never in my experience had the disparity between the breath-taking scale of our responsibilities and the paucity of our strategic direction been so acute; and I could not decide whether this expanse of clear blue water was a function of design or omission. I worried about systems and instinctively expected hierarchical solace, whereas this concerned Timm not at all. He did not expect to be looked after and rarely asked permission to do anything. His kind of American still had a bit of the frontier in him. It was a quality the British generally lacked.

We had inherited from the U.S. Marine Corps a body known as the Constitutional Council. It had once served as an assembly of sorts and a provincial-level interlocutor, and had been constructed by the Marines from a long list of 800 names, gathered from all corners of Wasit in what must have been a nightmarish selection process. This included religious leaders, political parties, union leaders, tribal chiefs and a host of others. In the interregnum between the Marines' departure and our arrival it had continued to meet and had grown unruly, while its opinion of its own importance had blossomed. Islamic party representatives had become increasingly dominant, and had devoted recent sessions to advocating the creation of a citizens' militia. They had heard of our intention to review Council structures across the province, and proposed a motion that this power of adjustment should properly belong to them.

I had not attended any of these sessions, not wishing to lend legitimacy to them till I understood the situation in the province. But while there was clearly more to be done to achieve this, we felt that we could no longer allow such meetings to continue. Although we quailed inwardly at the prospect of dissolving the only quasi-governmental structure we had, and the apparent impossibility of assembling another, we could not yet muster the power merely to modify it in the face of probable opposition. It had to go.

The province felt dangerously fragile: the stand-off in Badrah continued, although the Ukrainians had imposed a truce; the tension in Zubadiyah appeared to presage a more general movement by Sadr to exploit our weakness, for which we lacked any obvious remedy; and fighting had broken out between rival factions in al-Akhrar, a town 20 km. west of Kut, who now vied for control of its Council. The police force would do nothing, and the Ukrainians rightly saw the solution to these difficulties as being primarily political. While the idea of a militia, or tribal levies, seemed attractive in the short term to deal with urban security problems and boost employment, we feared that in creating them we would merely solve one problem and beget another; and I privately doubted whether disestablishing them afterwards would be easy. Meanwhile Wasit seemed caught in an arc of growing violence that ran from Baghdad to the holy cities of Karbala and Najaf in the west;

and on southward to Nasiriyah. At our backs was a border that was not worthy of the name. We needed to take control—quickly.

The Constitutional Council met on Saturday mornings in a room just across the hall from the Governor's office. Its raucous sessions, I had been told, often lasted hours. Our decision wholly to dismiss it was the result of careful consideration, but it made me anxious. In dissolving this structure we would be forced to create another, and in taking the provincial helm with our tiny team we could expect no early assistance. I was also entirely unsure whether the Council would obey my instruction to disband, and what effects might ensue from the order. I did not wish to use force, but had no choice but to do so if opposed. We could not afford to look weak now.

We had elected not to use troops, but had retained Ukrainian soldiers at the gates of the Governor's building who could rapidly be summoned upstairs. We had decided to give the Council no warning and no opportunity for comment; and to ask one of our interpreters to check first that it was fully in session. At 1030 we jumped into the CRG vehicles, and swept through the city and in through the heavy gates. I could hear the noise of the Council from the end of the corridor as if hundreds of people were shouting at once, and walked towards it as one might enter a gladiatorial arena, feeling little of the confidence I consciously radiated like a force-field. CRG went in first for dramatic effect; and as they moved left and right from the double doors I saw that the room was completely full— there must have been at least seventy people. All stopped talking. I walked through the crowd to the chairman and told him that I wanted to speak. He got up without a word.

Iraqi society, though it is underpinned by rigid social structures, can appear haphazard to an onlooker. Meetings are, by our standards, anarchic. I knew that Iraqi etiquette requires that one traditionally greets the members of a meeting as one enters the room, however late—not for them the guilty ignominy of the Westerner in joining such sessions after they have begun—and had done so brusquely. It is also traditional, however, for Iraqis solemnly to greet the guest again with right arm raised in welcome as he sits down, and this I had forgotten completely. My plan to cow this unruly Council with ten seconds of stage-managed glaring thus fell foul of a noisy and extended ripple of shouted greeting: '*Allah bil Khair*'.

As the noise died away I told them that we had travelled the province extensively, and seen in it a sense of drift and confusion. There was no faith in government; branch Ministries did not function properly; there was sewage and rubbish in the streets; crime, corruption, high unemployment and disillusionment among the young were rife. Much of this was due to misrule by Saddam Hussein, and some too was due to the war fought by us to depose him. I told them that it was time for us now to end this period of emergency, and to work to improve the lives of ordinary people on the basis of three priorities: the rule of law in all its aspects, reconstruction, and preparation for elections. I thanked them for their courage and hard work but said that we would need a new provincial structure for this period. This Council was not to meet again, and the doors would remain locked till its successor had been established. Some of the crowd nodded, and we left in silence. It was over. I later found that the Kut City Council had taken to joining the provincial Constitutional Council's sessions, and that I had inadvertently dismissed both.

We had given ourselves two weeks to create another. This was no arbitrarily selected period but the longest time we thought we could risk this representative void continuing before it was exploited to our detriment. We had determined from the beginning that we would not seek to replicate the 'Council of Notables' model that the Constitutional Council had been. At this distance from the end of formal hostilities the population had a right to expect more, and the relative judgements about individual worth that the selection process would inevitably require would make us vulnerable. We wanted the new Province Council to be as representative and democratic as possible within the limitations of political circumstance: we could not initiate elections, and the body had to be in place in a fortnight. Above all, we wished to tie the province to its Council in a way that would make disavowal of its activities difficult.

We decided on a crude form of proportional representation. Each District Council would supply two of its members to the Province Council, and each sub-district one. This would provide the basic foundation. There would be variations, but our rule was that each of these should be transparent and easily justified. The first was that Kut, because of its size (and the number of people we would need to placate) would be allowed four Councillors. The second was that we would impose women members because none would otherwise be selected in this post-war climate of Islamic conservatism, ironically more restrictive now than it had ever been before the war. The total number of district Councillors would thus be fourteen, and of sub-district Councillors eleven. We would add four women—all we thought the Council might accept, plus one, whom the Province Councillors themselves would select from the province. The Chairman would be chosen by Council vote and the vacancy then re-filled by the district or sub-district Council of the member chosen. The total figure would thus be thirty, out of a theoretical maximum of forty.

The third variation was more contentious. We debarred any district or sub-district Council from sending us political candidates, to avoid the risk of re-creating precisely the kind of self-sustaining political cabal that we had just dismissed. What we wished to establish was a cadre of the very people whose absence had proved so damaging to date: the educated middle-class. Once this was done, and a majority of such people had been established, we would add the components to make it properly representative using the ten vacant slots.

Meanwhile the Councils that were to provide these were to be subjected to careful scrutiny and adjustment. We saw the Sistani tradition as the best expression of mainstream thought in the province, and had agreed with Sheikh Abdul Jawad al-Qarawi's staff that we would draw on their knowledge of its districts and post-war structures. This would allow us the local knowledge we had so obviously lacked in the early weeks. We had also asked two political parties for their views, and the outgoing chairman of the Constitutional Council for his. Each of these four bodies provided us a list which, in its opinion, named the best Councillors available. Some were in Councils already, while others were not. These names were then combined in a master list after extensive discussion, designed to ensure that no one group—including the Sistani—got all that it wanted. These lists were to dominate our every waking moment. Our aim was to create Councils that were merely good enough to deliver us candidates for a provincial body—we did not delude ourselves that this was a perfect process.

We now had a selling job to do and drove through the province again, this time with the clock ticking. During our journeys I would look at our province in detail, and mark the seasonal changes. In the few moments when our work did not clamour for attention I daydreamed about long imaginary journeys into the empty spaces that I could only glimpse from the road. It was cold now, and the desert light was fragile. The sand, once grey and lifeless, seemed gold in the slanting sunlight; the blue-hatched areas I had once overlooked on the maps had gradually become seasonal lakes, which in spring would come to resemble inland seas that stretched from the road to the horizon. The desert birds that were drawn to them were magnificent: herons, oyster-catchers, pied kingfishers and egrets. I think we once saw flamingos as a distant pink line on flood-water.

Now that working life had become brutal, I came to treasure such moments. The British Army speaks of 'the loneliness of command', and that constant corrosive strain now increasingly affected me as that first winter enveloped us. Every little thing was so very difficult, and it took a huge effort to move us forward each day. The very word 'forward' was subjective. It was as if Wasit were pre-programmed for anarchy and decay, and nothing we did could deprive it of this basic birth-right.

The routine of these journeys was largely unchanging. We would arrive at a town without prior warning. Councils often used the same premises as the police, particularly in small towns, and our arrival would cause near-panic as two or three policemen would appear with their faces crumpled by sleep, pulling on the semblance of a uniform. I would sit on a chair in an office strewn with papers and cigarette-ash. They would offer me a seat at a desk, as befitted my status, but I would always refuse—this tendency to self-depre-ciation and humility they saw as nothing but folly. Why would any man renounce the trappings of power? They would quickly de-nounce the Councils they purportedly served as idle good-for-nothings, and plead for weapons. If one were to ask about security they would say that it was *very* good—anything else would imply criticism of their proficiency. Yet in the next district—well, they said, it was a catastrophe.

I would then castigate them for sleeping and doing nothing. They would say that the Ramadan fast was stressful and caused one fatigue. I would say that I was fasting and not at all tired. By this time a Councillor would have arrived, as well as a dozen or so other random members of the local population who were merely inter-ested in seeing what was going on. Each in turn would be noisily welcomed regardless of what point our conversation had reached. The police, the Councillor would later tell me quietly, were very poor indeed.

Each night Neil and I would sit late and document our impressions. These would then be compared with the lists and notes provided by the Sistani office and others. Councils were adjusted and encouraged, and the worst of their members dismissed. Some townspeople were persuaded to join. The kinds of people who might make members of the Province Council gradually emerged in the course of a frantic fortnight. Each Council was then asked to provide its candidates, whom we insisted they should choose themselves. Mainly they chose sensibly and with great care.

In all this time the CPA's future in Iraq had remained opaque. We believed, when we had time to think, that we would be in Wasit for a year or two, gradually abdicating power while strengthening the structures we had created. I had thought I might keep a micro-light aircraft at Delta and explore the desert that daily bewitched me from the Land Cruisers. Sergey supported all forms of aviation enthusiastically and had already beamed his assent. I wanted to see the holy cities and to speak Arabic fluently. At the same time, conditions were very difficult and the security situation was worsening, and the idea that this life would continue without remission was a strain.

The November 15 Agreement abruptly turned these plans upside down. It arrived without warning. The CPA would dissolve on 30 June 2004 and hand over to an interim Iraqi government. The shock of this was considerable, and I felt quite numbed by it. One could not mistake the general sense of relief which permeated HQ's announcement of the news—there was no appetite for remaining in Iraq among many in the CPA in Baghdad, and here at last was an exit strategy. We had seven months. On the CPA website there now appeared an automatic counter that calculated the remaining days to sovereignty.

We welcomed the new sense of focus, but dreaded the increased workload. We understood the political reasons behind it all, but my overwhelming feeling at the time was of professional shame. Gone were our projections about training and capacity-building, our carefully thought-through project work, and our plans to nurture each of the Councils and steadily reform the branch Ministries. We would run out of time. As the news filtered through, people adjusted to these new facts. Our local staff, who had run the risks of working with us, now knew that we would soon leave them. Saddam Hussein remained at liberty, and the possibility of retribution scared them. Most Iraqis welcomed the notion of sovereignty so long as an Iraqi was not in charge, and wondered, only half-jocularly, whether Bremer might stay. They feared the abrupt withdrawal of military and political power, and some feared civil war. The agreement would encourage the corrupt and inefficient, who might now attempt to avoid scrutiny; and doubtless the Police Chief and his Deputy had a quiet celebratory fruit juice in the limitless savannah of his palatial office.

One of my earliest memories as a child is giving a party to which almost nobody came because a powerful cabal of six-year-old girls at the Kuwait Anglo-American School had persuaded one boy after another to defect to a rival function. As the date drew near for the inaugural meeting of our Province Council, similar nightmares assailed me. Iraqis love the destruction of institutions, and our dismantling of the Constitutional Council had won favour with the rank and file. The Governor was ecstatic, and praised me extravagantly while wringing my hand. His political opponents who had so disturbed his Saturday mornings had gone from his building like the Gadarene swine, and he was alone with his fridge. But there is also a commensurate suspicion of any move to build something new in its stead, and every effort will be made to pull it apart at birth. Neil and I had proudly unveiled our draft list of Province Council members to our interpreters, who gathered around it with relish. After a moment one pointed to our most promising candidate and said

'This man is a mean and greedy thief'. The others nodded. This was undoubtedly true. 'And he', another said, pointing to a second name, 'accepted bribes in the Army.' A third said helpfully that at least three of them were practising Ba'athists, and the sister of one was thought to be a prostitute.

On the appointed day I sat in the Council room with my stomach in knots. It was cold and the power had gone. One could hardly imagine a less auspicious beginning, a room so devoid of spirit and life, or that any of the people we had encouraged so tirelessly could still bring themselves to believe in us. My childhood nightmares returned—the untouched jelly, the Twiglets inviolate, the balloons crisp in their corners, unsullied by small hands. The faces of the U.S. Military Police who guarded the entrance showed that same gentle concern that my parents had shown at the time, and CRG stood talking to one another in the empty room. By the start-time of 1000 only three members had arrived. I smiled fixedly at them. Two more came and sat disconsolately on a bench. Over the next half hour they arrived in twos and threes. Fourteen people—then eighteen—then twenty-two: the room gradually filled and warmed. Shyly, one member for Kut showed me a bundle of letters left to him by his grandfather. They were signed by Sir Percy Cox, who had assumed his duties as the British High Commissioner in Iraq eighty-three years before.

I welcomed them and asked who wished to be considered for Chairman. Seven people raised their hands. The rest prevailed upon them to describe themselves and why they stood. They did so, calmly and sensibly. We circulated a ballot paper on which all names were listed. We were determined to allow them to choose their own leader, but the consequences of error were potentially serious. The first vote was tied, so we did it again. And this time an English-speaking clinical pathologist, Dr Abdul Salaam al-Safaar, won by a clear majority. I got up from the Chairman's chair and gave it to him before joining in the applause. He asked for God's help in performing his task, and then smiled. We had a Council and a Chairman. Most important, we had allies.

Dr Abdul Salaam was about fifty and a good example of the kind of man who had previously walked to work at his hospital each day, head down, concentrating on this ritual and little else. Political issues and the situation in Iraq might be discussed at home, but generally not elsewhere; and at no stage had he contemplated direct action to effect change in one way or another. He was, the interpreters said disapprovingly, from a very small tribe and unmarried; in addition, his sister was a Ba'athist. But so far as we were concerned he was all we could reasonably have hoped for, and he had been elected by his peers from a representative Council. He spoke some English, and had learned Spanish from a Cuban girl who had worked in Iraq long ago.

We now established for him a small Secretariat of two people which Research Triangle Institute funded, whose job it would be to help run the Council, its documents and finances, and agreed to maintain the closest working relationship. We would meet formally each week on Mondays, before the weekly sessions of the Council on Tuesdays. We agreed that his Chairmanship would again be put to the vote in a month.

Each of the three principal power bases in the province—political parties, the tribes and Province Council—believed that they, solely, should be running its affairs. Dr Salaam saw the parties as trouble-makers and the tribes as obsolete windbags, and counselled strongly against apportioning power to either. They in turn saw him as a *parvenu* of no experience and an opportunist who did not know his place. In order to absorb these potentially damaging tensions and allow the Council to gain momentum and stature, we had long accepted that two other structures should be formed: a consultative group of political parties that included religious representation, and a tribal council.

We had hoped to use the Province Council as a quasi-legislature, and the two other groups, formed solely to assuage their ambitions, as councils of elders who might guide our thinking. In this I was doubly mistaken. The tribes were generally too polite to presume to proffer guidance and confined their debate to feudal issues, such as the supply of water, fertiliser and land disputes. Their view of the world was retrospective. The sweeping political issues of the day were of only limited interest to them, and they disapproved of overt politicking. The Amir al-Rabi'a, the head of the Rabi'a tribe, who lived in an airy mansion on the river bank in the nearby town of Al-Akhrar, quoted Ali, the first *imam*—'Oh God, make the borders between us and Persia mountains of fire'—and saw in the encroachment of Iran and its merchants a dangerous erosion of the tribal lore that had once secured Wasit. He confided that he was profoundly tired of clerical agitation.

The political parties meanwhile arrived in our offices each Thursday like a convocation of 1970s British trade unionists, exuding self-importance. Each spoke at length from prepared texts and would allow no interruption. Meetings were stormy and could not end till each had ground their way ponderously through their pamphlets. The Supreme Council for the Islamic Revolution in Iraq (SCIRI) and Dawa dominated these sessions, and each prefaced its interventions with a religious dedication.

These were difficult meetings, and our courtesies did little to disguise the innate antagonism between us. They saw me as an obstacle to advance, and politics as a chance not to serve but to lead. We feared, in their grand pronouncements and thin rhetoric, the worst of futures for Wasit; and devoted ourselves to controlling them. This was not easy. The CPA, in July 2003, had inaugurated a consultative structure of its own, the Iraqi Governing Council (IGC), with a rotating Presidency and limited powers. Its symbolic power, however, was substantial in a country where symbols are important, and these parties, most of which enjoyed IGC representation, were suffused with its warmth. The IGC was unpopular in the country, and exasperated CPA Baghdad with its meandering, but gave its constituent parties more profile than they deserved. Meanwhile, their local representatives, armed with up-to-date information from their IGC seniors in Baghdad, were often far better informed than we were because Governance was overstretched and we had no classified communications system.

With the advent of the 15 November Agreement and its newly compressed calendar, our workload towered over us. The days were exhausting, and each separate accomplishment required brute perseverance. It was cold. Rain fell unendingly from leaden skies, and the province was covered in red clay that regularly bogged the heavy vehicles and stuck to clothes and boots like glue. The roads were increasingly flooded, and the cities began slowly to run with rainwater in which sewage and rubbish mixed. To the frictions of the day were added a catalogue of systemic deficiency, error and omission such as I had never experienced before. We had no perimeter, few security lights, no classified communications systems and no operating budget. KBR presented, in its recalcitrance, an endless array of problems. The food was delivered erratically, always unpalatable and often cold. There was little hot water. The sewerage system was regularly overwhelmed. We had satellite telephones on which one could call home, but no other morale and welfare facilities of any kind, and no social life except each other. Meanwhile the security situation made every move out of the compound a potential hazard, and heightened our apprehensions. We both lived and worked at close quarters in a small building: the team, with security detachments, was now fourteen-strong, but the delays in the building and refurbishment programme meant that this crowding would persist.

The British had established a leave routine for their nationals of six weeks on and a week off, which, despite their best intentions,

now damaged a team that was at once too small and ill-matched to
its tasks. It was never again complete, and generally at least two
people were away at the same time. These portfolios would then be
absorbed by the others, who were already swamped by the scale of
their existing tasks. Timm, for example, in dealing with KBR and
the spectrum of provincial projects, was simply unable to do more;
he took leave only once in eleven months. Meanwhile each British
national going on leave was delivered to Baghdad and later collected
again by CRG in our only set of armoured vehicles, as regulations
required.

I did not dare show the strain of which I had become increasingly
conscious. The daily threat of attack, our flawed perimeter and this
cargo of undiluted responsibility now conspired with the rigours of
our political task to create a crushing weight. Each day was indistin-
guishable from its predecessor. Fatigue was evident in everyone, and
the team had become fragile. Timm and Neil, so long the motor of
our effort, could no longer keep awake in afternoon meetings, and
fell asleep as soon as they got into a car. I clung to the rigours of the
fast because it enabled me to impose a simple framework on the day,
as surely as the rigours of the day sought to impose themselves on
me and cleaved to the half-remembered personal standards of my
military training.

Each morning, as I walked the ten feet from my room to our
communal office for the daily brief, I threw on my leader's confident insouciance like a cloak. The rain and overcast skies now
seemed perpetual. The swollen river above the barrage was red
with mud, its surface creased by a sullen and gusting north-west
wind that rattled our doors and windows. We would coordinate the
day's events, absorb the night's bad news—there was rarely any
other kind—and work till evening. During many of these winter
days one could sense the low morale in the room like humidity; and
on a few, when a light of infinite clarity lit the river against the reed

beds, one felt the room lift. I wondered whether this was what defeat and failure felt like. Was this frantic perseverance mere human reaction to a sense that one lacked control of events? Was the CPA, after all, to be withdrawn ignominiously from Iraq? However dramatic it may now sound, we felt very alone that winter; and I believe that all that then stood between us and outright failure was the unrelenting application of will. During our nine months in Kut we were visited only once by senior Foreign Office staff based in the Green Zone, and then at my express request. This was a style of leadership unfamiliar to me.

On December 14 a contentious and difficult meeting of the political parties took place in the Villa. An apparently interminable speech by one of the Kurdish representatives was punctuated by sporadic gunfire from al-Ezah, a poor quarter across the river. This was not unusual, and he continued without a pause. In the next few minutes the firing became more frequent, till one volley joined another in a curtain of noise that reverberated around the streets of the city. I was determined not to react and carried on listening to the speech, which by now was mercifully faltering. Now explosions were added to the gunfire. I heard grenades and what sounded like bomb-blasts. An interpreter came into the room with a CRG security man. He told me quietly that Saddam Hussein had been captured. Kut was merely celebrating. I told the parties quietly and with genuine pride—the Coalition had achieved, in the end, what they could not do themselves. They were curiously silent as they left the room. I walked the SCIRI representative to our gate as stray bullets fell to the ground around us. Later, when we saw the first pictures of Saddam in captivity, one of our interpreters, with infinite dignity, said to me 'Sir, this is the most wonderful day of my life.'

I am often asked if I supported the war in Iraq and whether I felt morally exposed once it had become clear that its underlying rationale—the threat posed by weapons of mass destruction—was baseless. The truth is that once I arrived in Iraq I thought little about it. This was partly because our presence there was an accomplished fact and could not be undone; and partly because all I saw in my tenure—the echoing palaces, the profligacy and evidence of whole-sale persecution, the lack of development, the insane size and variety of his armed forces—trumpeted Saddam Hussein's defi-ciencies as a leader and made preposterous any notion that the region could have remained at peace with him in power. He was hated in the Iraqi south. Our mistake was to think that we would therefore be loved. A local man said to me: 'Saddam Hussein could be eliminated only by Allah or by the Americans, so we accepted the Americans—yet we are anti-American because of Israel.'

Saddam Hussein's capture appeared to create a strategic oppor-tunity. Perhaps more than this, it answered the question posed by the November 15 Agreement: how could we possibly have left Iraq with him at large? We now had an exit strategy, and we gathered in Baghdad to discuss it at a 'Commanders and Leaders' conference—my first. The power represented by those in the room was consid-erable. Ambassador Bremer, at the head of the table, ran the coun-try. General Ricardo Sanchez, to his right, ran the Coalition's military forces. On his other side was Britain's Sir Jeremy Green-stock. Around the table sat the eighteen Governorate Coordinators, each responsible for a province; and interspersed among us were the Divisional commanders, each mustering thousands of soldiers.

The meeting hinged on three topics: the capture of Saddam Hussein, the implications of the November 15 Agreement and the launch of the strategic plan that would govern our disengagement from Iraq. Bremer noted that there remained a core of hard men whom we would have to capture or kill; others, on the fringes, had been motivated by hope and fear, and now with Saddam Hussein's capture they had been deprived of hope and were no longer condi-tioned by fear. We had a time-sensitive opportunity, and our rate of project spending would rise threefold in the next three months in order to create jobs and cement political engagement. During this period a process of 'refreshment' would begin, in which each Council should be reviewed to ensure that it was sufficiently representative. Once this had been done, all Governors who had been appointed rather than elected were to be confirmed by Council vote. Councils would also be given new local powers commensurate with CPA's intention to de-centralise Iraqi government.

Despite the triumph of Saddam Hussein's capture, I thought the atmosphere in the room brittle. Bremer was a tough man and an assertive leader but he was also remote, and his lack of human warmth made it difficult for him to assuage the anxiety that lingered stubbornly in the room. Our problems at Governorate level were overwhelmingly practical, and these increasingly affected our political capacity. The capture of Saddam Hussein did not affect this fact one way or the other. For most of us security was a primary concern, though there were marked geographical variations. All hoped that this remarkable success would herald a change in this environment; meanwhile our ability to operate seemed to hinge entirely on the forces under General Sanchez's command.

It was U.S. military power that guaranteed our political transactions. We all knew it, and it was most in evidence when the American generals spoke. The silence that greeted their observations was especially eloquent—it was these people who would ultimately make a success or failure of Iraq. Dempsey of 1st Armored, Swannick of the 82nd Airborne, and Odierno of the 4th Infantry Division, whose soldiers had just captured the former dictator: these men, laconic and measured were the rocks to which we instinctively clung. The broad power they wielded was extraordinary. I had been told that Swannick alone had over $30 million—renewable—to spend on public infrastructure in his Divisional area. A Spanish general rose to speak, and apologised for his accented and halting English. 'Hell', said Dempsey, deadpan, lounging in his chair, 'that's OK. Swannick barely speaks English either.' General Swannick, well over six feet tall, and with a face like cracked leather, smiled suddenly and with affection. Confidence radiated into the room from these people like warmth from a log fire.

The 'refreshment' idea caused alarm. Already stretched, the GCs felt that this deliberately created more turbulence in provinces that already appeared fragile enough. Instead of playing our provincial hands in a manner that suited our circumstances, the 15 November Agreement now forced us all into the same political box, at a rate and pace driven only by CPA's proposed dissolution. For most of us the *ad hoc* array of councils and assemblies that characterised our province structures was the only social glue we possessed, and we were loath to tamper with it so soon; and to throw the Governor—the province figurehead—into the balance at so sensitive a time was to risk disaster. If Governance saw the imposition of a popular mandate on jerry-built local government structures as politically essential, we, thinking practically, saw it as a rash and laboratory-led experiment. These reservations were compounded by the intricacies of an accompanying 'Strategic Plan' which charted a process of systematic disengagement founded on the phased return of executive power to the Ministries, in some cases as early as January 2004. The idea that Wasit's police, for example, should shortly enter a cosy condominium with their cronies in the Ministry of Interior and wholly escape the cleansing fire of reform appalled me; and my colleagues' faces reflected that concern.

Everyone was right. Practically, it *was* too soon for such measures; yet, given the reality of the Agreement, Governance had no choice and the imperative was clear. The CPA's dissolution had initially been conditional on a preceding election designed to establish a government. This was no longer the case, and an interim solution was needed. Here was the real reason for the democratic overhaul of our ramshackle structures: the Councils would be required to help establish a caucus process designed to produce an interim Iraqi government; and any flaws in these components would cast doubt over the outcome.

This imperative, however clear, failed to eclipse the significant risks inherent in the process. The perils and frictions of our existing work would be compounded by these additional complexities as we kicked away one admittedly inferior prop after the other, and the time available in which to accomplish each step was compressed for us by the transition calendar. We sought now to impose ourselves more directly than at any other time; yet the power which alone enabled us to do so would be simultaneously withdrawn from us, as Ministries assumed their briefs and our opponents contemplated 1 July 2004 with mounting excitement.

The prospect of increased turbulence in Wasit was, we thought, inevitable, as these new facts were assimilated by the clans and interest groups that passed for civil society. In ascribing a date to our departure we would just as surely initiate a power struggle, whose effects would be made all the more dangerous by a lacklustre and criminal police force. In seeking now to pre-empt that struggle, we would be forced to act more speedily—and clumsily—than was appropriate for the political conditions. We risked a form of cyclical deterioration in the security situation and possessed no obvious remedy. I was more than usually thoughtful as we drove back to Kut.

Crisis after crisis besieged us in the following weeks. Ayatollah Sistani's opposition to the plan for indirect elections had been immediate. We foresaw a process in which Councils and local government structures selected a transitional assembly, which was then to choose an interim government. He rejected this notion and called for a direct ballot, which we deemed impossible in the time remaining. Negotiations were laborious because they were necessarily indirect—he had refused to meet CPA staff, but now exercised a growing political influence increasingly at odds with Quietist precepts. The spectre of mass opposition from the Shi'ia majority preoccupied us, and demanded, in its implied power to disrupt our plans, a form of accommodation.

We also experienced a full-blown fuel shortage in the province. The effects of sabotage elsewhere in Iraq, combined with run-down refinery infrastructure—and ironically compounded by traffic born of new prosperity as wages rose—now conspired to create queues of vehicles at the filling stations 2 kilometres long. Conditions at the pumps were made worse by a free-for-all as hundreds of people attempted to fill jerry-cans and motor-cycles in order to re-sell the fuel on the black market. The police, belatedly sent to keep order at the scene, confined themselves to taking bribes in return for offering preferential treatment, after which they were beaten up by the others and fled. One day a man entered the yard of a storage facility across the river holding a grenade and demanded fuel. It detonated and blew his hand off. The pool of blood was still there when we visited the site.

In a bid to avert what we saw as the likelihood of general insurrection we set up a fuel rationing scheme, issued an edict restricting cars to 30 litres and trucks to 50 in each station, and asked Sergey to enforce it. He did so with a mixture of soldiers and units of the nascent Iraqi Civil Defence Corps (ICDC). Timm abandoned all else and drove round the province with his U.S. Military Police to carry out spot-checks at the stations. Gradually the crisis eased, and we were left with the impression that there was more cohesion among the population than we had previously supposed. We wondered about its breaking-strain.

Our perimeter wall was completed in mid December, and our security lighting arrived on Christmas Eve. On the 27th nineteen people were killed in four separate suicide attacks in Karbala,

140 km. to the west. The concentration of these attacks—which were launched within minutes of one another—suggested careful planning and, more troubling, the active co-operation of elements of the Iraqi security forces. One vehicle had followed a convoy; another had driven across a playing field to the wire at the main gate of a military HQ. The dead included eleven Iraqi police officers and five Bulgarian soldiers. Almost every major Iraqi city had now been attacked by suicide bombers.

We were hampered by the inability of our police to carry out security tasks—even to run a single fuel station. With the odd welcome exception they were unable even to run their own police stations, and their principal pre-occupation appeared to lie in promoting one another: a recent visit had unearthed a sub-station in which the force consisted of forty-five officers and fourteen men; of the officers three-quarters were absent 'on business in Kut'. We judged it essential to reform them as soon as possible, and saw this as an early task for the Province Council. Ideally we wanted new senior officers in place before this process of refreshment and its associated turbulence began. I had meanwhile been told that the new city police chief in the southern town of al-Hayy had been threatened with a pistol by one of his sergeants, and took the opportunity of using this lever on Brigadier Abdul Men'em when he turned up unannounced during a meeting in the Governor's office.

The Governor had greeted me with what looked suspiciously like happiness, and endured my halting Arabic greetings with great courtesy. He responded to the news that his mandate would be reviewed by the very Province Council whose creation he had so recently welcomed with apparent pleasure, as our private convention demanded, and noted that the job and its responsibilities lay heavy upon him. We smiled at one another in genuine fondness, each knowing that only an explosive charge might successfully remove him from office. It was at this point that Brigadier Abdul

Men'em entered the room from a side-door. I immediately asked
him why a man who had threatened his superior with a pistol was
still in the force. He agreed that it was quite extraordinary, as
though we were discussing the beauty of a distant mountain range,
and sadly shook his head at this tale of human weakness. The
Governor chipped in helpfully—the very fact that this station chief
had not drawn his own pistol and killed the sergeant who threatened
him merely underlined his weakness and unsuitability for the job.
I tried another approach. Why were the new pistols we had given
them last week being sold in the weapons market in Kut? Brigadier
Abdul Men'em explained that this was because they were thought
of as gifts by the police officers to whom they had been given.

For the first time my temper frayed. Did he not see that the law
was all that stood between the province and ruin? Could he not
understand how important it was that the entrances to the city were
properly secured? These people—the pistol-packing sergeant,
Abdul Men'em's officers and their 'gifts'—would make fools of us
all. I told them with quiet exultation of the powers to be allocated to
the Council: of their power to dismiss Ministry officials and to
review province police forces and their leaders. I summarised anew
the plans to submit Governors to popular scrutiny. Both sat quietly
as my voice gradually faded away. The Governor looked at me indulgently, eyes twinkling. I had, he said, set an example for his people.
In all my time here, even when I had been hard with them, no one
had complained about me. I had never been accused of corruption—my imprint on the history of Wasit was permanent. In my
fatigue I was moved, but waved my arm dismissively. The Governor
reached over, took my hand and patted it. No, he said, Allah saw
everything. The Chief of Police smiled at me warmly. I had been
defeated. I told my interpreter on the way out that his people were
maddening. He said he thought it unlikely that I was the first Englishman to say so.

With the advent of the November 15 Agreement, 'refreshment' and the implicit diminution of CPA's power, the Iraqi Governing Council now asserted itself; and CPA gave it the right to review Councils at province level to ensure they met with their approval. To pre-empt the censure we thought inevitable we now folded in four political parties and three tribal members, the latter chosen by the tribes in council. The four parties we had chosen—SCIRI, two divisions of Dawa and the Communists—were selected on the basis of our own assessment of their effectiveness and power. The rest were asked to take up positions on Kut city council. They did so with the greatest reluctance, feeling that they had an automatic right to sit *en masse* at province level. There was not the remotest prospect that we would allow them to do so.

Dr Abdul Salaam, the Chairman, had accepted the expansion of the Council and its rationale with commendable wisdom and flexibility, but regrettably this body, in which we had invested so much optimism as an instrument of provincial reform, had largely failed to perform as we had hoped. Neil had been exceptionally patient with them, seeing potential. They had, for example, solved the problem of Badrah's Mayor. Yet I saw only the daunting series of hoops through which we still had to leap before transition. While they were content to discuss the issues of the day, they were loath to take decisions. This resulted from a kind of generational deformity: Saddam Hussein's security system had made such discussion, let alone action, unthinkable. Nor, in their anxiety, were they willing to accept my assurances that their much-vaunted new powers were imminent: they wanted see the legal documents that proved it and were most reluctant to advance without them. We applauded when they summoned the Chief of Police before them to discuss security, but their fear of the police was palpable; they had roundly denounced him and his indolent officers in their absence the week before, but they now congratulated him in turn. While none of them felt that Brigadier Abdul Men'em and his Deputy should remain, there were no obvious replacements; and CPA staff in Baghdad responsible for overseeing Ministries had no appetite for change at this distance from transition—rather, they understandably preferred such chains of authority to remain in place. The November 15 Agreement had begun inexorably to narrow our freedom of action and to cement Wasit's deficiencies. Yet the essential question for us—against which we measured all else—was whether the structures now in place would survive our departure. If not, we would have merely wasted our time.

The grove of palm trees behind the Villa was a place I had always found particularly restful. In summer the water that fed them flowed through a network of channels, apertures and tiny fountains of delightful complexity, fed by the over-pressure from a cracked stone basin in the corner of the garden. An old green pump, its patched hose buried in the river, filled the basin in turn. I often walked from the Tigris to the trees. Standing among them, listening to the wind in the fronds and watching the water bubble upward over the dry concrete, chattering and gurgling, felt like a tiny, repetitive miracle. In winter now that wind was very much stronger, and scoured the trees with rain and sand. Towards the end of December it stopped and on New Year's Eve we festooned the trees in coloured lights, hired a band from the city and had a party. Our American MPs set up a barbecue. The whole team gathered, strengthened by the off-duty members of the Ukrainian garrison force and General Bezluschenko, who came from Delta. The band used only drums and a wind instrument I did not recognise. I looked at our small group and the band, at every improvement to the site, and felt for the first time that we had made progress. But even Sergey's punishing round of toasts in Ukrainian vodka—to the CPA, to the Ukrainian Armed Forces, to our families, our children and holidays in the Crimea—failed to put me entirely at ease. After some hours he elected to leave but insisted on a last toast as a 'walking stick', as he put it. I proposed an eighteenth-century one from the Royal Navy: 'Confusion to our enemies and damnation to the French'. Sergey, visibly impressed, said 'OK!' and drained a glass of Jack Daniels before leaving in a long line of armoured vehicles for Delta.

At midnight the Ukrainian guards at our site opened celebratory fire with machine-guns from the towers and emplacements on the perimeter, and tracer leapt away into the night. Vladimir, their commander, came to me, saluted, and gave me a card from the Ukrainian President and an illumination rocket. I unscrewed the cap and pulled the cord, and watched it arc skyward through the palms before shedding a red parachute flare that trailed thick smoke as it sank slowly over Kut. Vladimir seized my hand and said 'S Novom Godom'—'Happy New Year'—and smiled. 2003 was over.

The next day we drove north with the head of the U.S. counter-intelligence team to negotiate the payment of blood money. One of the unit's soldiers had inadvertently killed a member of a powerful tribe in a traffic accident. Iraqis were wont to accept such events as destiny—this man had died because his time had come, no more or less. The phrase that so often infuriated my colleagues, 'Insha'allah', merely expressed the Iraqi belief that man's life was ordered by God. If one asked an Iraqi to come to a meeting at 0900 hours the next day he would nod and say 'Insha'allah', indicating that he would do his best but could not be sure what God had in store for him; though clearly the phrase also constituted a useful social device.

The ritual after the killing of a tribal member is clear, and tribal law is invariably followed. The family members of the killer go to the family of the victim, normally on the same day, and negotiate a period of adwa—generally no more than a month—to conclude negotiations, although an aggrieved tribe may deny this and initiate immediate punishment of the killer. During this period of adwa the killer must absent himself. If he is found he can be rightfully killed. Blood money will not be discussed in the early stages of these negotiations, *adwa* being rather a period of contemplation and arrangement. A few days before it ends an envoy from the killer's tribe is sent with money for food and expenses. Both tribes then attend a meeting in which a calculation of blood money is made after consulting a table of relative values held on paper or in the collective memory. A son might be held to be worth $7,000, and certainly more than a daughter; and a powerful tribe may demand a greater sum than is generally set. Each of these delegations must include at least one *sayid*, or direct descendant of the Prophet, which confers a sanctity and gravitas on talks that may improve the conditions obtained. The culmination of blood money negotiations is marked by a ceremony in which a holy banner is ritually pulled taut between the chiefs of the two tribes. It ends with lunch.

I explained all this to my American companion, who looked thoughtful. A speedy response in such matters was important, and the thought of an entire Iraqi tribe out for revenge tends to concentrate the mind. Yet we could not find the tribe, and the policeman whose help we sought could not do so either. We enlisted instead the help of one of our Iraqi engineers, who was a member of the tribe and offered to set up a meeting.

I returned, frustrated, to find a police officer from a town on our province boundary waiting at the barrier. He reported that fuel rationing had been proceeding well till that morning, when a disgruntled black-marketeer had fired a rocket-propelled grenade into the petrol station. As I scrawled a request to our liaison officer that the Ukrainians dispatch troops to the town, restore order and arrest the culprits, Timm emerged. Listening to my account of our morning and reading my note, he sipped his coffee and said 'Just another New Year's Day in al-Kut'.

There had long been a damaging assumption that some parts of Iraq were somehow pre-determined to be quiet, as though they were immune from pressure—the Coalition's gaze was drawn rather to the hotspots of Tikrit, Ramadi and Fallujah, where the steady diet of violence produced an aura of permanent menace. Kut had been judged by the CPA to be one of these 'quiet' areas. I thought this classification ill-judged and meaningless, but curiously the population too thought of their province with pride as an island of calm. I could never persuade them that we faced danger; violence to them was something imported by strangers and not home-grown, and in the seemingly anarchic bustle of the city's streets and markets a hidden order was at work. Kut's people knew everyone to an astonishing degree, and in the public mind the word 'foreigner' was often synonymous with criminal intent. A 'foreigner' would generally be spotted with extraordinary speed by Kut's citizens; he would then be gently interrogated and either ejected from the city or imprisoned if his answers failed to satisfy. These methods were unlike ours, and there was no set procedure in which to take comfort; but they seemed to work.

The three days of riots that took place simultaneously in Kut and in our neighbouring province of Maysan damaged these con-ceptions in the minds of CPA HQ and local Iraqis alike. The old cer-tainties that had underpinned CPA planning, such as it was, and Iraqis' understanding of their province proved outdated; and a new turbulence arising from a multitude of factors—a porous border, unemployment, political ambitions, CPA dissolution, envy and greed, the whole exacerbated by the weaknesses of our police force—was to overturn our assumptions.

Peaceful demonstrations were not unusual in Kut, though most were aimed at the Governor. After an appropriate period he would generally allow a small representative group of protesters through the gate and into his office, where he would agree with alacrity to each of their demands. In the ensuing excitement he would then sigh heavily and say that regrettably only Mr. Mark could turn these promises into action. The Governor would then allocate his visitors a police guide to display the authority with which he had now endowed them, and an excited procession headed by a corpulent and sweating police officer would then arrive at our site. Presented with this *fait accompli* by Nema Sultan I would telephone and berate him for his weakness, while he denied that he had agreed to anything at all. The crowd would trail increasingly slowly from one building to the other as the sun sank gradually over the river; and so the days would pass.

This was different. A crowd of about 200 gathered at our barrier on 11 January to complain about recruitment procedures in the border police, which we were now expanding in a bid to strengthen the border defences with Iran. This was a military responsibility, and Sergey had begun training and equipping a force of 650 at the request of Central-South. However, the precise division of responsibility in this matter was unclear. The Iraqi general who had been appointed to lead the force insisted on his sole right to do so, and had promptly gathered a large number of people according to long-established Iraqi traditions of patronage. Each of these then recruited the rest on similar lines. The allegation made by the crowd was that these last had been forced to pay for their positions. Such claims were not unusual and could rarely be proved one way or the other, but behind the crowd on this occasion lurked a senior SCIRI lieutenant who appeared to be orchestrating events, and unknown to us, and almost certainly to his party, a relatively minor piece of political activism would, in the inflammable atmosphere of Kut in January 2004, spiral quickly out of control. The next day some 500 people gathered at the Governor's building and attempted to break down the gate. They stayed there throughout the day, held back by Ukrainian reinforcements who blocked the two access points with armoured vehicles.

The next morning Neil Strachan and I drove to Tuesday's Province Council meeting in the Governor's building. We expected

Chaos: the provincial border crossing between Iraq and Iran at Arafat, near Badrah.

Interpreter Majed Mayat al-Kureishi at the front gate of the CPA base in Kut.

Blackhawk helicopters over the Tigris, departing from the CPA base in Kut. The barrage is just visible between two Ukrainian armoured personnel carriers.

Timm Timmons with Iraqi children in a crowded classroom during the provincial school refurbishment programme.

FACING PAGE

Above Ukrainian armoured personnel carrier from 'the Villa', the CPA base in Kut.

Below The author with General Sergey Ostrovskiy, commanding Sixth Ukrainian Mechanised Brigade, on the road from Kut to the Arafat border crossing with Iran.

Followers of Moqtada al-Sadr demonstrate at the front gate of CPA Kut, 4 April 2004. Their provincial leader, Sheikh Abdul Jawad al-Issawi, is visible centre-left in a white turban.

Ukrainian sniper returning fire from the back window of the Villa, Kut CPA base 6 April 2004.

Kut CPA team and security teams in Ukrainian Brigade's Delta Camp, 7 April after the 6 April attack. *From left* Frank Filmer, John McGough, Dave Fox and Bob Pease (team leader) of CRG; Timm Timmons, Rob McCarthy, the author, Reda Salem (kneeling), Colin Coyle, Graham Kerr and Nigel Massey of CRG, Neil Strachan, Nick Stronach (CRG), Malcolm Russell, Mark Purdey (CRG).

U.S. Army Lieutenant-Colonel Mark E. Calvert, commanding First Squadron, Second Armored Cavalry Regiment (1/2 ACR), May 2004.

The Villa in May 2004 after occupation by Moqtada al-Sadr's militia, the Jaish al-Mahdi.

At the inauguration of a new Province Council building on 26 June 2004, four days before the CPA's dissolution. *From left* CRG security team leader Russ Pulleng, chairman of Suwayrah Council Zamil Amash, CPA Deputy Timm Timmons, new Chief of Police Brigadier Abdul Haneen al-Umara, Projects Officer Colin Coyle, new Governor Mohammed Rodha al-Jaishami, the author, Chairman of Province Council Dr Abdul Salaam al-Safaar.

trouble but were confident in our ability to deal with it. We felt that if we once showed any public weakness we would no longer be able to operate successfully; to retain any kind of mandate we had almost to seek out trouble and meet it head-on, or risk political irrelevance. For this reason we disregarded every instruction to remain in our base because it was this anniversary or that, or deemed a time of general threat, unless we had received intelligence of specific danger.

A large crowd had gathered at the front, and CRG, having previously checked the route, took us round to the back. I went to see the Governor. Neil went to stiffen the Council—extraordinarily, most members had turned up. The crowd had meanwhile expanded rapidly to about a thousand, and began throwing what sounded like home-made grenades over the fence. The Ukrainians, who had already sealed the gate, now opened fire over their heads with automatic weapons, saying that individuals in the crowd had fired at them.

Inside the building the noise was deafening. The Governor turned pale, and his office quickly became a refuge for plump police officers of all descriptions as they fled from responsibility. By 1100 it looked like a form of Noah's Ark for security forces. Brigadier Abdul Men'em's contribution was to hover dramatically by the Governor's three phones, and at one stage he held a handset to each ear. The sound of automatic fire now reached a crescendo, through which the sound of Nema Sultan's clock and birdsong buzzer trilled at intervals. The crowd now surged into the adjacent city post office and began tearing it apart.

CRG, quite properly, requested that we be extracted in the cars, and I, equally properly, demurred. We had no choice but to try and resolve the situation confronting us, and called in a group of the demonstrators. The breadth of their demands reflected the extent to which an arguably legitimate cause of protest—unemployment— had been appropriated and magnified. They wanted 100 of 'their' young people employed in the border police, political party representation in the Province Council increased, all district and sub-district Councils abolished and re-established; de-Ba'athification accelerated and placed under the control of the political parties; and dismissal of the head of Border Guards and the Governor. It was risible—clearly we had begun to squeeze the political parties and it pleased me. It was interesting that the self-appointed representatives of the 'People' in front of me showed no enthusiasm for returning to them.

The Province Council meanwhile had got off to a shaky start. After the miracle of their arrival they wished to leave but Neil, commendably, refused to allow them to do so. This had a startling effect on their work rate: our once moribund Council now sped through the agenda as gunfire shook the windows. Motion followed motion at dizzying speed, the passage of each marked by a forest of raised hands and brisk nods of acquiescence. Recalcitrant Islamic parties grew briskly co-operative. The tribal chief who appeared congenitally unable to discuss anything apart from his hamlet and herds became Churchillian in his oratory, and the irritable barrack-room lawyer from Badrah, whose watchword had always been 'I vote yes—but with conditions' grew taciturn and decisive. Neil looked pleased.

The disturbances, which ended the next day, had a number of important effects. Miraculously only one person was killed and a half-dozen injured, but this was sufficient to create a conservative backlash of disapproval spearheaded by Sistani *wakil* Sheikh Abdul Jawad who railed against an emergent criminal underclass and urged draconian penalties. His anger was partly due to his anxiety that such disturbances might be interpreted by the CPA as a Sistani-led Shi'ia rebellion against the indirect elections plan; and the CPA, who had feared precisely this when the disturbances began, exhaled.

Again, it was what had not occurred that now seemed instructive. Despite the infrastructural deficiencies that were everywhere apparent—fuel and power shortages, pools of grey and sewage-contaminated water everywhere in the city, and above all the obvious deterioration in security—despite these factors a three-day riot with a seductively broad agenda had failed to rouse a population of 350,000. From this some drew comfort—here, surely, was evidence that the silent majority marched alongside CPA and its strategies.

In fact this tiny group of rioters had paralysed the city in security terms and exposed our grievous weakness in dealing with it. The Governor saw in this assault the 'hidden hand' of Iran and its political agents, an analysis with which Sergey agreed. We were less sure. While the default conservatism of Wasit was welcome, it was a form of conservatism *in absentia* exercised by a people who could not be engaged—not by our opponents, certainly, but not by us either. This curious absence of the majority from political debate allowed all factions to claim its tacit support in turn; and this very absence precluded public refutation. It was as if a small group of the ultra-Right had gone on the rampage in America or in Britain, and being unopposed thus claimed the support of the city's terrified inhabitants. The contradictions inherent in Iraqi society were apparent in the data we gathered: they wanted sovereignty, but 55 per cent of a group recently polled had said they would vote for no living Iraqi as their President. A majority, too, had a low opinion of the Coalition, but only a tiny minority had ever met its representatives.

For me the rocks and debris of the riots that littered the area outside the Governor's building for some days underlined a series of failures: of intelligence; of our domestic and Coalition security apparatus; and, above all, of our apparent inability properly to integrate the civil plan with military power. We now needed to take firm action against the ringleaders but lacked the intelligence information and military ability to do so. Meanwhile we ejected SCIRI's representative from the Council for inciting public disorder.

A few days later, the Governor and I sat together in his office drinking coffee. My spirits were at a low ebb: I had the sense of our being almost abandoned, lost somewhere up-river and out of radio range, and the battered post office just visible from the Governor's windows bore witness to my failure to manage the problems of the province. Nema Sultan watched me carefully, and said presently that I had a visitor. The bird-song buzzer trilled, and his secretary ushered in a U.S. Marine Corps major who seemed draped in radio equipment. He treated me as though I were the slightly deranged commander of an isolated fort deep in Indian territory. He said 'Hello sir. We've come to help you.' I thanked him, uncertain how he intended to do so. At that moment a great swelling roar filled the room and a black shape flashed past the window. An American fighter-bomber wheeled away across the Tigris. 'Air support sir. Thought we'd have a show of strength this morning. Remind the bad guys who they're dealing with.' The aircraft came round again at roof-top height and swept straight down the road in arrogant assertion of a transcendent and effortless power. The building shook. Trails of white vapour streaked from its wing-tips as it rocketed skyward at the end of its run. The Major laughed. 'We got no targets for now, but it sure feels good don't it?' Curiously, it did—and I felt a sudden bond between me, the Marine officer, Nema Sultan and the faceless pilot whose voice I now heard over the radio as he sped back to his base at 400 knots.

5

THE SADR UPRISING

In remembering the April 2004 fighting in Kut it is the luminous skies that followed winter, the profusion of white birds flocking to the river, and the emerald reeds that frame those memories. The natural beauty of our surroundings tinged the ordinary with drama-tism, and lent extraordinary events a resonance that etched the mind indelibly. The wind had blown unceasingly and did so still, but it was now cool, not cold; and these sensations on the skin after the dead hand of winter lifted our spirits. I had taken to sitting some-times at the edge of the Tigris in an old chair I had found behind the hotel, and watching the water in the sunlight. Black and white pied kingfishers hovered motionless above the surface in dozens, diving at intervals; and great flocks of duck bobbed between them. The water was alive, as it had always been, and its steady bustle had come to represent normality in the midst of the daily turbulence of our working lives.

Much had changed by the spring of 2004. We felt a sense of achievement, which partly eclipsed the fatigue and miseries of the preceding months. The brutal work of forming province, district and sub-district Councils was broadly complete—we intended to use these new bodies as springboards for further reforms. Tarawa House was at last ready, and we had established our offices in it. Our accommodation needs were largely met by the adjacent hotel, which lay inside our security perimeter and had been refurbished by

149

KBR. A few of us remained in the Villa, which now seemed like home after the passage of months. Its unusually strong concrete structure and ribbed design additionally commended itself to CRG as an emergency refuge. We thus, fatefully, retained it as a base, together with its original internet communication system. Our morning meetings now took place in Tarawa, and I would walk the hundred metres between Villa and office each morning along the river bank.

Our October beach-head had become a base. We were stronger. My route now took me past half a dozen armoured personnel carriers with turret-mounted heavy machine-guns, rather than the trucks the Ukrainians had previously used. We had watched the departure of Sergey and his Brigade with real sadness—they had been of incalculable help to us. We had given him a farewell dinner at the Villa and a painting depicting him as an Iraqi tribal chief. His replacement, General Sergey Ostrovskiy, had benefited from his predecessor's experience. His Sixth Mechanised Brigade had more armour and a Ukrainian Special Forces component, coupled with better intelligence-gathering facilities. Perhaps most significantly, two small formations of U.S. troops had been co-located with the Brigade: a Marine Corps air-liaison detachment of about a dozen, whose commander I had last seen in the Governor's office, and a group of about ten Special Forces soldiers. The Special Forces' tasks comprised their traditional skills of intelligence-gathering and covert operations.

We were a larger group. Colin Coyle, our Projects Officer, had finally arrived. I had last met him in Sarajevo in 1996. Originally from Northern Ireland, he possessed that quiet political acuity the region's troubled history so often seems to impart. Sally Bond, our administrative officer, had chosen to leave and been replaced by Rob McCarthy, an obviously competent man who ordinarily worked for the Ministry of Defence. These two briefly brought the CPA team to full strength before the leave schedule again took its toll. Although our invaluable team of U.S. military police had been posted elsewhere, we had additionally been allocated a military linguist, the American-Egyptian U.S. Air Force Sergeant Reda Salem. He had been trained as a pharmacist. We now asked this intelligent and able man to work alongside Colin on Projects, an area of activity that daily threatened to overwhelm us.

With us in Tarawa House was the Research Triangle Institute team, consisting of some eight internationals and the local staff whose description of Wasit's problems had so depressed me. In the Ukrainian building were fifty soldiers of the new Brigade, their numbers reduced to reflect the fact that we, at last, had a guard force: CPA had contracted an American security company, Triple Canopy, to provide a small international team to each Governorate. In our case they were to train a locally-recruited security contingent of about eighty. These enhanced security measures now allowed KBR to station three international staff permanently on site to run our facilities. Triple Canopy was not responsible for our mobile security—CRG would retain this task in British team locations. The Foreign Office had agreed that a second CRG team be allocated to us, and we placed this additional four-strong group in the hotel to secure CPA team members living there. Our total base strength with these additions was forecast to be 180. Overseeing this agglomeration of cellular agencies and individuals, and trying to ensure that their portfolios meshed satisfactorily with each other, had become increasingly difficult, underscoring anew the importance of coordination in interventions of this kind.

Our growing sense of the imperfections inherent in the Coalition effort in Iraq sprang from the fact that Wasit's CPA team had now gathered an unusual amount of experience, and was better able to judge the situation. The British Foreign Office had wisely sent its people to Iraq on six-month renewable contracts, an example the

State Department followed only in late 2003. Almost all my American colleagues in other Central-South Governorates had been on three-month placements and had now gone. Clearly this compounded the difficulties of constructing a consistent strategy in the field. Timm was one of the few Americans remaining from that period, and now one of the longest-serving. He had extended his tour till 30 June. While this hardly made us elder statesmen, it meant that we had more collective experience in theatre than most, and had been together for longer.

Despite the advances made by the spring of 2004, formidable difficulties remained, born in the main of our failure to create in Iraq a military-political system that worked. The glitches and gaps that we had once thought of as mere growing pains had now come to seem permanent; and CPA's imminent dissolution bred a sense of systemic fatigue that militated against their being addressed. This encouraged a patchwork operational culture and widened the gap between HQ and its satellite Governorates because HQ could so rarely proffer logistic or technical solutions. Wasit, certainly, was operating in almost complete independence by late 2003. My early surprise at this perhaps owes something to my British expectations of hierarchy: I believe Governorate Coordinators in the British sector to our south were more constrained. Actually our broad remit was the only possible approach in the circumstances, and owed much to a creditable American readiness in Baghdad and in Hillah to confer latitude on its provincial leaders. We reported twice a week. A weekly summary was sent to Regional Operations and Governance offices in Baghdad, copied to Mike Gfoeller in Regional Centre Hillah; and Bremer had initiated a system in which each Governorate Coordinator reported personally to him weekly. Inevitably this soon supplanted the former procedure, and once we grew accustomed to Bremer's style and working practises it proved a powerful tool. Yet even Bremer's support for a proposed policy was no guarantee that it would be executed, and I believe his frustrations at the endless frictional losses inherent in CPA policy-making were occasionally as pronounced as our own.

Overwhelmingly, the problem for which we eternally scrambled for an answer was security. It remained the first concern in Iraqi minds and this emerged repeatedly in our local meetings. The power and panoply of the Coalition that had so impressed me when I arrived in October obscured significant military problems. Chief among these was that the Combined Joint Military Task Force remained far too small for its task. This deficit affected every sphere of our work; we were unable to dominate our areas of responsibility, and great tracts of the province saw only one patrol in a fortnight. Being small, we could not quickly train border guards, police or any other of the Iraqi formations that might relieve this pressure and give an Iraqi face to the security sector; and, most damagingly in Wasit, our border remained wide open. In short, we failed to dominate our surroundings by failing to marshal the requisite resources, and we thus steadily lost the initiative.

On 2 March 220 people were killed in suicide attacks in Karbala and Baghdad during the *Ashura* festival that marked the death of *Imam* Hussein. Local leaders saw the roots of the disaster in Coalition negligence, and for the first time I met hostility in province meetings. One said 'You have occupied our country—it is your duty to protect us'; another that had we only allowed the broader use of party militias, such tragedies would never have happened. If I had been sufficiently confident in the Coalition to feel surprise at its emergent flaws, the instinctive faith of Iraqis in our overwhelming military supremacy made it difficult for them to contemplate the possibility of military failure. It was futile to highlight the difficulties inherent in countering terrorism because they believed, quite simply, that the Coalition was powerful enough to succeed at anything it chose to tackle. The truth was that six suicide bombers had struck in a crowd of a million people in Karbala; and there was no obvious military answer to the threat.

In Wasit we had long lacked the surgical military capability in support of public order objectives that military service in Northern Ireland had taught me was essential. The police lacked the requisite expertise for the task and were scared of retribution. The Ukrainians were too blunt an instrument, lacking experience and unable to move with the agility and speed required. For example, we had not imprisoned anyone at all after the riots, though my irritation at the fact was leavened by my knowledge that our failure was due to a lack of information rather than of will. The arrival of the Marine Corps and Special Forces contingents had led us cautiously to hope that we might now gain an initiative that we had never previously enjoyed, but it transpired rapidly that this would not be the case.

The American Special Forces contingent was headed by a young captain named Steve, and we saw a great deal of him and his men, whom we briefed exhaustively. They were polite, helpful and, I thought, professional, and might well have made a significant difference in a war other than the one we were actually fighting. They, like ourselves earlier, were largely fated to bounce off the hard outer shell of Iraqi society. There was simply no prospect of Caucasians, in or out of uniform, ever being able to conduct successful intelligence operations in the cities of Iraq without the most painstaking preparation, mastery of the language and careful and prolonged grooming of local agents. During the whole of my ten months in Wasit we failed to corral any of the major criminal leaders. This damaged us and retarded the political process. I attribute these failings not to Steve and his men, who did their best, but to a broader military complacency that permitted an approach to certain key issues so *ad hoc* as to verge on amateurism. While we welcomed the presence of the U.S. Marine Corps air detachment, one had to wonder whom, exactly, they intended to bomb. In short, the very manner of the Coalition's military response to public order crises suggested an institutional inability to grasp the nature of such problems and what had created them.

These difficulties were compounded by a fragmentary approach to intelligence-gathering. The Marine Corps, the Special Forces, the Ukrainians, the Romanian drone platoon and our resident counter-intelligence team were all now engaged in gathering information about the province. The only group to which this product was not provided was the CPA team running the place because we were not in the military chain, although we had been in theatre longer than all of them. Indeed we had been vetted and cleared to at least 'Secret' before deployment, but this made little difference. Nor could we task any of these formations in pursuit of our political objectives. While I understood the military's predilection for rigid security classifications and why it was all so difficult, their explanations were frustratingly unconvincing in practical terms.

Time and again the problems which we faced in our daily work could be boiled down to a single irreducible minimum—the inability of our local police force to carry out its tasks. This we had known since October, yet in all the months that followed we could not find a way of tackling it. The Council wanted the Chief of Police and his Deputy out, but could think of no suitable replacements. The institutional responsibility for the force was divided: the military were to provide them with equipment including uniforms, cars and weapons, and the CPA provided Ministry of Interior liaison and police training. Plan after plan was articulated at meetings and conferences, but in the province little changed. The bulk of our force was not armed, and those that were had little ammunition. Few of them had transport, or flak jackets, batons or radios. They had no winter clothes because these had not been centrally ordered—Timm eventually had them made at the textile factory. There had been only the most limited training since the force's inception, but we could not embed police trainers locally because of security considerations. Meanwhile the imminence of transition meant that it was especially difficult to argue for leadership change, and thus the Ministry of the Interior together with Brigadier Abdul Men'em's invisible protectors within it was daily strengthened. In March 2004 the Ministry promoted him to General and his Deputy to Brigadier.

In all of this time we and the forces ranged against us fought for the public mind. Moqtada al-Sadr's steadfast opposition to us had framed the ideological battle in terms of the poor unemployed, and we wooed them assiduously. Among the new weapons in our armoury was an American initiative of breathtaking scope: a Congressional appropriation of $18 billion. This colossal sum was designed to kick-start major construction projects across Iraq in every field—power generation and distribution, oil, irrigation, health, law and order, military infrastructure and roads. It was expected to create two million jobs and would be run by a new department—the Project Management Office (PMO). The plan was sold aggressively and the head of the PMO toured the country. We touted it around the province, attempting in so doing to describe a future infinitely better than the present. Yet the clans of Wasit responded as they had always done, seeing in the PMO a ladder for personal advancement and little else; the idea of national or even provincial prosperity remained no more than a concept.

Disseminating messages such as these was difficult, because the transmission range of the television and its co-located radio station remained limited to the outskirts of Kut. I appeared on television at intervals and talked through the issues of the day; and was often interviewed by reporters. Malcolm Russell and I had campaigned vigorously for money to enable us to expand this transmission range, but had failed. Two thirds of our population thus lay outside the reach of local media. Although the terrestrial network had lost viewers to satellite channels, to which Iraqis had flocked in great numbers, the failure to utilise stations such as ours to capacity merely compounds my suspicion that, from the beginning of CPA's tenure, the organisation had no long-term media strategy, and certainly nothing approaching the sophistication required.

While we trumpeted this new reconstruction plan we spent as many of our own project dollars as we could. The system we had adopted—using Iraqi engineers in the field, managed by our Polish staff—had proved remarkably successful, but controlling the flow of this money and accounting for it had proved difficult. Iraq in 2004 was riddled with corruption, and this immeasurably complicated our work. Iraqis regarded the embezzlement of government money not as theft but rather as a form of holy calling. Contractors would commonly form cabals before bidding and share any proceeds. One city's construction companies would attack any other who won a contract on their turf. Work was often shoddy and materials inferior. An engineer we sent to check a contractor's work might be bribed to keep silent; and he in turn might bribe anyone else whose silence he required. Nor could one rely on Western precepts of morality. Many of the schools in which children studied were in heart-rending condition—a child playing was killed by falling masonry in late 2003; yet I never met a head-master who did not vigorously insist that his own office should be refurbished before any other work was done. The head of a school we had virtually rebuilt complained to me that the contract had not included new doors, and indignantly gesticulated at the gaping doorways. By chance we had used the school in a promotional film the week before; Malcolm Russell was able to show them in place and subsequently prove that the head-master had removed them himself and sold them. These problems were now Colin's; newly arrived and professional to the core, he took the reins and fashioned the system we had given him into a machine that ultimately initiated 219 separate projects across the province for a disbursement of

$6.9 million; and Timm was able to give up a portfolio that had dominated his every waking moment.

Throughout these frantic months we watched over our new Councils, encouraged them and sheltered them. Dr Abdul Salaam had on the whole proved a good choice, and his authority remained largely unchallenged by political parties and tribes alike. I buttressed his role at every opportunity, and never opposed him in public. We met frequently and I began to take him with us in the cars. We travelled to each Council in turn, where I would introduce him and myself, summarise our concerns, and then sit silent for the rest of the session while sipping sweet Iraqi tea. Typically, he loved rhetoric and could talk uninterrupted for hours, alternately cajoling and berating his audience; now spreading his arms wide in appeal and now raising an admonitory finger, with his face set like stone. Stern, capricious, difficult and charming, he was a master of the art; and I would watch spellbound as this Iraqi tackled Iraqi problems with a strength and wisdom I could never have emulated, showing the extraordinary power inherent in the use of local capacity. Often, once a meeting had finished, I would venture an opinion: 'That Council seemed pretty strong.' He would laugh and climb briskly into the car. 'They are all thieves.' His methods never varied—he was prepared to spend weeks sending his tanks around the flanks of his enemies and would never undertake costly frontal assaults. In Province Council sessions he would attack me with great passion, eyes flashing, as a new dictator, red in tooth and claw and a devious schemer of the worst kind. Afterwards he would say sorry, but he could not have done otherwise and retained Council support.

Fundamental problems remained. These Councils were at the very heart of our decentralisation plans and would provide provincial adhesive during the stresses and strains of transition. Yet the order designed to enshrine their new local powers was delayed month after month. The Iraqi Governing Council did not want it, fearing, correctly, an erosion of its power; and it was rumoured that the UN did not like it either. Council salaries, so long promised, had not materialised. Meanwhile, increasingly muscular Ministries, buoyed up by the prospect of transition, began to block what were seen as CPA initiatives and appointments and contributed further to a general sense of anxious confusion. We were left in an invidious position: we had no choice but to exhort our Councils ever onward as the transition deadlines approached; yet were unable to supply the legislative foundation and salaries that alone might have confirmed our words and assuaged their fears. I do not believe that CPA Baghdad understood the damage this caused.

None of us truly believed that the reforms we had helped institute would endure. Life had generally improved for most people—the streets were cleaner, the markets more varied and vibrant, and a multitude of petty restraints had been lifted—and the broad outline of a political future, despite attendant controversy, was at least visible. Most important, Saddam Hussein's capture had demonstrated that there could be no return to his regime. Yet in our attempts to undertake those reforms which appeared to us crucial to success after transition, such as reviewing the police, I felt like a man shouting at the top of his voice in an empty hall. It was exhausting and difficult work, and I came to dread Province Council meetings and the inevitable frustration of our hopes, not to mention that damned pigeon cooing throughout in the air-conditioning duct. We had placed a lot of weight on this new structure, but it could clearly not continue to bear a load daily made heavier by the unyielding calendar of transition. Certainly the Councils were less weak; but they were far from strong, and this worried us.

To these concerns was now added a more personal strain. I received a curious e-mail in the spring from Sir Jeremy Greenstock's office, addressed to many people. It extolled the virtues of one of our small team of British GCs in rich language: his sterling contribution over the past difficult months, his steadfastness, his quiet courage, his dedication, his tousled good looks, and his commitment to a bright future for the people of Iraq. I knew immediately what this meant—all the hallmarks of the FCO at its most reptilian were there—and checked with the GC in question to make certain. Sure enough, he had been sacked.

In the mind of at least one of the FCO's staff in Baghdad I was to be next. During one of my visits to the capital I had been privately told by Andrew Bearpark at her behest that two members of my team had complained about my management style—that I was too hard, too driven and autocratic and, memorably, that I 'had not allowed X to be ill'. Although surprised by the way in which the complaints had been made, I said I thought stresses and strains of this kind were inevitable, particularly in the close environment of a Villa in winter under the daily threat of attack. Clearly, though, the team was of variable quality and there had in some cases been no selection procedure at all. Inevitably, not every face would fit.

A few weeks later Andrew spoke to me again. One of the disaffected had now written a formal complaint to the British office in Baghdad, to Regional Operations and three other addressees alleging misuse of funds: that, *inter alia*, we should not have bought local saloon cars for our engineers and that operations were being distorted for 'Timm and Mark's personal convenience'—he and I were criticised equally throughout. It also stated that our decision to remain in the Villa rather than move to the hotel was redolent of 'private personal domestic arrangements', and added, obscurely, that 'every day at mealtimes a member of our local staff is seen to fill three blue plastic bowls with food and take them to the [Villa]'. Timm, seeing that I often missed meals in the hotel canteen, had simply asked that food be kept aside for me to eat when I got in.

I thought this missive said more about the author than it did about us, and imagined that the Foreign Office would ignore this nonsense and take the requisite disciplinary action in concert with me. I was wrong. Andy, as bemused as me, next told me that my contract with the Foreign Office was unlikely to be renewed. I have rarely been so shocked. At no stage had any member of the Foreign Office spoken to me about it. I immediately made the dangerous journey to Baghdad that my employers appeared too busy to take themselves, and sought out the person who seemed to me to be the heart of the problem. I said to her that traditionally an accused person was at least consulted, and that such problems were discussed with the line manager. Given that I was both of these people I found the omissions odd. I explained to her the position and the operational realities. I noted that the Foreign Office, who thought 'staff morale especially relevant in difficult environments' had provided no welfare assistance at all—not even a set of playing cards. Nor had they sent any of the security equipment they had promised—indeed, one of the world's wealthiest countries had found it impossible to provide us with a hand-held fog-horn. When she then suggested that I send the team up for 'Baghdad film nights', I saw with awful clarity that she had no conception at all of what we faced on the ground, and wrote directly to Sir Jeremy Greenstock. The problem ended messily and I received a quasi-apology. In all of my time in Iraq nothing caused me greater strain. It took forty days for them to remove the author of the letter from our small team in Kut.

Ambassador Bremer planned to visit us on 13 March having cancelled an earlier February programme because of problems in passing the new Transitional Administrative Law, designed to enshrine fundamental rights and freedoms during the transition period. The caucus plan had been abandoned after Sistani's opposition in favour of a selected transition government and elections in January 2005. The visit was to be kept secret, and so I secretly dispatched a draft programme on my Hotmail account. I rather quailed at the idea and the organisation required, especially as there were few of us around: Timm had at last taken his first holiday in six months and gone to Ukraine with the departing Brigade. Neil and Colin were on leave.

A few days beforehand a pair of tiny doorless helicopters appeared over our complex and after landing ostentatiously on Tarawa's ragged lawn disgorged a posse of watchful men with spade beards, black machine-guns and sun glasses, who spoke an impenetrable language. I had asked that Brigade attach a permanent liaison officer to us. Greg, the security team leader, now asked him whether any 'indigenous vehicles were allowed ingress on-site'. Pavel looked blank. Greg looked carefully at him and repeated the question. Suddenly it came to me and I said 'You mean, are Iraqi vehicles allowed into the base?' Greg stared at me implacably—I had betrayed the Code and used plain English. Could the Ukrainians, he now asked, 'stage gun-ships on the bridge?' Pavel was again stumped. I interjected (I was getting good at this): could we put an armoured vehicle on the dam to close it if necessary? Pavel brightened—of course. Greg eyed me with flat menace and toyed with his knife.

They then reviewed our perimeter security. Local press could come in, one said, but a sniffer dog would have to check their vehicles at the road-side. They would then have to be body-searched. Iraqis detest dogs, believing them to be unclean, and regard the use of sniffer dogs as particularly insulting. They are no more enamoured of body-searches. I, knowing all our prospective visitors, wanted them to be exempt from these indignities, but the security man demurred, reeling off a string of incidents in which one august personage after another had been attacked by their visitors. 'Gentlemen', he said 'remember that even a sniffer dog is only 33 per cent effective.' 'Have you considered using three?' asked Rob McCarthy, our Administrative Officer, who had a very logical mind.

Protocol arrived in a large helicopter to pull together the programme and organise the media. They too brought with them a new dialect of 'press at the top', 'media sprays' and 'press avails'. Still haunted by my childhood non-party in Kuwait, I knew in my heart that none of those I had selected to meet 'our important visitor from Baghdad' would turn up. My dismissal was certain. Meanwhile I smiled encouragingly at Protocol, trying to delay my removal by a day or two.

He was due at 1000. The morning sunshine showed the river at its best. A warm wind blew from the north and great flocks of egrets virtually obscured the reed stands in mid-river. Greg and his helicopters came first, sending dust billowing across the site. Fifteen minutes later five dark shapes appeared low on the horizon before spreading out, and a growing wall of sound brought our local staff out to watch, no longer in doubt about the identity of our visitor. They drew nearer and now one could see three Blackhawks with an Apache attack helicopter on each flank, quartering the ground like buzzards. They spiralled into our complex simultaneously, thudding into position in a whirlwind of noise and dust. It was 1000 exactly. I walked to meet Bremer.

The day went well. Governor Nema Sultan harangued Bremer about the border with practised ease. Bremer, shocked by the *Ashura* bombings, promised additional border guards and stated his intention to close all but three border crossings with Iran. Ours would remain open. Sistani *wakil* Sheikh Abdul Jawad was marvellous, and waved his stick and his beads: 'I am ready to be a soldier at the border myself.' His secretary looked alarmed. He looked at me steadily and said 'I think of this man as my son.' Bremer's personal assistant made a note. I imagined it said 'Kut GC gone native—fire soonest'. I began, despite my imminent demise, to enjoy myself. Dr Abdul Salaam; the Council; Ukrainian General Ostrovskiy: all came and went happily.

At 1400 we lifted in a swarm of seven helicopters to fly to a project site on the Tigris, where we had overhauled and rebuilt two sets of irrigation pumps at a cost of $120,000. We flashed over the river and traversed Delta at 30 feet, the Apaches ranging left and right with the sun glinting from their canopies. I sat opposite Bremer, and watched the lakes and reed-beds slide below our machine as we jinked hard to avoid settlements, power lines and flocks of panicked sheep. Shepherds, alone in those expanses, waved up at us. We landed on the road in line abreast, surrounded by a cordon of Ukrainian troops. Out we jumped, press cameras flashing, to see villagers waving at us from the cordon's edge. A little boy kissed Bremer, who was genuinely charmed. The pumps gushed pure arcs of sparkling Tigris water into a channel. Bremer and his entourage moved swiftly from one site to the next and back to the aircraft. Bremer shook my hand. The formation took off again and flew low and fast to the north-west. It was over.

Bremer's visit and its air display seized Kut's imagination, and press descriptions of the day were glowing. I was struck anew by his coldness. Tireless, steely and professional—he was all these things, and he must have been under almost intolerable pressure. Yet we had exchanged no more than two or three personal sentences in our four hours together, and it was quite impossible to draw him out. When he left he said 'You seem to have a pretty good hold on this, Mark. Thank you.' In a European diplomatic environment this would herald the onset of conversation, but with him it was the reverse. I saw him strap himself in and begin reading a pile of documents. As the noise of his helicopters faded I felt a curious melancholy, as though Bremer's visit marked the culmination of our work in Wasit and hastened our departure.

But my suggestion that Sheikh Abdul Jawad should meet him and allowing that meeting to be photographed had been a political error. I had wanted Bremer to see how solid a relationship we had been able to foster with him at a time when reaching wider political accommodation with Sistani's followers had proved difficult; and

Sheikh Abdul Jawad's comment about regarding me as his 'son' was indicative of a similar impulse in him. Yet in publicising this alliance I damaged the Sheikh and strengthened his opponents and ours; and crude hand-written posters now appeared in the market denigrating him as a collaborator with occupation forces. These criticisms were judged by him to be so damaging that, although I met his staff often in our final months, he and I were never to meet again—it was regarded as too dangerous. His staff now asked for weapons permits.

The enemies they feared were the followers of Moqtada al-Sadr, whose opposition to the CPA was now entrenched. Our strategy within the province for dealing with them had bought us stalemate and nothing more: the place on the Province Council that we offered remained vacant; and the town of Zubadiyah, where we had endured their sermon, remained generally calm. Neil Strachan and Malcolm Russell saw their young leader, Abdul Jawad al-Issawi, irregularly, and skirmishes continued over access to the television station's daily hour of local airtime. I had never met him, regarding this step as something to be linked to progress on the disestablishment of their militia and illegal *sharia* courts. Still, it was arguable that we had contained them and that this truce might persist: there was no evidence to the contrary.

It is clear in retrospect that we had failed to chart the growing influence of Moqtada al-Sadr's followers over the minds of ordinary Iraqis. If some actively supported him, he inspired fear in many more; and such was the potency of his brand of Islamic nationalism that few dared criticise him openly. His militia, the Jaish al-Mahdi, did not concern the Coalition much. Our attitude towards it— certainly my opinion—was that this was schoolboy amateur dramatics and no more than a faintly amusing irritant. For much of our time in Kut, Iraqis themselves took the same position—these were young people, they would say indulgently, occasionally intemperate, and not to be taken too seriously. CPA's political view, however, had hardened, and it was clear that those pushing for action against him were in the ascendant.

Two incidents in Wasit in March had indicated the extent to which Moqtada al-Sadr's influence had increased. Among the first projects funded by Congressional money was a provincial site destined for a new Iraqi Army barracks. We had attended the inaugural ceremony on 18 March and invited a visiting Governing Council member, Mowafak al-Rubbaie. He arrived late, and our vehicles crossed outside the barracks as we left and he entered. His power drew the great and the good of Wasit like wasps to jam, and his motorcade was simple vaudeville. Following him Mayors, Directors, police officers and other notables swept past in cars, mini-buses, trucks and on motorcycles. Sirens wailed and blue lights flashed. They spread across the road in a solid phalanx. We saw General Abdul Men'em and the Governor as they passed us and one branch Ministry head after another; and there, unmistakably part of this convoy, were two black-clad Sadr militiamen with a medium machine-gun placed on the cab of a pick-up. How could an Iraqi Governing Council member, together with the province Governor and his Chief of Police allow themselves an escort composed in part of Sadr's Jaish al-Mahdi?

For many months now, despairing of gaining full access to local military intelligence, we had been developing our own information network. The man to whom we chiefly spoke was well-connected and apparently fearless. He had worked for the Americans in one form or another for years. He hated Ba'athists and the followers of Moqtada al-Sadr with equal vigour. I asked him to see me urgently. He showed no surprise at my description of the events at the construction site, but said that it was a lot worse than we imagined. He passed me a document dated 9 March, written by General Abdul Men'em to his superiors in the Ministry of the Interior, stating that a group of 'terrorists' had been arrested 4 March on the province boundary by a mixed patrol of police and Jaish al-Mahdi. After their interview at the police station the militia had demanded custody of the suspects, and the police had agreed. No one now knew where the suspects were, but it was thought they might have been sent to Sadr's *sharia* court in Najaf.

For the second time that day I was taken aback. Not only had the station commander formed a mixed patrol with an illegal militia, but he had handed over terrorist suspects to them as well. His superior, General Abdul Men'em, had done nothing about it except write to his Ministry in Baghdad, which had done nothing either. Our source said he was certain that General Abdul Men'em had been there at the time. He left me the document, walked to the door, and then turned. 'Mark, believe me. Be careful of these people. Watch your interpreters. Be very careful.' He shook my hand, and walked quickly into the night. I had never before seen him frightened.

We dismissed Police Chief General Abdul Men'em and his Deputy, Hassan Thuwaini, on 3 April after the most careful preparation, in the teeth of opposition from the Ministry of the Interior and from CPA Baghdad. I knew that our case was cast-iron and that this collusion with Sadr had given us the lever I had long looked for. The Police Chief said quietly, eyes brimming: 'Can't you see that we have to work with these people or there will be a war?' Hassan Thuwaini was quiet, but looked broken. On the collar of his starched uniform shirt, now devoid of badges of rank, was a small writhing caterpillar.

On 4 April we appointed their successors. Both were military. The police advisors in CPA Baghdad objected to this. I could not get them to see that we had already failed, and that the time for some woolly notion of community policing had long gone. Despite repeated entreaties for help with our police for the last six months, nothing had been done. Now we needed strength. The new Chief of Police, Brigadier Abdul Haneen al-Umara, was the former commander of anti-aircraft forces in southern Iraq in the 2003 war, and a well-connected member of the regal Rabi'a tribe. His Deputy, Colonel Ali Riba al-Kureishi, a huge man, was a former member of Iraq's Special Forces. Dr Abdul Salaam had said simply, 'It is time for such men.'

CPA headquarters had meanwhile moved against Moqtada al-Sadr. On 28 March the Sadr newspaper *Al-Hawza* had been closed for inciting violence against the Coalition. On 3 April, the day on which we at last dismissed our Chief of Police and his Deputy, one of Sadr's aides, Mustapha Yacoubi, was arrested for complicity in murder. The Sadr leader in Wasit, Abdul Jawad al-Issawi, who had already gathered his followers once at our gate to protest against the closure of the paper, assembled a crowd of 500 on the morning of 4 April and again made his way to our site.

Our interpreters had heard of this plan in the market, and we had accordingly enhanced our crowd control measures by digging ditches and topping them with barbed wire. Triple Canopy had placed their local guard force, now trained, armed and uniformed, along the outer perimeter. The inner cordon was provided by Ukrainian troops. Within this circle were our two CRG teams. We had created a second vehicle gate near the hotel, and each had long had a vehicle placed across the entrance as an anti car-bomb measure, moved only for access. I was satisfied with what had been done, but conscious of the inexperience of our guard force and how dangerous any loss of control might prove. I asked CRG, which included highly experienced former members of Northern Ireland's Royal Ulster Constabulary, to oversee events.

A well-organised group of three hundred people waving placards and flags, including a group of Sadr clerics, blocked our main gate at 1100 hours. A further group of two hundred sealed the second and only other exit point. I recognised the cleric from Zubadiyah, who rallied the chanting crowd with a loud-hailer. Sheikh Abdul Jawad al-Issawi stood beside him. The demonstrators now scrambled on to our concrete car-bomb chicanes and unfurled banners emblazoned with political slogans. They demanded to see me.

At 1500 we agreed that we would allow a small group into the base to deliver their message. I did not imagine that they would accept—Sadr had always refused to enter our base before, seeing any such move as redolent of collaboration; but a group of five clerics now entered the Villa, headed by Sheikh Abdul Jawad. His request to bring a cameraman was rejected.

I thought the abandonment of my long-established refusal to see him justified by the fact that he had entered the base and made the running; and that we had thereby established a measure of moral ascendancy over him. I determined that my meeting with him and his companions would be brief and the language tough, and walked downstairs. Timm told me *en route* that CPA Najaf had called in an air strike on a Sadr demonstration that had turned violent.

The deputation sat on black sofas in our meeting room. Sheikh Abdul Jawad, bearded and fresh-faced under his white turban, looked impossibly young. Next to him was a white-bearded cleric of sixty. I recognised two others from our travels. The fifth was our friend from Zubadiyah, whose resemblance to Rasputin now seemed uncanny. They formed an incongruous group. I began by saying that throughout our time in Kut we had tried to reach accommodation with Sadr, believing that there was room for all points of view; yet this had been made very difficult by their insistence on the use of militia and establishment of parallel government structures. Sheikh Abdul Jawad pulled a copy of the Koran from his black robes, raised one finger and said that the Jaish al-Mahdi was not a militia but God's army. He crossed his wrists as though bound, and adopted a martyr's pose, head thrown back. Why did we arrest clerics? What did we fear? I interrupted him to say that the rule of law bound every-one, regardless of position, and all accepted that murder was a crime. If Mustapha Yacoubi were found innocent he would be released.

It was clear from the outset that the group was implacably op-posed to us and would be persuaded of nothing. Once, when Sheikh Abdul Jawad rose to his feet and raised his voice, I reminded him that I was older than he was and that a man of his education should be prepared to listen to others as I now listened to him. He sat down immediately and apologised, bowing his head and briefly touching his brow; yet this mock-obeisance and the conversation that prece-ded it amounted to no more than crude melodrama. Till the con-clusion of this heated debate I had not realised that there was no battle to be won, no intellectual redoubt to be stormed by our infantry. I do not know what they thought of me. They left abruptly, and none but the Zubadiyah cleric shook hands. He did so like a soothsayer, who could see a future that was hidden from me.

I saw in the followers of Moqtada al-Sadr a large sect with its own discrete rituals and beliefs. I had not fully understood that it was also an aggressive sect which unhesitatingly used intimidation when mere sermonising failed; and that its influence had grown. We fear instinctively what we do not entirely understand, and for me these men and their black-robed Puritanism exuded an indefinably malign presence. Their supporters had picked out interpreters and mem-bers of our guard force present with Political Adviser Neil Strachan at our gate, and told them that they knew who they were and where their families lived. My interpreter, who had relayed one unpal-atable sentence after another during my meeting, was visibly shaken. Their threats were like a voodoo spell, and those marked by them were inconsolable thereafter. Timm, with his instinct for the heart of the matter, had proposed that we simply arrest them all and hold them at one stroke. I demurred, but wondered ever afterwards whether he was right.

CRG were not immune to this sense of contagion, and searched the room carefully after the group had gone. As these clerics relayed to a jubilant crowd the series of victories their leaders had just won over the CPA—'He told us to disarm! We told him that *he* must disarm!'—they now carefully examined the black sofas. Tucked down the side of one was a black negligée. We had bought the sofas second-hand in Kut. Despite our difficulties, we laughed for the rest of the day.

I awoke early on the morning of 5 April with the blunt certainty that somewhere, in the barrage of almost imperceptible sensations that continually inform the human mind, something was very wrong. Dressing quickly, I walked into the sun-lit compound, tense with premonition. The city seemed quiet, almost leaden; and the daily traffic jam at the barrage was missing. As I watched, I saw a convoy of three Ukrainian armoured vehicles cross the river on their way to Delta, and was partly reassured.

Majed arrived at 0745. Concerned, I walked to meet him at the gate. He told me that Sheikh Abdul Jawad al-Issawi had addressed a group of 200 armed men outside the river-side Sadr office that morning at 0200 hours, and again at 0700. Shortly afterward a bus had allegedly rammed a Ukrainian vehicle in the city, and a U.S. Special Forces vehicle had been hit by a rocket-propelled grenade—both its occupants were injured.

Over the next sixty minutes our Province institutions began to fall apart as though they had never properly existed. Bad news flowed into our base like an incoming tide, littered with the wreckage of our efforts. Less than half of our local staff came to work at 0800. The morning shift of our new guard force failed to report, leaving us at half strength. Ministry officials stayed at home. The police, I was now told, had deserted their posts, as had the paramilitary Iraqi Civil Defence Corps.

It was difficult to think. Clearly some form of Sadr coup was in train. We had to stop it, but we would need troops. I immediately

briefed the others, and asked our Ukrainian liaison officer to call
General Ostrovskiy. It was imperative that we strengthened the key
points of the city—the government building, the bridges and above
all the television centre. Without these locations Sadr had nothing
worth the candle. The liaison officer looked uncomfortable. Majed
then told me that there was no Ukrainian presence in town at all,
and that their vehicles had been withdrawn across the bridge to
Delta. I had seen the last of them go. The liaison officer, visibly
frightened, said he did not want to call his General. I marched him
to the Ukrainian garrison radio myself.

More fragmentary messages came in. The police station was
empty, Governor Nema Sultan had co-signed a document with
Sadr, and the Sadr office had appointed a new province police chief.
We turned on the television. Moqtada al-Sadr had called on his followers to 'terrorise your enemies'. The Ukrainians had abandoned
the city without a word of warning to us and the province appeared
to have simply collapsed. For a moment I felt absolutely paralysed.
What in God's name was one supposed to do?

We had to know more. I quickly briefed CRG and got into the
cars. Bob, who was again team-leader in Russ's absence, did not hesitate; nor to his great credit did my interpreter. I elected to go alone
and to leave Timm in charge. We knew each other well enough for
there to be no need of further words. We considered taking a
Ukrainian escort but discarded the idea. I wanted speed and agility,
and they were as likely to get into trouble as we were.

We sped out of the main gate into a deserted city. There was no
one on the steps of the police station and few cars were on the road.
We crossed the intersection and accelerated across the dam. Turning right, we now ran parallel to our base as we drove under the
grain silos on the opposite side of the river; and there, as we slowed
to cross the lock gates at the river junction, we were suddenly
among a dozen heavily armed men. All gazed at us steadily, their

kefiyas wrapped tightly around their faces. Some wore sunglasses. Others were in uniform, but I could see neither badges nor insignia. Rocket-launchers lay propped against a nearby wall. I saw two medium machine-guns on tripods and piles of grenades beside them. All these men held Kalashnikovs. We were in their midst before we could react. Bob said over the radio 'Keep going' and we moved steadily through them and over the lock bridge to a point 100 metres beyond. They did nothing. I saw, incongruously, a group of three uniformed police sitting together in chairs and stopped the cars. They made salaams cheerfully as though these circumstances were quite normal. I asked them about the identity of this militia. 'Jaish al-Mahdi', they said. Why had they not removed these people? 'We have an arrangement with them.'

I was about to berate them for their folly and ineptitude when I realised that we were in serious trouble. The militia blocking position was now between us and the CPA base, and there was no certain way back except along that same road. I was cut off from my team, and it was clear that this emergency had just begun. We might need these fools again; and so, face set, I congratulated them on their professionalism and vigilance. CRG drove us the remaining kilometre to Delta as I sat in the back with ice in my heart. Where were our new Chief of Police and his Deputy?

I found General Ostrovskiy in his office, and asked him levelly what had occurred and what he had done. He said that because of disturbances in other cities like Najaf and Karbala, Sadr followers had said that the safety of Ukrainian forces in Kut could not be guaranteed. These had accordingly been withdrawn from patrol as a precautionary measure and to avoid bloodshed. He was due to meet a Sadr delegation shortly in Delta to discuss the matter. Would I like to attend? I heard myself say no, and that this was a time for strength not negotiation; but I felt powerfully as though an alien power had seized control of the minds of everyone I met and turned them into dissembling automata.

Aghast at the scale of this secret capitulation we drove to meet the American Special Forces and Marine contingents inside Delta. I briefed them in their quarters as they huddled around me with radios crackling. They told me that intelligence indicated that Sadr had placed explosive at the lock gates, and that their check point had been strengthened in the last hour to prevent any attempt by the Coalition to move forces back into Kut. I asked what they intended to do; I expected them to call for air support and clear the road. There was a long silence. One said 'There's not much we *can* do'. I said we had no choice but to return, and left the building.

I felt very alone. I found the Ukrainian withdrawal astonishing, and was equally shocked by the apparent paralysis of these two elite American units. Every minute that we permitted militia to remain in control of the city damaged us terribly. I briefed Bob about what I had learned and said that we had to go back; to leave the CPA team isolated in these circumstances was unthinkable, and I could not contemplate staying where I was. I said I thought it would be very dangerous, and quite understood if he wished to say no. He got into the car without a word. At that moment I felt something akin to love for my security team. They had every right to refuse. We drove without further conversation to the front gate. The lock was visible ahead, and the empty road that led to it shimmered in the unseasonal heat.

At the gate were Steve and his Special Forces troops, in full combat gear, mounted on open Humvee vehicles bristling with heavy weapons. It was not clear why. Had they decided, after all, to fight? I talked to him. Tension crackled in the thick air around our small group like summer lightning. Every movement and word seemed suddenly to be of great consequence in these moments before departure. I asked him what he intended to do. He said that two of his soldiers had been rocketed that morning and momentarily looked down as he spoke. Nothing. The word lay unspoken between us.

I shook his hand. We called Timm and said we were coming back. I got into the cars and we drove out of the gate toward the lock.

The road was entirely empty. We were on our own and no one else could help us now. I thought the chances of our being killed or injured were high, yet could neither contemplate the humiliation of merely surrendering to events nor conceive of the idea of abandoning my team while I skulked in Delta. I firmly believed that we must pick up this gauntlet or face political defeat. I could imagine the FCO's dry post-incident report: 'Inexplicably the GC now decided to return through the Sadr position.' I could surely not expect cover from that quarter.

We stopped at the lock. There was no sign of explosive. The police said that Sadr had moved to the area of the grain silos ahead. We debated whether I and a small CRG group should walk ahead of the cars and negotiate passage, or try and drive it. I favoured the former course. Then an extraordinary thing occurred: a garrulous Sadr supporter who spoke perfect English walked up to me at the lock. He said his name was Sammy. What did I think of all this? I said I thought it was a scandal that CPA had closed Sadr's paper, and it was clear that Mustapha Yacoubi was innocent. I had never seen the town as well-run as it was this morning, and was eager to report this to Ambassador Bremer but regrettably, the road was blocked, making this impossible. Might Sammy consider getting us through? He beamed. It would be a pleasure. He jumped in beside me. Was it a trap? We did not know. We were committed.

We drove around the corner slowly in a two-car convoy. Neil radioed that he had us in his binoculars from the office across the river and could see the checkpoint ahead. I now saw it myself—it consisted of about twenty people—and could also see at least four RPG launchers, all pointed at us. As we closed with them one man tried to wave us down. Bob said calmly 'keep moving'. I opened the door on the move so they could see Sammy, who now jumped out of

the rolling vehicle and attempted to calm the leader, who gesticulated wildly. We inched onward. Two RPG men now knelt in firing
positions, with the weapons at ranges of 25 metres. Point blank—
we would have no chance. I was struck by the terrible anonymity of
this kind of violence, and imagined lying hurt in the dust. Neil said
urgently, 'They're taking up firing positions.' Sammy was now
shouting at the group's leader who shouted back, and then, as suddenly, turned away. Sammy turned to me, shouted 'No problem',
and ran back to the car. We accelerated gingerly, watching the rear-
view mirror. Someone said 'Fuck-ing hell'. We were through—and
returned at high speed across the dam. I heard months later that
Sheikh Abdul Jawad al-Issawi, hearing that we had been allowed
through by his feckless militia, flew into a rage, saying we should
have been either killed or captured.

We now stopped at the police station. Sammy and I said goodbye.
I do not know what happened to him. I walked down its empty corridors with CRG. A man sat at a desk reading a magazine. I asked
where our new police leaders, Abdul Haneen and Ali Riba, were.
He flicked over a page, looked at me without interest and said he
had never heard of them—there was a new Chief now, appointed by
the Sadr office. I returned to base, light-headed with adrenalin reaction, and reported to Baghdad that we had lost control of the city.

We now applied unceasing pressure to the Ukrainians, both
directly through their liaison officer and via CPA HQ. Not a vehicle
moved. Rumours of an attack by militia on our compound at 1600
proved groundless. In the early evening an ashen-faced Dr Salaam
came to see us; he seemed to be on the verge of a break-down. We
sent him home. An hour later I received a telephone message from
Deputy Police Chief Ali Riba: he could re-assert civil control, but
there would be bloodshed. What were my instructions? I told him
to do nothing, believing that the police were incapable of carrying
out the task. The Coalition would have to do it, and I could not but

believe that their intervention was imminent. At 1900 I was told that four militiamen had seized the television station and begun broadcasting Sadr material. Four! Could we be so pathetically weak? BBC Monitoring now reported that the Jaish al-Mahdi had assumed control of al-Kut. I briefed everybody in my office. Triple Canopy and CRG organised a permanent guard roster through the night. I finished writing my reports late that evening and lay awake till 0400, seething with anger and humiliation.

I was woken up just before seven by birds tapping at the reflective blast-film on my window. I could hear aircraft. I ran up to the roof of the Villa. Two American fighter-bombers circled the city. On the bridge were Ukrainian armoured vehicles; the military, at last, had moved. Again we sped into the city. Ukrainian soldiers and vehicles were at each intersection. They had re-occupied a deserted Kut at 0530 without resistance. Our new police officers were behind their desks at the station as though my visit of the day before had been a day-dream. Sadr had melted away. In the government building Sultan wore an air of confidence like cheap scent—one could smell his fear through it. It was clear that he had folded. Dr Abdul Salaam strode from his office, beaming and clean-shaven after his shambling performance the previous evening.

We now wholly doubted the evidence of our senses. Sadr had slouched from the reed-beds, forced an entire Brigade into humiliating surrender, and vanished again. Kut, so far as one could see, had returned to normal. Yet who could we now trust? The Governor? Dr Abdul Salaam? Were our new police officers backing Sadr too? And what about our interpreters? I was no longer sure of anything, and remembered our source's words to me at the door that night.

We needed first to ensure there would be no repeat of our catastrophic military performance of 5 April. I decided to go and see Ostrovskiy again to make sure we perfectly understood one another.

We went to pick up our liaison officer at the base before going on to Delta—he needed to be conversant with the plan. We returned to the site to find an additional protective cordon provided by the Iraqi Civil Defence Corps; and to hear that an arrest warrant had been issued for Moqtada al-Sadr.

Our liaison officer was unenthusiastic about his work. Although we had thought that establishing the post was important in enhancing civil-military co-ordination, the concept was novel for the young captains of the Brigade; and so devoid of authority were they in these centralised formations and so afraid of their autocratic commanders that they were of limited operational use. Ours now ran to collect his helmet, flak jacket and rifle which, typically, were scattered around the complex. I chafed at the delay. His inefficiency may have saved our lives.

As I looked idly at the dam over which we were about to travel a rocket-propelled grenade (RPG) hit the road next to one of the armoured vehicles picketing the route with a sudden explosion and black smoke drifted swiftly away across the water. The birds on the river scattered in a white cloud. A burst of machine-gun fire followed from the river's western bank. A second Ukrainian vehicle engaged the supposed firing position with its heavy machine-gun. Two more sped toward the firing. The gunfire rolled around the city. All this happened in thirty seconds. It was 1100 on 6 April.

What had begun as a skirmish rapidly became a full-scale battle. A group of Ukrainian armoured vehicles moved to the western end of the dam, 500 metres from us, and poured torrents of heavy machine-gun fire into a black-flagged building in a poor quarter of town. The building shook as it was struck by shell after shell, the tracer wheeling off the walls through a haze of dust. A car beneath it was hit and caught fire, billowing black smoke. Within minutes a growing roar blanketed the sounds of firing as two grey American fighter-bombers appeared overhead. Our radio crackled—'fast movers inbound'.

My initial reaction to the spectacle was shock, followed by quiet exultation that we were at last using the military power on which we had long traded, in circumstances that were clear-cut. This feeling was shared by most of us, particularly after the humiliations of the day before. We watched from the Villa's roof as the battle continued. Yet I felt an additional tension to that which had dogged me since the demonstration. Despite the brutal punishment meted out by Ukrainian machine-guns the fighting no longer appeared localised after the first few moments. It was as though sparks from the firing had been carried far into the city. Sporadic shooting broke out on our side of the Tigris. Shortly afterward I saw an explosion about fifty feet above the middle of the river; and then another on our river bank which sent water and red mud across the road. The reports were very loud. They were RPGs at the very limit of their range, and the first had self-detonated at the end of its flight. These were not overshoots—there were no Ukrainian forces on the line of flight—but a deliberate attempt to hit the base.

The sound of firing came steadily closer from the city. Again I watched Ukrainian armoured vehicles as they sped over the dam away from us and towards Delta. This was not the reaction I had hoped for. I asked the liaison officer to get me an update and spoke to CRG. As we had decided in our contingency plans, we now divided civilians on base into two groups, placing staff with operational tasks in the Villa and non-essential staff under cover in the hotel protected by CRG Team Two. Neil Strachan, Timm and I remained in the Villa with CRG One. Numbers in the base were larger than envisaged—the U.S. counter-intelligence team, who had moved back to Delta when we occupied Tarawa, had been visiting CPA that morning and were trapped by the fighting. Our Polish military staff who worked in the GST had also visited us that morning. All were now gathered in the hotel.

We divided responsibilities. Neil would handle the tactical reporting of events to Baghdad by e-mail. I would deal with CPA

Baghdad by satellite telephone in an attempt to work out some kind of strategic response. Bob and the international members of Triple Canopy would coordinate security between them. Timm would oversee the Ukrainian garrison force and liaise with Bob. Each of us took hand-held radios. Rob McCarthy meanwhile wiped the hard-disks of our computers in Tarawa and we destroyed sensitive files. I reported to CPA HQ that we were under attack by what we presumed to be Sadr militiamen.

The situation worsened steadily as the sounds of fighting worked their way towards us. By 1500 it was clear that insurgents were on the roofs of the houses behind us and as though in a dream I heard our CRG team begin firing from the roofs of our own complex, and a Ukrainian sniper break the glass on the upstairs landing of the Villa with his rifle butt and open fire. The reports were deafening in the confined space, each followed by the rattle of an ejected cartridge-case as it hit the floor and bounced down the stairs. RPGs were now being launched into our compound from adjacent houses at ranges of no more than 150 metres. I saw one hit the wall above Triple Canopy's office and the tail of another spin smoking to the ground outside our kitchen—we moved the gas bottles inside. During the intervals between explosions we could hear a steady and eerie chanting from the minarets of the city. Triple Canopy now told me that our entire local guard force except for two had run away, and left their weapons and uniforms scattered about the compound. The Iraqi Civil Defence Corps cordon had got back into their vehicles and fled.

I remember realising at that moment, on an otherwise unre-markable Tuesday afternoon, that we had run out of options, and that all the accumulated inefficiencies and frictions of the preceding six months had simply coalesced. We were now in serious trouble. This was not a re-run of yesterday, when we had been forced to decide whether to remain at the airbase or return to the CPA site through the Sadr position. Now we had no choice: the fighting had come to us and could not be avoided. If, the day before, I had feared the prospect of death or injury in a Sadr RPG salvo, I had overcome it by consciously electing to meet it. Now the element of decision had gone, and it was this sense of helpless inability to influence events that robbed me of courage. For the first twenty minutes I felt afraid. I do not know whether it was obvious to others. I sensed in myself an inability to think or function—I strode about and asked questions but was wholly unable to process the information. I was simply overwhelmed by sensation: one simply stood, receiving momentously bad news second by second with no possible escape or remedy. Every explosion and rattle of automatic fire underpinned the reality that we were now trapped in our base with nightfall no more than four hours away. Yet after this initial paralysis my brain began gradually to re-exert control again and produce solutions. At 1515 we asked for air support by sat-phone and e-mail.

The firing into our compound was now almost continuous, the report of RPG warheads exploding mixed with the concussion of mortar shells. The noise was very loud and the echo in our confined spaces was deafening. We had two communication systems only in the Villa—a hand-held satellite phone that I had to go on to the roof to use, and our Internet in a Box. Neil sent regular situation reports by e-mail including grid references of the militia's firing positions. I added my views at intervals. Timm and Bob tried to coordinate resistance using the garrison force and CRG.

In all our contingency planning we had relied on two key elements: defence by the Ukrainian garrison force until we were reinforced by Brigade at Delta, and the presence of a site guard force. I could see no sign of any intention by the Brigade to break through the Sadr position and re-open the road; and our guard force had run away. Our only additional help had been the chance arrival of three Ukrainian armoured vehicles under the command of Deputy Brigade

Commander Kumilov, which had been securing the television station before being ordered to withdraw. He was now trapped as we
were. He told me that all other Brigade vehicles had returned to
Delta, which our liaison officer now confirmed; his manner indicated that he did not think they intended to return. We were alone
with no prospect of rescue.

Under normal circumstances the site would prove a difficult
place to attack and seize: we had Ukrainian troops, our own security
details, a twelve-foot wall on one side and the Tigris on the other.
Yet any reassurance this might have afforded was largely delusory.
The site was large and these defences would retain value only if
overseen by armed men. I detected limited enthusiasm for the fight
among our Ukrainian soldiers. Some were in firing positions, certainly, but many were not; and a few had quietly absented themselves. Our CRG teams were too small to fill the gap. The very size
of the site thus worked to our disadvantage, and the notion of fighting these people inside the complex and its scattered buildings was
particularly unattractive. The Ukrainians could not remain inside
the perimeter observation towers—these were too exposed and
had already been repeatedly targeted from the houses across the
road. They had not been properly prepared for defence and thus
were untenable at the time we most needed them—so we were
blindfolded as well. Triple Canopy now consisted of only the three-
strong international core that had first arrived. Their former links
with U.S. Special Forces had encouraged the U.S. contingent across
the river to leave them a radio, and lacking any kind of official radio
communications system, we now relied on this as a military link.
Overwhelmingly the assistance we now needed was air power and
reinforcement, yet we were powerless to speak to the aircraft we
had requested because we had no ground-air radio system. The
Marine Corps contingent whose only task this was remained in
Delta, 4 km. away, along with a Special Forces group whose skills

would at last have proved particularly useful and a Ukrainian contingent of hundreds of troops. None left the base. I thought this inexplicable. The prospect of nightfall under these circumstances was unpleasant.

The uncertainty and fear that now permeated the compound rapidly eroded a CPA-led team structure that had never been properly formalised. Our staffing roll betrayed its rushed and patchwork origins; within the compound were international and non-international, CPA and non-CPA, military and civilian staff, and responsibility for these groups was divided among six separate organisations, four of which were sub-contractors. Most of them had their own communication systems, through which they reported to their own command chains. This multiplicity of reporting greatly complicated our task in those early hours as we strove to fashion and coordinate a response to the assault on our site. It was not till CPA Baghdad relayed a lurid KBR report back to us by e-mail, sent by the KBR team from its office some 50 m. away, that the scale of this problem became apparent. This period of confusion cost us hours of daylight as CPA HQ received one conflicting report after another.

The deterioration in morale was steady and marked among the disparate groups in the compound as each separate agency turned in on itself. Fear, once it takes hold, is deeply contagious, and it spread quickly in the confines of the darkened hotel. The noise of mortar shells, RPG rounds and small arms was deafening, but, as so often when they are used against buildings, the effect on the mind exceeded the physical damage done. When I walked across to the hotel in late afternoon I was shocked to find that the majority appeared to believe they would die if they were not rescued. Privately one had to accept that this possibility existed, and anxiety about this hidden enemy was compounded by the fear of an Islamic militia made more merciless by religious fervour. It was this fear that now conspired to paralyse. Despite Timm's best efforts to rally the

Polish military contingent and the U.S. counter-intelligence team, neither was keen to take up fire positions to defend the compound, and it was sufficiently difficult to get the counter-intelligence team to monitor the radios with which their vehicles were equipped that we had to offer to do it ourselves.

The clamour of the attack, physical and mental, threatened to submerge all attempts to think. During my satellite phone calls to Baghdad from the roof, rocket-propelled grenades swept regularly overhead momentarily eclipsing the sharp reports of small arms fire; and I saw a sand-bagged position on the roof of Tarawa House shatter as one struck home. The Villa had proved a good choice—it was difficult to hit and masked at the rear by the palm grove. In a hurried discussion Neil Strachan, Timm and I established a simple set of core principles after first examining the proposition that Sadr had returned for their negligée. The first was that we would not simply give up the site: to do so would make no sense since apart from dealing a substantial blow to the Coalition's prestige it would force us to re-take the complex at greater cost. Withdrawal was anyway a chimera. Leaving the complex now would be hugely dangerous and inevitably lead to casualties, and the buildings behind us would first need to be cleared. We would stay. Yet we were weak, and nightfall would make us weaker still. We had to be given reinforcements, but it was clear they would not come from Delta.

I told Timm that as a Parachute Regiment lieutenant my first company commander had been an American officer, of the U.S. 82nd Airborne Division, who had greeted each dawn with the words 'What a *great* day to be a paratrooper!' *Zulu*, a film about the nineteenth-century British stand at Rorke's Drift in South Africa, had cult status in the Regiment at the time and he had thus been forced to watch it repeatedly. He adored the film, and like everyone else learned chunks of the script and used it in briefings. He would have loved the situation I was in now: the native levies had indeed run away, and the part of the missionary cleric who shouts 'You are all going to die' was presently being played by KBR. All we now needed was a member of CRG to report levelly to me from the front gate: 'Sadr sir. Thousands of them.'

We understood that far from planning rescue our Ukrainian garrison troops were considering unilateral withdrawal. I had intervened strongly with Kumilov once this suspicion hardened; he had merely said that it was not his decision. I inferred that the government in Kiev was anxious. We reluctantly agreed a second principle—that if the Ukrainians left, we would be forced to go with them. It was clear that any attempt to hold the site with two CRG teams alone would present an unacceptable risk to our staff.

We passed our recommendations to CPA. I asked for helicopters to reinforce us with soldiers from Baghdad in the knowledge that British and American Special Forces squadrons were based in the city, together with dedicated airframes. The aircraft that brought our reinforcements should fly out non-essential staff at the same time whom it made no sense to retain in a dangerous situation if they could not affect the outcome of the fighting. We envisaged the operation taking place during the night, if necessary via Delta, with the landing covered by Apache helicopters. Neil Strachan had already provided grid references of points from which we had been fired on during the day. While waiting for a response we drafted a list of non-essential staff—both American and Polish military contingents asked to be on it. I heard Timm asking them to leave behind their weapons and ammunition.

As evening drew near we faced the prospect of ten hours of darkness under these conditions with concern. In the hours since 1100 the Coalition had proved unable to summon a response to the attack, largely because of a series of damaging failures of communication. The first was that military HQ in Baghdad doubted the accuracy of our reports, in the belief that civilians were unable to evaluate such matters. This cost hours. The second was that they were issuing orders downward to a Ukrainian Brigade that to all intents and purposes had ceased to heed them: thus Baghdad believed for many hours that its orders to initiate a rescue package were being followed, but they were not. Finally, I detected an inherent belief in the military that air-power was the answer to our problems. It was part of the answer, of course, in that it might buy us time pending Ukrainian action to reinforce the complex and clear the houses of our assailants; yet the prospect of that action, unknown to Baghdad, remained fantasy. Air power would not solve the problem on its own.

American fighter aircraft had initiated a series of low passes along the river in the late afternoon. I was asked whether they should drop bombs in the river to intimidate our opponents, but I thought it would merely demonstrate our impotency. I could tell that Triple Canopy staff, via whose Special Forces radio the offer had been made, disagreed with me. To their credit they did as they were asked, and relayed the response. An hour later at dusk two Apache helicopters made their way slowly and deliberately across our compound and adjoining houses at 150 feet. Their sinister presence imposed an instant ceasefire. They circled us for forty minutes in the dying light and then broke away across the river to refuel. Firing began again almost immediately.

The appearance of Colonel Abdul Haneen, our new police chief, at our site seemed so improbable that I wondered whether he too was a Sadr nominee. Looking haggard he said that Sadr was offering terms and wanted to meet us that same evening. I saw an opportunity to buy time and demurred, saying that this was too complex a matter to be dealt with so soon, and that I would need to confer with others. I suggested 0930 the next day, which might secure a fragile stalemate till the next morning—surely the Coalition could move by then. He smiled in a gentle way, and I thought that, with or without Sadr, his first days in his new assignment must be proving burdensome.

It now seemed certain that we would receive no reinforcement before nightfall, and I did not see how we could withstand a determined attack. Our enemy appeared dedicated and to have plenty of ammunition. Probably all of us believed we might have to fight these people house-to-house in the dark—we had under-estimated them. Each of us now prepared personal weapons and magazines. As darkness fell we turned the Villa lights off, and I sat alone in the dining room on the ground floor with the radio and tried to think. The firing died away, as though a tap had gradually been turned off. Then in the silence I heard Triple Canopy report that eighteen armed men were walking towards us down the approach road. It was as I had feared. I asked CRG to confirm the information. Bob said, in his laconic manner, that there was no one on the road at all. We sent an exhausted Triple Canopy member to bed.

The night was alive with shadows and one retained the ability to think logically with only the most steadfast application of will. The silence was worse than the firing, and the darkness seemed a thing of velvet malevolence. Neil now told me that he was receiving heart-wrenching pleas for help on the telephone from a house not 500 metres away occupied by Hart Security, a team charged with protecting power lines from looters as they were slowly re-built. Sadr had attacked the house and killed one of them; the others had gradually withdrawn to the roof and were now trapped there. Sadr had entered the building and was calling through the door for them to surrender. I again pleaded with Kumilov for troops from Delta. He said he had asked the same question repeatedly, but in vain. We relayed the situation to Baghdad, and Neil remained in contact with Hart for hours till finally losing communication with them in the early morning. We did not tell the rest of our team—it could hardly have improved morale. The same fate awaited us if we did not hold the site.

If each hour seemed interminable I judged every minute that passed and brought dawn fractionally nearer without shooting to be a tiny victory. I sat in my bedroom-cum-office in the Villa with the curtains drawn and the wardrobe dragged across the window, writing e-mails with my flak jacket on and a pistol on the desk. The whole of my floor was occupied by Ukrainian soldiers resting, and the giant figure of Colonel Kumilov lay stretched out on a camp bed. Neil Strachan next door lay under his desk relaying situation reports on his laptop in his helmet and flak jacket. I did not like being without air cover—to sit here in this sprawling and ill-defended compound at night was uncomfortable.

Timm entered the office, and I reflected to myself as I saw him that if there was ever a place where one needed a bearded Texan at the barricades it was in Kut on the night of 6 April. He asked me to listen carefully; and there, just above the chorus of frogs from the river-line and the sporadic shooting from the city was a steady rhythmic drone. I walked up to the roof, from where one could just see a black crucifix orbiting the city, occasionally obscured by wisps of cloud. We had an AC-130 'Spectre' on station: a modified Hercules aircraft of considerable complexity which carried radar-directed 40 mm. cannon and a 105 mm. howitzer. It flew an endless oval pattern at unvarying height. Something in its robotic circling of Kut breathed power. We quickly spread the news and there was a palpable improvement in morale.

Triple Canopy now radioed the news that Steve's Special Forces team was 200 metres from our gate, and asked that we open fire to draw a response from the Sadr positions. 'Spectre' would then fix the firing positions and engage them. I could see no sense in this— better, I thought, to allow this relative calm to continue and infil-trate the Special Forces in silence. We could cover them in. I vetoed the idea. In retrospect it is apparent that there were many on site who saw us as at war with the city of Kut—I never read it in that way, knowing that a passive majority had been intimidated by a minority. I could not see how destroying their houses and killing those caught up in the crisis by wild exchanges of fire could advance our cause or help us recover from this debacle. Again, I could tell that the leader of the Triple Canopy team disagreed with me, but he did as I had asked. It quickly emerged that the group was 200 metres from Delta's gates and nowhere near us.

At about 2300 I was sitting on the ground floor in darkness with the CPA team. All I could see around me was the red glow of ciga-rettes. That steady drone above us had continued for hours. I heard a salvo of machine-gun bullets pass over the roof of the Villa; then, very distinctly, what sounded like a cannon firing slowly and delib-erately at one-second intervals. I raced up the stairs to the roof: there, across the river at the far end of the dam, a cloud of white dust hung suspended in the air, suffused with moonlight as it drifted slowly over the luminous water. The aircraft had fired, and what-ever had been there was there no more. That black crucifix con-tinued its implacable circling of the city.

So accustomed was I now to the sound of that aircraft and the implied power of its presence that I noticed instantly when it flew away. As so often during this confrontation, we were engaged almost immediately afterwards by machine-guns from the grain silos across the river. I ran up to the roof to find Timm there by the parapet. As we watched, the gunner fired again and dozens of red tracer bullets made their way slowly towards us. Time seemed to slow as we watched them come, unmoving. In those few seconds that seemed like full minutes of concentrated sensation I at once felt an overwhelming exultation. Something urged me forward into the fire: I wanted to climb the parapet wall and stand framed by it, arms outstretched, and step into the darkness. It was a kind of madness which now infected my mind as surely as fear had done all those hours ago. Then the crack of the bullets was all around us as it swept overhead. Seconds later the Ukrainian armoured vehicles at each corner of the Villa returned fire; and two great silver streams of tracer made molten arcs into the enemy positions opposite. The Sadr machine-gunner did not stop firing—I could only admire him. For those brief moments I was transfixed by the scene—the red clusters of the oncoming tracer, the avalanche of noise, and the colours on the Tigris; and Timm in front of me framed by plunging comets of Ukrainian bullets. It was almost as if the mind, saturated by this cascade of sensation, momentarily allowed one a moment of detachment in which peace flowed from a complete absence of fear. I saw the steady passage of incoming fire but the brain blocked the calculation of cause and effect and allowed me to marvel at its eerie splendour like a child. In our shared experiences over these terrible months and particularly in that moment of shared danger, I felt a profound bond of kinship with the American beside me on the roof. I feel it still.

Throughout the night we had used every means at our disposal to encourage intervention by the Coalition but by midnight it was clear that Ukrainian political resolve had become fragile. The British Office in Baghdad was deeply concerned about the fate of this predominantly British team, and had sent a terse message prohibiting partial evacuation: the team was to evacuate in its entirety if an evacuation effort was to be made. The message added 'It is not a civilian's job to hold ground.' I then received two further messages asking me to acknowledge both the order and the sentiment but ignored them. One sensed the Coalition's inherent structural weakness seep through the ether. It was clear that evacuation fever had begun to grip everyone, and as it grew our ability to influence events waned.

The decision to withdraw us came by e-mail, and its tone brooked no argument—its transmission by deployeddaddy@ald.com merely emphasised the amateurism that had characterised the CPA communications system from the start. The question-mark over the plan was whether the Ukrainians were intended to withdraw as well. One could at least understand a move to extract civilian staff while the military restored stability, but full evacuation was strategically incomprehensible and I could not imagine that Bremer or General Sanchez would have agreed to it. It was not clear that either had been consulted—if they had, my suspicion was that the Ukrainian Brigade was not listening. Kumilov told me that he had orders to withdraw his soldiers in convoy at first light. We called General Ostrovskiy and he confirmed that he had orders to withdraw—he did not say from whom. Now, as the hours ticked away, we tried desperately to find out whether CPA was aware that the military garrison intended to leave too.

Kumilov meanwhile lined his vehicles up in convoy on the perimeter road; it was clear that he was going to leave as ordered and that we could not stop him. As we had long ago decided, we had no choice but to go with them—we could not gamble on being rescued by the broader Coalition if we attempted to stay behind. Everyone began to throw possessions into bags and load them on the vehicles. I felt bitter.

We had been told to expect a rescue package but none materialized and it was soon clear that this would be no more than the Ukrainians leaving our gate. Evacuation fever now swept the camp, and all semblance of order vanished. The first Ukrainian vehicle began to edge towards the barrier. I found Kumilov and stopped it. KBR jumped into our CPA vehicles and we ejected them. Near-panic gripped some people, terrified that they would be left behind; I tried to control it but failed—no one was listening any more. I was horrified at the proposed withdrawal—this was a far more risky manoeuvre than remaining. There had been no accommodation with Sadr, there had been no clearance of routes, and none of these vehicles could have withstood an RPG strike. Above all, we had a rump Brigade just four km. away, plus American specialist troops. It was madness, but we had no choice but to follow. All the Ukrainian vehicles had now closed up at the gate, engines running. There was no pretence at protection—this was a Ukrainian withdrawal with everyone else trying to keep up. I watched Timm throw his computer in the river. I walked the line of vehicles, jammed with people, shocked by the proposed abandonment not just of the site but of personal discipline and pride. Kumilov was now waving his arms as next to his armoured vehicle a pair of Apaches appeared over the lightening river. I called Baghdad and told them that it was too late—we would have to go. They told me that the Coalition commander General Sanchez had ordered the Ukrainians to stay. I ran up to the lead armoured vehicle and told Kumilov, but these were not his orders. Vehicles now drove around me to get out of the site, headed by the Ukrainian convoy. I checked so far as I could in the chaos that we had all of our people. I was proud of our own CPA team, who had behaved calmly and bravely throughout. I got into the car. Bob suggested blocking the Ukrainian military vehicles but I said no—I am not sure that it would have made any difference, and we might well have had a mutiny on our hands.

We threaded our way through the main barrier. It was a cold spring morning and the city was deadly quiet. I sat next to Timm numb with shock at what had been done, listening to Bob describing this humiliating surrender on the radio to CRG Baghdad. All our work overturned. We drove a 55 km. diversion route to Delta under Apache top cover. At the outskirts of Kut we moved to the front of the convoy and blocked it in order to check that no one had been left behind. It was like trying to slow a runaway bull. Few cared about anything at that juncture but themselves, or showed any signs that they were conscious of the political gravity of this capitulation.

We needed to intervene forcefully in Baghdad. Once the team was safe in Delta, Bob at my request quickly pulled a composite security team together, and we left two hours later. We drove north at high speed. No one had taken any rest for some twenty-eight hours, and Timm rapidly fell asleep beside me. Perhaps it was fatigue, or my long and exclusive concentration on Kut, but I had not fully grasped that this insurrection might not be confined to the city. The province was deserted; and as we sped northward I began to wonder why.

We were ambushed thirty minutes later outside the town of Numaniyah by Sadr militiamen with Kalashnikovs and an RPG. Bob accelerated and shouted 'RPG right' as the air filled with the sound of bullets. I watched one man attempt to aim a rocket launcher and another empty his automatic rifle at us at a range of one hundred metres. Incredibly, they missed both cars. Ahead of us the road was blocked by the town market. We raced through a poorly-sited ambush, but they were now just behind us and there was no way forward. Car Two now shouted route instructions to us over the radio—astonishingly they knew a back-route through the city. We careered left and ran at high speed through labyrinthine alleys to the open road. I asked CRG to take us to the nearby compound where we had attended the construction ceremony so long ago—we needed to take stock before driving further. For the first time I realised that we had lost control of the province.

6

RETURN TO KUT

The Foreign Office withdrew the British members of the Kut CPA team to Britain on 13 April. We would not return for a month—at the time we were unsure whether we would return at all. They gave us suites in the Kuwait Marriott Hotel and flew us out business class. This compulsory holiday engendered in some of us a sense of comfort and relief; others felt anger and frustration. For me the antiseptic veneer of my hotel room and coyly curtained British Airways window seat compounded an acute sense of dislocation and alienation. The Marriott's complimentary fruit bowl with its plastic cover 'for your protection' quietly enraged me; and the everyday concerns of life outside Iraq seemed impossibly banal. The change in our environment had been abrupt. I no longer knew who I was or where I properly belonged. I temporarily lacked the language to re-integrate myself into 'ordinary' existence, perhaps because it seemed difficult then to imagine a life freed from the regular threat of violent injury or death. One saw that it was not only modesty that urged reticence on those asked to speak of their experiences of conflict, but the futility of attempting to describe that onslaught of sensation. Overwhelmingly I felt as though we had been militarily defeated; and my humiliation and determination to redress the balance eclipsed what was undoubtedly a large measure of fatigue and strain.

After our withdrawal from Kut and subsequent ambush at Numaniyah we had remained overnight at the construction site to rest and gather information. I wrote a post-action report for the Foreign Office and spoke to the rump Kut team by satellite telephone. I remember feeling as if I were describing events that had been experienced by somebody else. So pronounced was this sensation that I found it difficult at first to complete my report; and what delayed progress most was my reluctance to continue this unwarranted impersonation. Discomfited by this sense of duality, I left the claustrophobic confines of the construction site Portakabin and walked for a while in the evening to escape the clamour of the generators, lighting sets and air conditioners. I bathed my face in a desert breeze that would have relaxed me but for the knowledge that we must leave this site again or risk being permanently cut off. In considering this latest gambit I again felt my skin prickle and adrenalin stir. I realised then that the transformation the mind and body undergo in moments of extreme danger—that sense of implacable focus, the suppression of extraneous stimuli and the way in which the simplest event seizes and secures the mind—was both logical and comprehensible, and that the people whose actions I had so balked at describing were, indeed, ourselves.

Still I felt like a fraud. The military campaigns I had studied and the history I had read were full of heroism and suffering; and we had run away after an attack that would have merited no more than a single line in a Second World War company diary. I spoke to Timm about it, who told me that I was ignoring the human evolution that had occurred since that twentieth-century watershed; and that what might once have seemed a virtual irrelevance was significant now.

CRG had meanwhile been looking for cross-country routes out of the province but had found nothing suitable—all potential tracks we explored petered out in the desert. I saw no alternative but to keep going. The militia knew where we were and might block the exit route; we could not allow ourselves to be trapped. We left just

before dawn next morning, 8 April, and joined the main road as the
first hint of sunlight began to dispel the darkness. We had been
running the gauntlet continuously for three days; and the long
shadows at the edges of the empty road ahead mutated into black-
clad assailants as the sun rose. The danger of further incidents was
acute. The roads were arrow-straight and despite our high speed,
we knew that any blocking position would have ample warning of
our approach. There was silence in the car save for the roaring of the
engine and the chatter of our communication systems. For forty
minutes, as we drove hard for the province boundary, my eyes
remained fixed on that road and the earthen banks beside it as our
high-frequency radio wailed. Scattered groups of banner-carrying
pilgrims en route for Najaf and Karbala on foot momentarily transfixed us and were gone, and I did not sleep until we had joined an
escorted American convoy heading north to Baghdad on Route
Tampa, which was halted twice to allow Apaches to investigate
suspected mortar positions.

I stared through the car's window at the looking-glass world of
the Green Zone as if I had never seen it before. The towering flanks
of American Bradley armoured fighting vehicles at the checkpoints,
their cannons levelled along the road; the white sandbagged watch-
towers and their black machine-guns; the impassive and taciturn
American soldiers; and the constant to-ing and fro-ing of pairs of
helicopters low over the palms: these drifted in and out of vision as
though it were all a dream. We were debriefed by British officers in
a quiet meeting room in one of Saddam Hussein's guest houses;
deftly and expertly our experiences were transmuted into times,
numbers, rounds fired and casualties. There were bodies lying behind the Kut compound—no one was sure what had killed them.
The Hercules 'Spectre' aircraft had fired twice. It was unclear
whether the Apaches had fired at all. The Hart security team that
had been besieged by Sadr had lost one dead, but the others had

jumped from the roof, commandeered a car and got away. I asked whether consideration had been given to a military intervention mounted from Baghdad but was told that the British Office had not been fully cognizant of the existence of a British Special Forces stand-by squadron there, and that no thought had been given to the issue till it was too late. Nor had British forces reconnoitred our complex and landing site in the months before the attack.

The large television outside the meeting room was on permanently, and one of the first pieces of news we saw covered Kut. The film had been taken from across the river and the compression of the telephoto lens imparted an indistinct, sinister quality to the images. Abdul Jawad al-Issawi and his followers had occupied our site a few hours after our departure. They must have been exhilarated by our unexpected and precipitate retreat. I was told some months later that the militia had run out of ammunition that night and called from the mosques for more. Black banners hung from the buildings in which we used to live, and oily smoke drifted from one corner of the Villa. A small group of figures in black robes could be seen walking along the river bank. It is said that one can taste defeat, and my mouth now burned with it. Yet Kut had been the first casualty of a much wider rebellion: Moqtada al-Sadr's followers had launched a series of coordinated attacks across the region and in Baghdad with a determination and ferocity that had caught us unawares. The coverage was lurid. The road between Baghdad and the airport had been temporarily closed, and of all my memories that day the most poignant was the procession of casualty evacuation helicopters flying low over the compound to land at the military hospital in the Green Zone.

These reverses made all too evident the fragility of our command over Iraq. Our discharge of the functions of government had been possible only by the consent of ordinary Iraqis and it appeared this consent might now be slipping away. The concern engendered by this supposition naturally encouraged reflection on the nature of our hold over the country. Our military power was real, but it could not be steadily applied in all areas at once—no army can be strong everywhere. This weakness was compounded by the composition of our military force being predicated on political considerations rather than practical requirements. This reduced capability had been tacitly accepted in areas deemed to be 'quiet', indeed had provided much of the rationale for stationing the Polish-led Multi-National Division and its Ukrainian Brigade in Central-South. But these central and east European armies suffered from a whole series of deficiencies. Among the foremost of these was demonstrable inexperience in handling civil populations in a way consistent with preserving that consent. If one allows the existence of a honeymoon period after interventions such as the Coalition's, where the promise and opportunity implicit in a proffered new order briefly match the heady expectations of the people, then we had squandered a large part of it by failing to muster the requisite number of troops to pursue our objectives. And we eroded this climate of consent still further by attempting to fill the gaps with what an American officer once described to me as 'Rent-an-Army' schemes.

We now saw that these deficiencies in Central-South were more fundamental even than this, because these armies, in the main, were not fighting units either. They and particularly their governments saw their role as peace-keeping, and they had arrived equipped accordingly. Sadr's urban insurrection now promised conflict of the bloodiest kind, and underscored the fact that counter-insurgency in such circumstances presented the most difficult of all operations of war. One government after another began to wobble, as the Ukrainians had done, and we absorbed anew another of history's lessons: that if military power is often delusory, it can delude those who wield it more completely than anyone else.

Bremer was bullish, and bounced from his chair to shake hands as Timm and I entered his office. The meeting was businesslike. I was embarrassed by our failure, considered the abandonment of the site the utmost folly and was haunted by the thought that we might have done more. Could we have helped Hart Security fight off their attackers? Might we after all have refused to leave and thus coerced the Ukrainians into remaining? When I said that I was sorry we had lost the site Bremer merely replied 'We're going to take it back.' We described to him what had happened and he listened in silence. The press was already labelling the upsurge in fighting the beginning of the long-feared Shi'ia rising but to his credit Bremer gave the idea no credence at all. These were the followers of Moqtada al-Sadr and no one else, but if this were true, it nevertheless seemed inconceivable at the time that this fighting would not spread, and that we could combat these determined bands with the vigour required without making the conflict worse.

We had no magic antidote for this uprising, which few had expected to be so broad or ferocious. I wryly considered the irony that we had been unable to marshal that same determination and courage on our side in the Iraqi police and civil defence forces. Yet there remained in CPA some who stubbornly saw our salvation in tribal power, believing their brand of conservatism and tradition might yet provide the spine for the Iraqi body politic. That power certainly existed—during our tenure in Kut we had seen it for ourselves— but it was a selfish and self-aggrandising impulse that by its very nature could not be conscripted for national ends. During the fighting in Kut we had telephoned the Tribal Council to see if there was anything it might do, though with no real hope of its intervention. Two representatives went to Sadr's office and condemned their actions, but nothing more was done. Had the foe been merely a criminal gang, the tribes might well have offered resistance; but the Islamic platform from which Sadr sprang precluded effective opposition.

Mike Gfoeller, the Regional Head in Hillah, was a proponent of this tribal role, and had urged it on Bremer. I agreed that some of these tribal chiefs were of sufficient calibre and stature to be useful, but did not see this as sufficient justification for embracing them all. There was, anyway, no 'all': the tribes themselves could rarely agree, and each Association of Tribal Notables or equivalent would invariably dismiss parallel groupings as impostors and charlatans. Bremer now said to us that 'the tribes are on the march', and entering Wasit province from the north. Stirring though this declaration sounded, there was no truth in it. Actually there was plenty of evidence that two or three major tribes were collaborating with Sadr in Wasit. The majority of them admittedly disliked Moqtada al-Sadr's followers, but this did not imply counter-action; indeed it had made no difference to our fate. The tribes more or less remained themselves during this emergency, and their 'armies' marched neither in our province nor in any other. The last vestiges of romanticism about them later died away in CPA, and we reluctantly disposed of the idea that the tribes were a political force on which one might rely in national terms. The fact that it was allowed to gain renewed momentum in the face of so much evidence to the contrary illustrates nothing more than the extent of our unpreparedness and need at the time.

The way in which Bremer dealt with this crisis again exemplified his no-nonsense approach. Although he was under considerable pressure he showed no sign of obvious strain. I had seen him testy and sometimes brusque, but I had yet to see him show any sign of inherent weakness. It was accepted that we would return to Kut as soon as practicable. He did not ask how we were, or what we felt after our withdrawal. The discussion hinged rather on the analysis of events and prospective solutions. I do not know whether this dispassionate drive in him was due to a lack of humanity, some rigid inner discipline or an abiding faith in the precepts of the 'War on Terror'. He and other Americans I met in Iraq rarely wasted time on ideological discussion, seeing their work as a brutally practical matter.

The extent to which this 'War' shaped the thoughts of ordinary Americans in Iraq was striking, particularly in the Armed Forces and among blue-collar sub-contractors like KBR. Had the present endeavour supplanted another great cause or had the nation simply lacked a battle-standard since the demise of the Soviet Union? In a conversation I heard between Rob McCarthy, our Administrative Officer, and Reda Salem, our U.S. Air Force pharmacist, Rob asked why he was in Iraq and Reda replied that it was to make the world safe for his grandchildren. Rob laughed, as any Briton would—the British deployment in Iraq remained unpopular and most of us are cynics. Reda, of course, was deadly serious. European reservations about the existence of this global foe and the very existence of an 'Axis of Evil' merely reinforced the widespread American notion that in the end they could rely on no one but themselves.

Timm and I made plans to return quickly to Kut. The task of re-capturing the city had been given to Major-General Martin E. Dempsey's U.S. First Armored Division. Its 1st Squadron of the 2nd Armored Cavalry Regiment had been on its way to Kuwait and home to Louisiana at the end of its deployment in Iraq. These plans were cancelled, and the Squadron was diverted to Kut. Their soldiers, Abrams tanks, Bradley armoured fighting vehicles and armed helicopters had assembled at Delta Camp. The Americans would first secure Kut's three Tigris bridges, then the CPA site, and finally the rest of the city. Phase One was slated for the following day, 9 April, when we would be taken to Brigade HQ in Baghdad to discuss arrangements for our return.

I was rapidly disabused of any such idea by the UK's new IRAQREP, who had re-placed Greenstock after his departure in March. There were, he said, no circumstances at present under which Britain would allow its staff to return to Kut. Even now, twenty-four hours after our withdrawal, he looked ashen and dishev-elled and it was clear that having extricated a predominantly British team from danger he would not readily entertain the notion of allowing us back again. If my surprise at this instruction sprang partly from my failure fully to appreciate the political consequences in Britain of losing a UK team in Iraq, it also derived from fundamental differences of opinion. The British Foreign Office must have seen a Kut team as little more than tokenism, believing that our presence in Central-South merely showed a readiness by Britain to play its part in the broad spectrum of international endeavour in Iraq rather than simply in the south. Believing this, it saw no genuine rationale for return, particularly at a time of risk. From our own point of view this stance implied a striking lack of knowledge of our work in Wasit and conditions on the ground. There seemed to be no tradition of seeing the area for oneself, in the military fashion; and this, together with the constraints imposed by the security situation, made these decision-makers and their advisers dangerously isolated and created a gap in understanding that our written reports had clearly failed to bridge.

This conversation further persuaded me of something I had long suspected: that the Foreign Office, for all the demonstrable calibre and intellectual ability of its staff, was out of its depth in Iraq. Whether we had looked for it or not, we were now fighting what amounted to a counter-insurgency war against the followers of Moqtada al-Sadr, for which we were ill-prepared. We had lost one site and were in danger of losing others. In abandoning Wasit we had lost our links with its million-strong population, together with a great deal of prestige and credibility, and it seemed to me that the case for return was so powerful as to permit no sensible counter-argument. We needed not only to reverse the consequences of our withdrawal, but to re-assert our political authority quickly and firmly. I fully accepted that this might well prove impossible but I thought it essential to try. This was not a time for discussion but for action. I saw another factor: that, as a leading member of the

Coalition we, the British contingent, needed to carry our share of the burden and be seen to be doing so. The Foreign Office was liable to greet such arguments with the undeniable fact that our input in Iraq was dwarfed by the American preponderance of soldiers, matériel and money, as if somehow our principles and moral courage should be commensurately re-configured to match this relative insignificance. I thought that this was wrong and ignored the political importance of our participation—and certainly no American I ever met in the field thought it anything other than substantial. Were we now to simply fold because we had been attacked? The idea appalled me.

The Foreign Office in Iraq, lacking operational experience was, at heart risk-averse, while their military counterparts were trained to accept risk and manage it. They lacked practice in handling operations on the ground, and despite their traditional strengths of analysis and reporting these qualities could not alone compensate for this deficiency. The British establishment's commitment to the Iraq venture had been lukewarm from the outset; and its fragility was now most obvious when the risks that had always been implicit in the enterprise were most evident. I thought this damaging, and a strategic fault that Britain ought to have rectified at an early stage. The discussion about whether we should or should not have intervened in Iraq was over. Britain needed firm and resolute leadership in the country and this should properly have come from a political appointee tasked to mould the British effort and fashion a united strategy from disparate political and military considerations.

I had not expected this opposition; and my hastily-assembled arguments for return moved IRAQREP little. It was reluctantly agreed that I could return for a brief period to assist the U.S. Army in restoring order to Kut, but that I was not allowed to leave the Delta compound where the American force would be based. After ten days I was to leave and take a break in Britain. Taken aback by the

British reaction but mollified by this concession, Timm and I began the search for a helicopter to take us south. There were none—and I remember suspecting, almost certainly wrongly, that the Foreign Office had put the brakes on me. Such were my frustrations at the time.

Our meeting at the U.S. Second Brigade Combat Team HQ, based in one of the smaller palaces in the Green Zone, was re-scheduled for the morning of 9 April. The professionalism of the Brigade staff was striking. The 1st Squadron had been in Iraq for twelve months. During their relief-in-place in Baghdad by other American units on 4th April they had become embroiled in combat operations against Sadr militia. With much of their equipment packed the Squadron had moved to another camp on 7th April before its road-move to Kuwait, then had its leave cancelled and been given new orders that same evening to re-take Kut. There was no sign of these operational stresses—we were greeted with elaborate courtesy and I heard not a single complaint. One sensed a deep-rooted and peculiarly American personal commitment to the war in Iraq that was probably unique.

There was inevitably a considerable void between this Brigade's breadth of capability and that of the Ukrainian Sixth Mechanised Brigade. The Ukrainians had come to perform a traditional peace-keeping task while the Americans had come to fight and retained the requisite equipment. Despite their expected preponderance in weapons—they had attack, reconnaissance and troop-carrying heli-copters, tanks, armoured fighting vehicles, artillery and mortars—this capability was evident above all in their offensive state of mind and in the American soldier's casual acceptance—indeed, expec-tation—of the extraordinary combat power and reach at his army's command. It was as if American military resources lay in some giant and apparently inexhaustible reservoir, and that all one had to do to meet a specific challenge was to open a tap by the requisite number of revolutions. This was of course delusory—no army cancels leave lightly—but their self-confidence was such that the delusion had great power to persuade. Equally noteworthy was the fact that an incessant flow of casualties had failed to dent their resolve. At this point the Americans had lost over 600 dead in Iraq and 3,000 wounded. Only 138 of these deaths and 542 cases of injury had occurred during the March–April 03 period of hostilities.[1]

As impressive as this mental resilience was the technology supporting these forces. Much of their equipment was 'digital': namely, each weapons platform was electronically tracked and portrayed on digital maps displayed on flat screens to within a few metres of its position in-theatre, together with its call-sign: hence the battlefield could be 'read' from a screen in Operations. Indeed, it was possible to send text messages to individual vehicles from HQ and from vehicle to vehicle. The screen now showed four blue shapes in the CPA compound in Kut.

The Deputy Brigade commander told us that these were American tanks. He could not have been more than thirty-five years old. He was tanned and fit. He had perfect teeth. His uniform was crisp. He radiated a wholesome expertise and discussed the night's combat operations in a manner so detached as to be unsettling, as if this were no more than an expensive three-dimensional arcade game. In crossing the dam into Kut in the early morning from Delta they had been sporadically fired on from the police station opposite, which they then hit using rockets fired from helicopters. The Sadr office had also been destroyed by missiles—the Brigade was uncertain how many people it had killed. The Squadron had then re-taken the CPA compound using tanks. The Deputy Commander then noted the militia's attempt to flee, and I thought I saw him frown slightly at their presumption. His speech sounded like that of a machine. 'Some people were egressing. We took them out with airpower

---

[1] These figures include non-combat cases.

rotating above the battle-space.' There had been no further resistance. I sensed regret that Sadr had not put up much more of a
fight. The Squadron would move further into the city during the
day. I knew that unless the Americans remained in Kut the British
would not allow us to return. The Brigade assured me that they
would be staying.

All that day Timm and I pushed for a helicopter south but to no
avail. Part of the rationale for our immediate presence had already
been eroded—Neil Strachan and the rest of the team in Delta had
been able to provide any guidance the Squadron had needed in
moving back into the city, and the Brigade now gently relayed the
news that their Squadron commander, Lieutenant-Colonel Mark
E. Calvert, wanted to get a thorough military grip of the area before
restoring civil authority. I conceded defeat. A British Royal Air
Force helicopter picked up the remainder of team Kut from Delta
Camp and flew them to Basra. We booked ourselves on a Hercules
aircraft to the same city the next day. The aircraft's interior was partitioned by a black curtain. I was told that we were carrying the
body of a British citizen.

Timm and I were re-united with our team at the airport in Basra.
We hurriedly discussed a possible way forward in Kut but hesitated
over the Governor's future. He was clearly lamentably weak, but we
remained uncertain whether it was possible to do better, particularly in these new circumstances. Moreover, was the Province
Council sufficiently strong to oversee an election for his successor?
It seemed unlikely that there would be anything left of the old
structures at all. Timm and Reda Salem returned with CRG to
Baghdad the next day. The Americans intended to send the two of
them back to Kut as soon as there was an opportunity.

The weeks in UK passed slowly. I saw the Foreign Office's Iraq
Policy Unit, and at its request described the events that had led to
our withdrawal from Kut. They sat around me in a quiet circle in a

small room and listened without comment. As I talked about those moments where clear choices had been available to me—the return through Sadr's road-block on 5 April; our dispositions and tactics on the 6th; our move to Baghdad and ambush on the 7th; and our arrival in the city on the 8th—the silence seemed particularly concentrated. I was unsure whether this indicated praise or censure, and never found out.

I was asked to see the British Foreign Secretary in his office a few days later. We sat alone together and had tea. The Political Director later joined us. Discussing the fall of Kut and wider events in Iraq in these circumstances had an historical resonance I should like to have bottled and taken away with me. I thought Jack Straw courteous, approachable and practical. I asked that he write to Timm in recognition of his contribution during the siege. He did so a few weeks later, and copied the letter to the U.S. Secretary of State.

Timm returned to Kut on 13 April with CRG and a temporarily loaned reporting officer from Baghdad. Our sub-contractors—KBR, Research Triangle Institute and Triple Canopy—did not return then or later. He accepted this formidable task without demur. Mark Calvert and his men had secured the CPA compound with tanks and an American platoon. First reports indicated that our site had been looted and partly destroyed by Sadr's militia. Timm and the commander of the Second Armored Cavalry Regiment walked the length of Kut's central market road, slowly and deliberately while a phalanx of infantry secured the city centre. He gave interviews on television daily; and slowly our local staff began to return to work. Shortly afterwards he fired Governor Nema Sultan for collusion with Sadr and gave the job to his Deputy in the interim period. The Governor, who had long made much of this arduous public service and repeatedly threatened departure, fought his dismissal tooth and nail. In the end he had no public support save from his own tribe and returned to his farm.

The Foreign Office's Iraq Policy Unit telephoned me in late April to say that they had been passed a memo written by Kut KBR staff which was critical of me and my handling of Sadr's attack. It alleged that I knew of the impending assault, and had deliberately 'downplayed' the threat and the number of our assailants, refused to allow the establishment of a blast wall between our complex and the river, and attempted to control the flow of information leaving the site. The official who delivered this message told me that the British press had a copy and would probably publish an article on it in the next few days. I asked—imagining that the Foreign Office would welcome the chance to counter this aggressively—whether I could be confident of its support, and what they now intended to do. The first part of my question was ignored. The last is a question a Foreign Office friend of mine used invariably to receive with an expression of deep gloom and the lugubrious rejoinder 'Ah, yes—the D-word'. This sense of uneasiness with action was apparent. I despaired of these people—in these uncertain days I sought above all unequivocal support on which I could wholly rely. I submitted a report to the Unit dealing with each of the issues raised and heard no more of it till the allegations were repeated in an American journal that autumn.[2]

Among the most interesting of them was the suggestion that I had 'downplayed' the number of our attackers—this from a KBR employee who spent the entire attack in a darkened hotel corridor. I saw not a single militiaman that day and I spent many hours on the Villa roof. What one could see—and clearly—was the overwhelming effect of fear on the unfettered imagination, the resulting temptation to immure oneself behind blast-walls and the damaging consequences for the political mission. These walls, I noted in my subsequent report to the Foreign Office, would have provided scant

[2] Stokes, David, 'Al-Kut, Iraq: After Battle Report', *The Middle East Quarterly*, Fall 2004, Vol. XI, No. 4.

counter to the fire of mortars, RPGs and machine-guns directed at
our compound because the mortar is a high-trajectory weapon and
the others had been routinely fired from roof-tops; but would certainly have precluded the kind of retaliatory response employed by
the Ukrainians when Timm and I were on the Villa roof that night.
How was it that we had allowed ourselves to get into a situation
where we had always to negotiate with our sub-contractors over the
substance of our task?

The Foreign Office had stated that there could be no return of the
British team to Kut for as long as the Ukrainian Brigade alone was
responsible for our security. The British security adviser in Iraq
instituted a security review of the site, and the Foreign Office
sought and received assurances from the Americans that American
troops would remain in Kut until the dissolution of the CPA. We
lobbied hard for the re-insertion of the former CPA team and
chafed at the delay as the Iraq Policy Unit considered the situation.

We returned to Iraq on 5 May. The whole team returned with
me, something that moved and impressed me equally. Timm had
asked the Armored Cavalry Regiment to pick us up in their Blackhawks. Two of them appeared over the Green Zone's Washington
heli-pad at midday on 9 May in a barrage of noise.

The helicopter in which I flew had a pair of crossed cavalry sabres
painted on its nose and a large polystyrene cut-out of a waving Bugs
Bunny wedged against the window in the starboard door. The door
gunners waved us in and we settled amid a mountain of our gear and
equipment. One had a patch on his helmet that said 'Blackhawk
Down—Leave No Man Behind'. The other man's helmet bore the
legend 'BOHICA'. As crew chief he had the right to name the helicopter, which was identically titled. Timm had once told me that it
stood for 'Bend Over, Here It Comes Again'. Probably the latest
cancellation of their home-coming and unlooked-for deployment
to Kut fell into that category.

We swept exhilaratingly south-eastward for Najaf and Kut at roof-top level over the suburbs of Baghdad, descending to twenty feet as we left the city, vaulting over power lines and scattering birds, over the irrigation channels and settlements, our wheels brushing the fronds of the palm groves and tracing the turbid waters of the Euphrates. In the desert one could still see stubborn pools of winter rain, and the fields of the strip-farms over which we flew remained a vivid green. The slip-stream tore at our faces. Again, the strength and power of the American military machine imbued one with purpose, yet despite this heady stimulant and my conviction that we must return I feared that we would prove to be marginalised in Kut.

It seemed to me most unlikely that anything could realistically be salvaged after so disastrous a reverse, which our five-week absence seemed to have made more pronounced as if we had somehow accepted our opponents' terms. I thought it made us look like cowards and, despite all our rhetoric, showed the limits of our commitment to Iraq. We had just over six weeks before transition: six weeks to re-invigorate the province politically, find a new Governor and gather our belongings once more and depart for good. The work of our fragile Councils would be central to success, although it seemed certain that Sadr's intervention had weakened their resolve. The police force remained weak, the Ukrainian Army was now largely prohibited by Kiev from any form of offensive operations, and an acting Governor tentatively held the ring with Moqtada al-Sadr dominating the political agenda. As we sped over the palms and hamlets, scattered flocks and sentinel shepherds of southern Iraq one bleak fact after another jostled for attention in my mind, and I steeled myself for what lay ahead.

Looking down on the bomb-scarred perimeter of Delta Camp one could see that militarily much had changed. The rubble and wreckage of two wars remained, but the once empty expanses of concrete dispersal areas had now been pressed into service by the newly-arrived Americans, who had also created accommodation and offices from the hardened hangars that once housed Saddam Hussein's aircraft. There were helicopters everywhere. In a gesture that exemplified the courtesy and commitment of the American officers I met in Iraq, both Lieutenant-Colonel Mark Calvert and his Najaf-based Regimental commander were waiting for me on the tarmac.

Mark Calvert was a wiry, tough-looking career-soldier in his forties from Athens, Georgia. He wore the 'high and tight' haircut favoured by American units, which was no more than a patch of hair atop an essentially shaven scalp, and had this remaining island of hair cut uncompromisingly every week. He exuded the same undiluted sense of mission I had seen in Timm, Bremer and the clutch of American generals at our Baghdad conferences. In each the mission shaped the man to such an extent that the task and personality merged, and this had inculcated a focused asceticism which in Calvert was compounded by the values of Southern conservatism. We agreed that we would talk through matters at length once we had re-occupied our base. His commander, Colonel Bradley W. May, pulled me to one side and shook hands. He said 'I've given you my best man.'

Our site was a ruin. The Jaish al-Mahdi had virtually destroyed the complex by detonating artillery shells and gas bottles inside the buildings and next to the staircases. The Villa had collapsed and burned. The central sections of Tarawa House and the hotel were likewise gutted. Storehouses had been ransacked, and Triple Canopy's armoury of Kalashnikovs blown open and looted. Almost everything left behind during the withdrawal had been stolen. In some cases Sadr had changed into our clothes and shoes on the spot, leaving those they had been wearing in a heap on the floor. They disappointed me—I had imagined a more principled opponent. Some of CRG's wardrobe, left during withdrawal, was untouched; and the fact that some of us owned clothing insufficiently fashionable to merit theft by an impecunious militia gave us something to laugh about for some days. Timm, with the help of CRG, had once again shovelled debris from the buildings in our absence, creating make-shift offices in Tarawa from what remained and fashioning steel staircases in Kut's metal market to by-pass those Sadr had destroyed. He had also managed to resurrect one wing of rooms in the hotel. On Tarawa's roof Timm had hoisted an Iraqi flag, flanked by those of Britain, the United States and Texas. He had been keen to employ the negligée as a battle-standard but it could not be found. His message was upbeat: the Americans controlled the city; our police officers had made progress in re-fashioning the police force; and the Province Council was conducting its affairs as though there had been no turbulence at all. He had done extraordinarily well.

I had not been long in Kut before I realised that my expectations of the effect on the public mind of Sadr's sudden rebellion were almost entirely erroneous. I had always been conscious that we had never managed politically to engage the middle class. If fear was one reason why none chose to mount soapboxes in the parks, appear on television or volunteer for public duty, simple cumulative fatigue was certainly another. The dangers of assuming profile appeared to them as great now as they had always been; and the majority of ordinary Iraqis simply remained at home with their families. I had always imagined this failure to be essentially our fault: we had failed to engage them forcefully enough, to exploit adequately that finite honeymoon period after the war, to get our message right.

If there was no doubt that we could have done much better in these key areas, I had not understood at all that this same group had remained just as unmoved by the siren-song of Sadr, who had under-estimated the resolute political immobility of Wasit's middle classes and an air of burgeoning unease about the activities of Sadr's militia in the holy cities. Many felt that Moqtada al-Sadr was now staining his revered family's reputation, and viewed the possibility of armed conflict in holy places such as Najaf, where he had taken refuge, with alarm. Wasit's innate conservatism had worked against Sadr as surely as it impeded us. If we had proved unable to stir them, they had done no better. The Jaish al-Mahdi had danced briefly on a largely empty stage, having pursued the mirage of popular uprising that had beguiled us all. I was also told by the interpreters that seven Sadr dead had lain in the streets behind our compound on the morning of 7th April after our withdrawal. It is a Muslim tradition that corpses should be immediately covered but none of the house-holds close to the scene had done so. When Sadr representatives came to the neighbourhood and asked for sheets for that purpose they had been met by refusal. One father allegedly refused to bury his own son. Their local leader Abdul Jawad al-Issawi was on the run and his offices were rubble. Calvert's men arrested anyone who visited the site or picked through the debris. Posters of Moqtada al-Sadr were simply removed; and the unemployed poor whom he had wooed were now offered jobs by the Americans in city-rehabili-tation schemes.

It became apparent that the events of April could be turned to advantage. It is simplistic to suggest that the attack allowed the people of Kut to peer into the abyss and turn away; and still more so to suggest that the turn was in our direction. Yet in denying Sadr mainstream political support they implicitly strengthened the *status quo* that CPA represented, however vocal their public criticism of our shortcomings and mistakes. Sadr's brief reign in Kut had tested whether the new structures we had emplaced were resilient enough to withstand pressures of this kind. Some, clearly, had failed. Others had not. In this sense the rising had provided a useful dress-rehearsal for transition. We now had an opportunity to make the requisite changes.

Overwhelmingly, the thorniest of our political problems was how best to select a new Governor. Although Bremer had long insisted that the Governor of each province should submit to a vote of confidence by the new Province Council or a similar body, we had always fought shy of it, fearing the public effect. So too had the Province Council itself, for three reasons: it was nervous about the exercise of its new power, and could not yet bring itself to believe in this de-centralisation; it had lacked Bremer's legal order confirming such local powers and felt exposed without it; and, like us, was unsure whether it could find anyone better. It had accordingly voted to examine Governor Nema Sultan's performance anew after a month; and I, mindful of the political leap forward in Iraqi terms that even this pragmatic decision represented, had agreed. That month had proved a turbulent one, and now we had no choice. The former Governor had gone, and the province could not be restored to its people after transition without a replacement.

Although we agreed that the ideal process would be one in which we did not interfere at all, it was apparent that any procedure which opened the most powerful position in the province to quasi-democratic competition was fraught with danger. The seat offered a salary, genuine power and the chance to shape province affairs, and we could expect it to be contested by tribes, political parties and warlords alike. A win by any of these partisan groups was unlikely to improve the prospects of Wasit's people, yet the alternatives were equally dangerous: the Deputy Governor who at present carried out the function was unpopular, and would simply be removed if we failed to initiate the process; and the political climate had changed sufficiently post-war that any attempt by CPA to sponsor the selection of an individual directly would fatally rob the process of credibility.

Our particular concern was that, by initiating this procedure we would provoke a popular reaction that we could not control. Not only would we have to accept the outcome, however unwelcome, but we would have to accept the possibility, even the likelihood, of those Council members involved in reviewing candidacies being subjected to intimidation. I feared that, having regained at least the semblance of control over the province, we would be placed in a position of having either to honour an unpalatable result or, in seeking to overturn it, to risk violent opposition from supporters' groups. In each case we would lose control as surely.

The principal reason for this careful evaluation was that, despite Moqtada al-Sadr's failure to marshal majority support, we were much weaker militarily now than before the April rising. It was arguable that the rapidity of our military collapse showed how delusory this semblance of strength had been; but we now lacked even this façade. The Ukrainians, whose rules of engagement had been dramatically narrowed by Kiev, could no longer be treated as an effective military force. Although their provincial distribution remained unchanged, they remained largely confined to their barracks and carried out only point-security tasks. Patrolling activity had all but ceased; and although Sergey Ostrovskiy remained the senior officer in the province and hence Calvert's superior, the Americans operated independently and at will. I saw no instances of this resulting in American-Ukrainian tension: rather, the mainstream U.S. military view seemed to be that the so-called 'Rent-an-Army' scheme had not worked, and that the root of the problem was a political refusal to commit the requisite numbers of American troops in the first place. U.S. forces in the first Gulf War had totalled some 695,000 soldiers of which approximately 400,000 had been ground troops; approximately 150,000 soldiers had taken part in Gulf War Two, of whom some 140,000 remained. This weakness could not be blamed simply on Multi-National Division Central-South, in whose defence it must also be said that their rules of engagement were often restrictive. If it was instructive to see how much activity the Americans could generate with a compara-tively small unit, it was always clear that Mark Calvert and his men could not alone compensate for this deficiency, although they tried hard to do so. The makeshift U.S. camp at Delta resembled a great hive, with vehicles and soldiers ceaselessly radiating outward from it. They patrolled at all hours of the day and night with a broad remit: visiting schools, investigating the state of utilities and grain supplies, checking on bridges and talking to bystanders. They initiated civil rehabilitation schemes and maintained an intelligence watch on Sadr's former premises and affiliated mosques. Above all, they dominated their environment: they carried out artillery practices in the late afternoon in great salvoes of fire that rattled the windows and echoed through the city; at night they patrolled with tanks; and, each evening the deadly little Kiowa helicopters took off in swarms from Delta to patrol the city and its surroundings. This gave a sense of firm military control of the city that we had not previously felt.

Despite this energy and drive, however, it was clear that, except for Kut, we could not dominate the province in the manner re-quired. Since the rising, Wasit had become a more turbulent place and its people more fearful. But now, although it was above all things what we needed to do, we could not re-assert our authority. There were too few Americans to do it, and the exigencies of the Sadr crisis meant that reinforcement was impossible. Although we could enforce stability in Kut, it remained a qualified stability be-cause our enemies—not merely Sadr but the full spectrum of op-portunists who saw advantage in renewed anarchy—had sensed weakness and become bolder. We had been forced to effect tran-sition swiftly, and time and security constraints had all but pre-cluded the package of training and capacity-building that would normally have accompanied it. The CPA's departure made the future too uncertain a prospect to bind the disparate elements of the province together, who now sought only to strengthen their own positions. The security situation had worsened. There was a sharp increase in instances of intimidation of Council members, local staff working at Delta and our own interpreters. A small hard core of people, almost certainly Sadr followers, attacked American patrols in Kut at least once a week with improvised roadside bombs. These were generally ineffectual because they were principally directed against tank patrols. Calvert wondered whether the destruction of an Abrams tank was considered a trophy. One, having been hit twice by shrapnel that left jagged holes in its external storage boxes, was re-named 'Bomb Magnet'.

Other towns in Wasit, together with the roads that led to them, were therefore outside our reach and could no longer be considered safe. We could assert control in such places but would then be forced to cede it in others. Any travel we undertook outside Kut would generally have to be with an American military escort. This made the formulation of a political strategy difficult—we could not personally rouse the province as we had once done, or support the district and sub-district Councils in the way that was needed. Yet these constraints and the remorseless passing of time forced us again to rely on local capacity, and Council members increasingly came to us. We began a complete review of each Council in turn.

We had learned that stability in a district or sub-district hinged almost entirely on the competence of the local Mayor and his police chief, who in turn were able to use their power to support nascent Councils. Where these pillars were in place and strong, one had a civic structure that could withstand turbulence. It was astonishing to see the difference that a Mayor could make. Just before April we and the Province Council had installed a powerful Mayor in the northern town of As-Suwayrah, Wasit's second largest, against the wishes of powerful local factions who, in a flawed election held illegally and entirely under their own auspices, had installed one of their own. We removed him, and when the Council protested

Dr Abdul Salaam harangued them and threatened them with dismissal. Here, despite these local fractures, Sadr's militia, implacably
opposed by the Mayor and a group of hastily-gathered relatives, had
failed to make a dent. The same was true of the border town of
Badrah, where Sadr had no prior purchase. Clearly Kut would stand
for as long as we propped it up and no longer; and it was clear that
the southern city of al-Hayy was lost. Indeed, a film was circulating
in the market showing Sadr dictating terms to the departing
Ukrainian garrison. Another, entitled 'Our Victory', showed the
fall of our own site. The Mayor of Numaniyah meanwhile assured
me that there had been no trouble in his town. I told him that, having
been attacked there myself, I could personally refute his claim.

Calvert was careful not to interfere in political matters, despite
his thirteen months' service in Iraq. I was just as careful to discuss all
of our plans with him—he was clearly very able and had been in Iraq
longer than I had. He had daughters of eighteen and sixteen, and a
son of eight—American units had not endured this kind of sepa-
ration from their families since the 1950–3 Korean War. I had
always believed in the importance of the most careful fusion of
military and civil strategy at all levels in such interventions, and we
did our utmost to cement the closest of working relationships. I
fully expected Sadr to attack us again, and in the first of our conver-
sations we talked about the U.S. response if there were further
assaults on our compound. Calvert said flatly that if this happened,
he would unhesitatingly 'go to where the firing is' and launch an
attack on these positions with his soldiers. In answer to my request
for more detail, he merely said that his firm intention in all cases
would be to attack the enemy, and we could tie up the fine detail at
the time. In the unlikely event that withdrawal was again necessary,
we would be taken out inside the tanks. He also told me that, in his
last post at the National Training Centre in the Mojave Desert, they
had used the film *Zulu* for debriefing about defence. He was a man

in whom it was easy to feel confidence, and one inevitably wondered what might have been done in the province with an entire American Brigade.

Our return to Wasit was the first time I had worked at any length alongside the U.S. Army. At first I found it curiously difficult to separate the product from its Hollywood brand, and my impression is that many of its soldiers did too till mounting losses in Iraq made the distinction clear. There is no doubt that Britain was nervous about what was seen as an American predilection for early and profligate use of firepower, and feared the political consequences. If the British feared spiralling violence as a result, they lacked the leverage a larger military commitment to Iraq might have given and found themselves unable to influence, let alone control, their much larger partner. A bold plan was mooted in the spring of 2004 to increase the number of British troops in Iraq and absorb responsibility for parts of Central-South, including the sensitive holy city of Najaf. At a stroke this would have bought the British more political traction with the Americans, allowed them to export their particular style of community soldiering to a pivotally important city, and released U.S. troops for other duties. To my lasting regret and disappointment this was not done.

As a lieutenant I had once asked my American commander his opinion of the British army. He said that we would spend hours deciding how best to outflank a hillside position, while the Americans would simply remove the hill. If the British argued that U.S. methods in Fallujah, for example, were counter-productive, American officers I met were adamant that if they had only been allowed to 'flatten' the city they might have broken the insurgency. In purely military terms it is difficult to decide who was right, and there is no evidence that a more gentle approach would have worked. It is true that the readiness of U.S. troops to shoot to kill in Iraq generally eclipsed that of their British counterparts, but when there had been important lapses of U.S. discipline in this area, these were roundly condemned by American commanders whose soldiers were forced to endure the consequences of a worsening security environment. My own impression was that such lapses were born of inexperience, procedural failures exacerbated by an over-stretched U.S. Army's enforced reliance on raw reservists, and a damaging lack of interest among Americans about the region and its people. This allowed Iraqis to be de-humanised in their eyes. Most Americans I knew were suspicious of the Arab world and its principal religion, and in some this amounted to phobia. If some of this sentiment was imported, much was also the result of experience: the shock felt by American soldiers in finding themselves under attack by those they had come to liberate was profound, and it was still evident in Calvert's soldiers when I first met them.

His Squadron was a strong force and the more impressive given its thirteen exhausting months in theatre and the sudden extension of its tour. Despite the unexpected cancellation of their leave and the fact that the bulk of their equipment had been packed for departure—indeed, half of their tank force had already gone—they had reconfigured themselves, re-fueled and re-armed, executed a 150 km. road-march to Kut and secured the city, all within a period of little more than forty-eight hours. I am certain we would not have lost our site had the unit been in Kut before April. If Mark Calvert was unusually able—and I cannot know if this is true because I saw no other U.S. army formation from so close—it was impossible not to admire the conviction, commitment and courtesy of American officers and soldiers alike. American morale remained generally high despite almost unprecedented tour-lengths and high casualties, and this must have been because most soldiers were led by intelligent, well-trained and educated officers who took the same risks. If they still had not fully mastered the techniques of dealing with civil populations in difficult circumstances they themselves would be the first to admit it; and if the American soldier sometimes appeared to a European posturing and gung-ho, there must have been as many times when their partners appeared pompous and infuriatingly cautious.

April's fighting, together with the imminence of political transition, now imposed an uncompromising clarity on the issues of the day. The mental clutter and background noise that had driven us well-nigh mad in the early days now ceased; and if this was partly a by-product of our hard-won experience it was also because the key issues were apparent to everyone. The selection of a Governor capable of steering Wasit through transition was essential, and dwarfed all other considerations. To fail here was to fail everywhere else. We would initiate the search through the Province Council and it was they who would set the criteria for candidacy, manage the campaign and select Nema Sultan's successor. We could allow three weeks for the process and no more. The incumbent had to be in post and settled before our departure. It was additionally clear that the new Governor must have a province police force that was as loyal and strong as we could conceivably make it in the time remaining to us. Mark Calvert would make this his priority. He liked what he had seen of the new police leaders, and told me that Deputy Ali Riba had taken to sleeping at the police station to make sure his officers performed.

If the exigencies of the moment imposed clarity on our working lives, they also conferred a refreshing simplicity on our existence in our diminished base. The site was not without a certain battered charm, and a powerful north-west wind made the thick stands of green reeds at the river bank rustle like silk. The team's experience and cohesion showed, and we needed very little support to remain working in this way for some time. The Americans brought food for us from Delta and many of us had anyway developed an inexplicable affection for our boxes of American combat rations. We picked up mail on our visits to Baghdad. Life was austere and difficult but the team prospered, and all looking back would regard this period of their work as their most satisfying and productive. They would be equally unanimous that the absence of most of our sub-contractors was beneficial.

It is idle to suggest that there is no room for sub-contractors in endeavours of this kind, but equally one cannot simply lump such companies together in an operational environment and hope for the best. The sheer disparity in their quality was striking. CRG's performance, for example, had been first-class and it had become an integral and indispensable part of our team. Britain did not have the national resources to establish this kind of protection without employing the private sector, and this pragmatic solution demonstrated Foreign Office thinking at its best. Our CRG teams were the envy of other nationalities and a formidable resource. The principal reason for this success was undoubtedly the calibre of their people, its operational culture and the resulting understanding that one cannot easily serve more than one master. In short, CRG did as we asked it to do and, so far as was possible, subordinated its discrete company procedures to our own. Bob's agreement to return through the Sadr checkpoint on 5th April was a case in point.

Our experience of KBR was less positive. The calibre of its people was variable, and their security standards were unrealistic. Our KBR team leader was once stranded at Hillah for a week because no one could assemble sufficient military hardware to meet the rules governing his two-hour journey to Kut. When I offered my own CRG detail this was rejected as insufficient because we did not have crew-served machine-guns. A KBR plumber needed a level of protection that surpassed Sir Jeremy Greenstock's. One can applaud this attention to personal security, but also see the difficulty of using such people in a fast-moving political environment from which one could not simply distil the risk. Friction of this kind coloured our relations because it made them unreliable; and look-ing back over our time in Kut I can say unequivocally that dealing with KBR's people was our single biggest operational headache. Of all the projects they undertook for us, all over-ran and many were not completed at all. The irony is that KBR was supposed to be the answer to many of our problems—but in giving a single company so much administrative power we also gave it command; and hence implicitly subordinated our operations to its policies. KBR prom-ised to return after April, but did not. So absolute was its control that CPA teams had never been given any form of operating budget; and during KBR's absence we could neither recruit nor pay local staff, which was obviously absurd. KBR may have been good at maintaining large logistical bases for the military and discharging the support functions this required; but the error lay in attempting to extend that expertise to small and exposed camps such as our own. If the creation of CPA Governorate Teams was an afterthought, it is not surprising that the issue of administrative support to them appeared haphazard. KBR could not do it—the role should have been discharged by military engineers. We placed far too much re-liance on a single company, and its monopoly became an embar-rassment. In our nine months in Kut KBR were unable to provide my staff with a single hot meal on site.

Research Triangle Institute (RTI) also proved an awkward fit. An American company that had been sub-contracted by U.S. Aid, RTI was to carry out the 'democratisation' component of CPA's work. This field had not been delineated, and it was thus left to the organi-sations on the spot to set working parameters. Our experience in south-east Europe had shown just how difficult it is to define the roles of those engaged in 'democratisation' and it was no different here. We assumed, for example, that RTI's main task would be to assist us in forming Councils and establishing rules of procedure. At this stage its team consisted of specialists in subjects such as women's rights, agriculture and water supply: they knew nothing about Councils or any of the fields that were pressing priorities for us at the time. Had we been asked what we needed, we would have begged for experts on the police, the courts and local governance but no one did so. My ability to make the necessary changes was limited because I had only a form of implied authority over the company's representatives on site, and they found it difficult to alter course having already recruited internationals for the job. The quality of these people was variable, and I believe that their team leaders were as frustrated as we were.

These difficulties complicated our working lives enormously. In my judgement, the failure of some of our principal sub-contractors in Iraq to work to their full potential was due to both systemic difficulties and the variable calibre of their employees. The age-old lessons about coordination had not been absorbed by the Coalition, despite the full force of experience in, say, the former Yugoslavia—and one was left with a raft of largely unaccountable companies with their own sets of rules and security procedures, arriving at intervals, whose roles had never been properly defined or harmonised with CPA's political objectives. The risks inherent in Iraq forced such companies to pay high salaries and to overlook patchy CVs to meet the quotas for which they had been contracted. This hotchpotch of ill-defined objectives and individuals of variable capability was then merely dropped into theatre without benefit of a defined chain of command or an over-arching strategy. Shortly thereafter the emergence of the November 15 Agreement forced the entire jumble to produce results in seven months flat rather than over a period of years as originally envisaged. The outcome, predictably, was chaos; and CPA teams like ours, which had thought we would launch ourselves from the shoulders of our sub-contractors, found reality to be quite the reverse. The system CPA had inherited was too complex, fragmentary and inflexible to function properly under the pressure of difficult circumstances, and could not make sudden changes of direction.

Our relations with the Ukrainian Brigade remained warm, and neither party referred again to the events of April. We were careful to brief General Ostrovskiy and his officers regularly and ensure that he was kept up to date with political developments; but in fact he and his men were now largely militarily irrelevant. Only at the border did the Ukrainian role remain unchanged, and we continued our programme of refurbishment of the frontier forts that had been built during the Iran-Iraq war so that the border guards could use them. The Ukrainians often invited us to dinner. Historical anniversaries were celebrated with great gusto, and the quantity of vodka drunk on Ukrainian Armed Forces Day and Victory in Europe Day was numbing. General Ostrovskiy had a Russian-style *banya* built in an outhouse; and if I found the sensation of standing naked above a similarly nude and shrieking Ukrainian Deputy Brigade Commander while beating him with eucalyptus branches a trifle unusual, nothing in Calvert's lexicon of Southern traditionalism equipped him to deal with such revelations when I described the event to him the next day. No power on earth could have led him into that *banya*. He walked away shaking his head.

Despite our dismissal of the former Chief of Police and his Deputy and the compelling reasons for it, our difficulties in confirming their successors officially at the Ministry of the Interior vividly illustrated the internecine political tensions of the period. We had installed them in early April, and exhaustively explained why we had done so to the CPA and the Ministry. They had begun, with our encouragement, weeding out the weak and corrupt from a grotesquely swollen force, of whom only a minority ever reported for duty. After initial review they recommended the dismissal of fifty-five officers and men. Timm showed me two intercepted documents. The first, dated 4th May and signed by a Deputy Minister of the Interior, told the new Chief, Abdul Haneen, that he was to grant ten days' 'ordinary leave' to his discredited predecessors. The second, headed 'Secret and Immediate' and dated 5th May, informed the Police Chief that he was 'not to obey the orders of the British coordinator'. The Ministry refused to confirm the new Chief and Deputy in post, and said that their attempts to reform the force must stop; indeed that only the Ministry could initiate such steps. The names of any officers deemed to have failed in their duties should simply be sent to the Ministry, who would judge how best to respond. Given that it was now beyond doubt that a group of the Emergency Police, allegedly among the best in Wasit, had attacked our compound alongside Sadr—led spiritedly by the unit's commander—one wondered whether this procedure would match the obvious requirement. This officer had been wounded during the fighting and watching him limping around police HQ irritated and pleased me in equal measure.

The gap between Baghdad and the regions now yawned particularly wide, not simply between CPA HQ and the Governorates but between province institutions and their parent Ministries. The key reason for this was the security environment, which made travel to the field increasingly difficult and robbed Baghdad of sensation. The short time remaining before transition demanded that CPA divest itself of Ministerial control, when it was quite clear that some could not shoulder their responsibilities with competence. Yet the process of divestment had to go ahead because the transition time-table demanded it. It was a muddle. An American soldier and I found ourselves looking at a policeman lying asleep in a plastic chair outside the station one afternoon. After a few moments he said 'Seems to me we need to start at the bottom and invade these guys again. Maybe we'll get it right this time. Hell—a *plan* would have been good.'

We sent our intercepted documents up to CPA HQ. Calvert began equipping the police with extraordinary speed through the

U.S. command chain. Pistols and assault rifles arrived, together with flak-jackets, handcuffs and batons. The police had long contended that these things alone were insufficient to combat the heavily-armed criminal groups responsible for a wave of thefts on the desert roads and the attacks on American vehicles but, for the first time, they were given a small allocation of RPGs and heavy machine-guns. It was clear, however, that Calvert judged that our new officers were not vigorous enough in their pursuit of those responsible for our worsening security situation. He harried them, and in mid-May conducted a series of joint raids with his Squadron and the police. The changes we saw—cars waiting quietly at functioning traffic lights, police officers at their posts, armed and uniformed police on patrol—were probably maddeningly small to him, but we saw them with incredulity and rejoiced.

The Province Council saw these improvements too, and felt proprietary pride in them: it was they, after all, who had supplied the names of the two officers and proposed them as candidates. Here too one could see change: the order confirming the Council's powers had at last arrived and all of them had begun to receive salaries. If the prospect of having their weekly sessions filmed for Kut television had once been unanimously opposed, the Council now eagerly embraced publicity. They had become increasingly muscular, and in their second session after the fighting dismissed the turbulent Council of As-Suwayrah in its entirety. They assembled a committee to visit each district and sub-district Council to assess its breadth of representation and competence. I found scheduling appointments with a busy Dr Abdul Salaam increasingly difficult, but took a perverse pride in it: he had grown in stature. The interpreters said that we had created a 'new Saddam'. I smiled wryly—these were positive signs. Actually, our battles with Baghdad had strengthened our relationship with the Province Council because we were fighting a common foe.

We saw the functions of the Governor of Wasit as incompatible with membership of a political party, believing that the political process in the province was not sufficiently mature to allow the requisite level of independence on the part of the candidates. Dr Abdul Salaam agreed. The post should go to an independent. Our discomfort with establishing this prescriptive process was eclipsed by what was at stake—and this we saw as being nothing more or less than the immediate future of the province. If we could have been sure that no political party could command the requisite number of Council votes to win we would have thrown the contest open, but we had no such confidence. Past experience showed that the political parties, particularly the Islamic ones, were feared by Council members and intimidation seemed a real possibility.

The political parties in Wasit had become stronger, a power gained largely by their opportunism and our caution. The largest retained former government premises and arms; and CPA, particularly now, did not feel strong enough to confront them. In Central-South we had pushed hard for a code of conduct for political parties that obliged them to uphold the law, but because of the shortage of time we had not been able to deal with this important matter. We would also have welcomed training for such parties in areas such as the development of manifestos, campaigning and internal rules of procedure. However, the scramble towards transition governed everything and no one wanted to take principled stands now. Dr Abdul Salaam, despite his acquiescence in the exclusion of political candidates, was wary of announcing the condition on his own; he preferred it to come from us, to which we agreed.

The Province Council, whose task was to formulate criteria and run the campaign, did so with real enthusiasm, and the media ran the contest prominently. We had made it clear from the outset that this could be no genuine election; rather, it was for each Council in the districts and sub-districts to promulgate the criteria on which the Province Council had decided, to review the requisite nominations, and to forward them to the Province Council which would sit in emergency session till a short-list of three had been decided upon. The Council would then vote in secret on a winner.

The criteria selected by the Council in a noisy but almost unanimous session combined conservative precepts with a measure of paranoia. The requirements for a degree-level education, experience of administration and a clean record were clearly sensible. I thought their insistence that the candidate be at least forty-five was excessive and said so, thinking that we should seek to be as inclusive as we could. Dr Abdul Salaam said we needed a figurehead, and no one younger would do. I deferred to him. If the next criterion, that the candidate should either have been born in Wasit or have lived in the province for twenty-five consecutive years, was an unalloyed twin attack on Iranians and political parties that had taken refuge there, the next was a sop to them: that the candidate should have had no connection with the Ba'ath party or its internal security systems. While logical enough, this last condition deprived us of the only people in the province with administrative training, since they alone could possibly have received it.

The Deputy Governor now beckoned me from the Council chamber and confided in me that he wished to be considered as a candidate. Inside the chamber meanwhile, the Chairman announced that the CPA wished to restrict the contest to independents only. The political parties immediately rebelled, and the Chairman asked Neil Strachan, in my absence, to confirm this ruling. There was confusion: Neil deferred to the Chair, and Dr Abdul Salaam promptly performed a nimble volte-face and said that he saw no difficulties at all in political candidates taking part. Neil did not wish to overrule him in public and the moment quickly passed. We were now committed to an open contest. I was appalled. A queue of political figures assembled to thank CPA for its progressive and open approach;

I mumbled platitudes and did my best to resemble the enlightened pragmatist they now took me for. Occasionally I would say truthfully 'You should thank Dr Abdul Salaam'.

The Governor's selection began in early May in a process devised by the Council. Each candidate was to display his candidacy papers in his local Council offices for his peers to examine—I could only imagine the enjoyment with which this would be done. While the local Council ensured that the applicant met the criteria, the candidate would then travel to Kut and deliver his bid on paper and in person.

By mid-May fifty people had done so. Each of the political parties had fielded a candidate. One was the head of the Communist Party, a professor at the local College. Two were from the Islamic parties, and one of these was the self-appointed leader of a committee that had vowed to bring the town's Ba'athists to 'justice'. The Council asked all fifty to appear in a televised session, introduce themselves and state their manifesto. Some were teachers; and many had military experience. One, white-bearded man of about sixty stood with quiet confidence and said that he would simply work hard and uphold the law—Majed told me that he was a former Iraqi Special Forces commander who had been held prisoner in Iran. Another said that Saddam Hussein had killed three of his brothers. At least a third of them had lost a relative in this way. As always, I was struck by the composed dignity of so many Iraqis in the face of what appeared to be overwhelming tragedy. My pleasure at seeing the process catch the public imagination was however eclipsed by the risks of the contest. Dr Abdul Salaam remained determinedly unruffled. He told me that he had asked for a suggestion box to be placed at the doors of the Government building so that concerned citizens might deliver information relevant to the selection procedure.

The procedure itself was effective but distinctly Iraqi. Each candidate was treated by the Council as a vaulting opportunist. The

Chairman would gather the list of nominations on the table like an executioner's roll, read out a name, and a string of people would invariably denounce that person in ringing tones. This man was a thief. 'And an Iranian' someone else ventured. The Council members would nod sagely. After a short period of contemplative silence someone else would add 'He is a Ba'athist'. After this period of ritual abuse was judged to have done the candidate sufficient damage, Dr Salaam would search his suggestion box for additional material with which to damn him in a silence thick with excitement. If he found something he would read it through silently, perhaps raising a single eyebrow at the sheer horror of his discovery, then say 'I am not sure these comments are appropriate for public discussion—let us vote on whether this man should remain.' The axe fell swiftly. One cited his administrative experience as gained in the supervision of a brick factory. 'Then let him remain with his bricks' someone shouted. The Deputy Governor rather grandly said that he had been too busy with province affairs to put his name forward earlier, but he was doing so now. He was summarily dismissed. At the end of a session in which some 20 candidates had been both disqualified and roundly abused, I would ask Dr Abdul Salaam whether he was satisfied that the procedure were entirely fair. He would look astonished at my naivety and say that everyone knew how unsuitable the twenty had been, and they had been lucky to be considered at all.

In the final week of May the voting became more contentious and Dr Abdul Salaam looked much less comfortable. Five candidates remained, of whom two were political. One of these was the Communist Party professor, whom I considered dangerous only because of his unsuitability for the task. Though charming, he had once confided to me that in political meetings he said 'anything that came into his head', and he could speak on a broad range of irrelevant subjects at length. The second was a Supreme Council for the

Islamic Revolution in Iraq nomination, Jaleel Mohammad Habeeb. I was distinctly uneasy with SCIRI's anti-Ba'athist portfolio of division, apparently unleavened by other plans. The Islamic parties, particularly, hated Ba'athists intensely. Others in the city were less committed, but feared condemnation as sympathisers. In the southern city of Amara the townsfolk had hanged a number of them post-war, a phenomenon that had not been replicated in Wasit. I thought the re-building of Wasit's civil society a more compelling vision than a protracted witch-hunt. Here was a man devoid of practical experience, who if victorious might well divide the province; and I resolved to remove him if he won, regardless of the fuss that might ensue.

I occasionally wondered if I was right to think in this way. Judgement calls such as these were difficult. What relentlessly drove our actions was the agenda of transition and the structures it required. If we had been given more time I would have used it and embraced a measure of experiment. As it was I saw the essence of our work as establishing unambiguous control of our environment and the subsequent promulgation of a new order, followed by a progressive abdication of the power we had needed to achieve these steps. The pace of this abdication should not be so rapid—or indeed so slow—as to prejudice our political aims. Democracy, in whatever form, was the product we sought, and not necessarily the means by which it was to be achieved. Conditions generally precluded so ideal a transition: the Governorate Coordinators were, I suppose, a group of political order chefs, serving stolid utilitarian fare with closing time imminent and one-third of the staff on holiday. Mistakes were inevitable, and cultural misunderstandings were frequent. It was clear, for example, that our moral talismans and theirs were not necessarily the same. Even tolerant religious leaders demanded the harshest penalties for miscreants, and when they described Saddam's habit of hanging criminals and displaying their decomposing bodies in the city they did so with a certain fond ambivalence. I once suggested to Majed, our interpreter, that he should enter politics. He looked thoughtful and said 'Perhaps. I would kill a lot of Iraqis. A *lot* of them.'

In May these contradictions became clear in our bid to corral Moqtada al-Sadr and erode his public influence. It is unclear how many of his militia had been killed in the fighting in Baghdad's Sadr City or in Central-South in April, but the consensus was that militia losses amounted to thousands. Calvert's men had been in Sadr City on 4th April preparing for hand-over before their leave when at 1740 hours 'all hell broke loose'. The Americans there suffered 8 dead and fifty-five wounded. Trusted police officers simply joined the militia. Calvert told me of a soldier who took cover behind a car next to an Iraqi policeman who then shot him. He judged that his soldiers had been opposed in his area by up to 1,000 fighters; and on the basis of visits to morgues and hospitals the next day believed that his soldiers had killed about 350 of them. The American military now appeared unanimous in its view that Moqtada al-Sadr should be dealt with. He had been isolated in his offices in Najaf by troops, and surrounded by overwhelming military force. It appeared inconceivable that he could continue to absorb losses on this scale, but we remained wary of his latent power. General Dempsey of First Armored, whose units were in Najaf, saw a potential future problem of greater magnitude that urged an immediate solution; and drew the military ring still tighter around him.

The effect of Moqtada al-Sadr's imprecations on the public mind remained difficult to quantify. Parts of Wasit province and others had not only risen in sympathy but exported young fighters to the holy places. Many of them had been killed, and their bodies were returned to their families in Kut and elsewhere. This damaged Sadr's standing. The Mayor of Suwayrah, exhausted by the violence, said 'Everyone suffers from these people. I am one. I have wasted my life in wars.' Sadr's remaining militia simply melted away after the fighting, as they had done in Kut. He had steadily lost influence in Wasit since 6–7 April, if anecdotal evidence and mosque attendance were anything to go by, and it is probable that the violence attendant on this 'rising' was partly responsible for the erosion of any initial popular allure. It seemed unarguable that a substantial majority in the city broadly preferred the path articulated by CPA and others. Yet various factors robbed this notion of strategic comfort: that support remained determinedly tacit, and it would be dangerous to assume that it would ever become active—direct action remained too uncertain and risky for ordinary people to embrace it. Also, the complexities of the population's reactions to the fighting in areas such as Najaf militated against active support: in the end, with or without the militia, clerics were revered and Iraqi deaths mourned, and the fact that they were being killed by foreigners created intellectual anxiety in Kut. Finally, the ways in which the Coalition and Iraqis saw the Najaf stand-off were fundamentally different: where the Coalition saw strength and forbearance in carefully corralling the Sadr leader, the Iraqis in Kut saw an emergent heroic quality in him as he walked to prayer under American guns, and commensurate weakness in us. We never found Abdul Jawad al-Issawi, although we were told that he regularly came to Friday prayers in Kut; and, if Sadr did not attack our base again, the city's population never handed him in either.

On 29 May the Council, in a tumultuous slanging match, voted to remove two of the remaining five candidates from the short list: my bête noire and one of the independent candidates. I was surprised by their courage—SCIRI was the most powerful party in the province. On 1 June, the remaining three were put to a secret vote in what I felt to be a defining moment after all our months of struggle. I saw that the Council had voted overwhelmingly for an independent candidate, the white-bearded former Special Forces commander Mohammed Rodha al-Jaishami. The Communist candidate had only five votes of a possible thirty-eight. Dr Abdul Salaam looked exhausted. The Council had come of age. The Chairman and the new Governor were the people who would now replace us. I congratulated both of them, and then quietly asked Dr Abdul Salaam how he had been able to marshal the support to remove the SCIRI candidate. He said he had told the Council that there were no circumstances in which I would accept him.

The key for us now was to ensure that the Governor's position was strong. Under the heaviest pressure and after Bremer's direct intercession, the Ministry of the Interior confirmed both the new Police Chief and his Deputy in post. In the most telling expression yet of the Province Council's new standing no one questioned the Governor's selection process, and all accepted the final decision and the man it produced. I watched the Governor, the Council Chairman and the Police Chief talk together in one corner of the room as the press gathered around them, and realised that our work was complete. Why this sight made me feel an almost unbearable sense of melancholy I did not fully understand; and perhaps I displayed it briefly, because the Governor caught my eye across the room, placed his hand on his heart and gave me a smile of infinite compassion.

We left Kut on 28th June 2004, and Mark Calvert and his Squadron followed a few days later. Neither we nor they were replaced. The Ukrainians remained, albeit without change to their restricted rules of engagement; and despite repeated intercession in Baghdad, we failed to persuade the State Department to station officers in Kut. They would instead be based at a new consular 'hub'—the old Regional Coordination site in Hillah. Up till the end these former CPA sites, so long a strategic anomaly, had clung to a policy role and fought their own Governorate teams for staff and matériel in pursuit of this centralist delusion; neither prospered. They now exercised a lingering hold on hard-pressed State Department planners.

What was needed was a small diplomatic team in each of the provinces, supported and protected by the military, and reporting directly to Baghdad. Such teams were cheap and effective and ensured a sense of continuity throughout the turbulence of transition, where we feared two principal threats. The first was renewed violence by the Jaish al-Mahdi, and the second was that newly-independent Ministries would seek to overturn 'CPA appointments' and undo nominations made on the basis of hard-won experience.

This regional plan struck me as misguided, and an attempt to justify the continued existence of a flawed system. I did not see how one could hope to monitor the evolution of events in a province of a million people from a hub two hours away, and said so at our final Baghdad conference. A political situation of this complexity could not be mastered through day-trips, particularly given reduced military efficacy. Any deterioration in the security climate would merely preclude travel from such hubs. I failed to win this argument, and Bremer later said that I could not have won it: resources were insufficient. The conference was thinly attended—a number of the GCs and Regional Coordinators had already gone. General Sanchez spoke of a 'very tough' security environment, and noted the importance of increasing Iraqi security capacity. Bremer said that the right to make mistakes was an attribute of sovereignty. The sound of patrolling jets and helicopters in these last days of the Coalition Provisional Authority drowned many of the farewells.

During my final week in Kut CRG drove me once more to the Iranian border. We stopped by the side of the main road, which runs north-east across the desert on top of an earthen causeway. I stood there in the heat and looked out at the low flood-plains left by the winter lakes, now receding. The vestiges of these shallow seas glittered with that same mystery and promise to which I had thrilled all those months ago. Creeks of dark blue, flanked by their stands of trembling reeds, wound away into the cracked sand. That ever-present wind ruffled the surface of the water, bent the reeds low and lifted small particles of gravel around my feet. I was beset by a profound feeling of transience, as though our work and its supposed achievements had been some elaborate fantasy. CPA had never hit its stride; and our functional weaknesses had dogged us stubbornly from beginning to end.

Interventions of the kind undertaken in Iraq in 2003 are brutally difficult, and impose the most ruthless of audits on the plans and the individuals assembled to prosecute them. War is often simpler than the reconstruction that follows it, and strategic failure in this sphere may risk the very object for which the conflict was launched. The claim that participating states had not properly appreciated the difficulties of fabricating a new Iraq has become a cliché; but—extraordinary as this may appear—our nine-month tenure in Kut convinced me that this was indeed the truth. One accepts that such operations are complex and demanding; that there was no international consensus on political strategy; and that the nature of Iraq made the Coalition's task especially hard. Yet these mitigating circumstances do not explain how the United States and its principal partner Britain, both permanent members of the Security Council and with the experience they had gained in former Yugoslavia, could have got themselves into this position.

The canvas of the Coalition effort was so large that it was difficult to separate cause from effect; and because each region was different in character and treatment from the rest, any specific deduction about the situation in Central-South might not be generally applicable elsewhere. There were clearly damaging rivalries, most notably between the U.S. Departments of State and Defense, and this political schism made the combining of civil and military arms difficult for the Coalition as a whole. One sensed too a certain intellectual distaste for the Iraq venture among the intelligentsia of the State Department and the British Foreign Office, as though it were somehow possible to divorce departmental posture from that of the governments they ostensibly served—in the State Department's case it is arguable that they were actively prevented from taking a key role. The United States showed complacency, certainly, and perhaps arrogance too, about Iraqis and their reaction to occupation, and, in their frustration with existing security structures such as the United Nations, simply ignored the accumulation of practical experience gained by such organisations in similar ventures. If it cannot be proved that this atmosphere of miscalculation, rivalry and dissent exacerbated CPA's practical difficulties, the empirical evidence for the charge remains strong.

CPA was never properly staffed, and few Governorate Teams ever reached full strength. Those, like my own, that did took months to do so. Too small for the task and incorrectly established for the demands of nation-building, such teams increasingly bore the cumulative effect of planning error above them—a British commander in the southern province of Maysan later described the provinces as the 'clutch' of the Coalition apparatus, or the point at which the planning process met basic truth. Despite the existence, in the British Foreign Office certainly, of comprehensive data bases of people with long experience in relevant theatres and disciplines, these were never, to my knowledge, drawn upon. Key offices such as Governance in Baghdad remained badly under-staffed, which produced commensurate deficits of information and policy at field level, exacerbated by the extraordinary absence of any form of classified communications system. Logistic and administrative procedures failed early: vehicles and equipment never arrived, dining facilities were never built, and security arrangements remained patchwork to the end. So absolute was the monopoly enjoyed by largely unaccountable sub-contractors in these spheres that no alternative solutions to such deficiencies could be found at field level. These damaging voids, gaps and incidental errors might in the end have been rectified, despite the constraints created by the burgeoning insurgency, and the requisite lessons learned, but the November 15 Agreement had the effect of both preserving and prolonging them till dissolution.

It may be that CPA was responsible for some of these failures but my impression is that it had simply to play the hand it was dealt. However, it is clear that its travails were worsened by the political failure to commit sufficient military strength to Iraq, and CPA battled with this grievous deficiency throughout its short existence. This flaw transformed the already substantial risks of intervention in Iraq into a perpetual and dangerous gamble. The establishment of an inexperienced, ill-equipped and fragmentary Polish-led Multi-National Division in the Central-South region was an error, and any political capital gained by it was eclipsed by the operational disadvantages. The use of military power in the civil role is a science, and it is a fundamental mistake to imagine that any military force can accomplish such tasks—Mark Calvert and his men eloquently, if unwittingly, charted the sharp differences in capability and commitment that existed in the Coalition. Without the rule of law— that indispensable first building block—civil reconstruction in all its guises became a matter of hazard and chance. We could never assemble the civil or military resources that we needed, and in the end were forced to entrust the future of Wasit province to the three key Iraqis whom we had helped to appoint and hope for the best. This seems an extraordinarily haphazard way of attempting to secure advances so painfully won.

It remains astonishing that the CPA and broader Coalition was able, despite this catalogue of errors, to stay the political course, challenging and demanding and beset by abrupt changes in political policy and associated time-lines as it was. It is also testimony to the uncompromising rigour with which the Americans, particularly, pursued their objectives, and the abilities and determination of those involved.

Overwhelmingly, however, any success the Coalition achieved in Iraq in 2003–4 was due to the resilience of the 'ordinary' Iraqi citizen. It is ironic that the weaknesses I describe forced us to rely in Wasit on the Iraqi population earlier and more completely than we had at first envisaged; and despite our failure to engage completely with the educated middle class, the results of a gambit that seemed dangerous at the time now emphasise the enduring power of local capacity and the durability of the democratic ideal. The inhabitants of Kut and the wider province bore our errors and inadequacies with endless courtesy, dignity and grace. They were ambivalent about many things, particularly the occupation of their country; and saw no contradiction in thanking us with great emotion for toppling Saddam Hussein and as passionately asserting their right to be left alone, independent and in peace.

Just before we left the city, I placed a letter, some photographs and my prayer beads together with pages from my diary in an old ammunition box, and buried it in the compound for my children. Saying goodbye to CRG and our local staff was very difficult. I walked with Majed once more in the palm grove and watched the water run through the channels at my feet. The trees were heavily laden with the date crop. We gave the site to the police, together with as much of our equipment as we were allowed to leave. Our saloon cars were given to the branch Ministries. We left Kut early in the morning in a small military convoy that Mark Calvert assembled for us. I rode with Timm, on whose unwavering support I had relied for so long. The vehicle gunner put on some music. The driver said 'That is the most gay-ass shit I *ever* heard.' He took it off again. Timm looked stolidly out of the window at the sun rising on the far bank of the Tigris and said simply 'You know—it just could have been done a lot better.'

When I said goodbye to Wasit Province Governor Mohammed Rodha al-Jaishami, he kissed me on the cheeks, took my hands in his and said: 'Thank you my brother. You have come from a long way away. You have built something with your own hands for our future, for our people. May God protect you.'

INDEX

243